PAPAL DIPLOMACY
AND THE QUEST FOR PEACE

PAPAL DIPLOMACY

AND THE QUEST FOR PEACE

The Vatican and International Organization
From the Early Years to the League of Nations

Robert John Araujo, SJ
and John A. Lucal, SJ

Cover Design: Eloise Anagnost

Printed in the United States of America.

Library of Congress Control Number: 2004090917

ISBN 1-932589-01-5

Table of Contents

The presence of papal diplomacy in the world may appear to be a peculiarity. In turn, the peculiarity raises questions about the nature of the Holy See as a juridical person. The Holy See is a unique entity that enjoys international personality under law. Moreover, the Holy See exercises a unique sovereignty as a unique juridical person. This chapter explains the nature of the Holy See's personality and sovereignty.

The previous chapter explained, by examining legal concepts and history, the juridical nature of the Holy See. This chapter, through historical examination, demonstrates how this personality evolved from the Church's interest in and labor to achieving universal peace in the world. The strong, even unchallenged, role of the Holy See in achieving the *Pax Christi* throughout the world was undisputed through the fifteenth century. However, with the rise of the strong national state and the Protestant Reformation, the role of the Holy See underwent alteration. The Peace of Augsburg in 1555 signaled the erosion of the Holy See's strong, if not quasi-monopolistic, control over efforts toward securing international peace. Moreover, the *jus gentium* that had largely been developed by the Church and its strong reliance on natural law was now undergoing a transformation reflecting the role of positive law. In addition, the emerging strength of national monarchs replaced the earlier predominance of the Empire and the Holy See with powerful states that now found themselves in aggressive military and commercial competition that threatened world peace. Moreover, the Enlightenment and revolutionary fervor of the eighteenth century also served to dispute the preeminence of the Church and the Holy Roman Emperor. By the early nineteenth century, even the security of the papacy and its temporal possessions were at risk. Still, the Holy See continued to play important but altered roles in this world of flux. Its status as an international person whose goal of peace remained largely intact and was evidenced by its activities in international diplomatic exchange, arbitration, and continuing contributions to the development of legal concepts.

Chapter 3
The Holy See in an Age of Transition: 1870–1914
With the Italian unification and the loss of the Papal States, the Holy See was unable to argue that its juridical personality and sovereignty were essentially linked to temporal authority. Nevertheless, it succeeded in maintaining its international personality and sovereignty. The 1870s brought not only a change in the temporal authority of the Holy See, they also saw the election of Leo XIII to the papacy. The Holy See's intellectual and other endeavors demonstrated that it was still very involved with the problems of this world that threatened peace and social and economic security. Moreover, it increased its activity in several important international arbitrations and mediations. In addition, the papacy emphasized the nexus between peace and issues of economic and social justice. As the winds of the First World War began to grow, the Holy See did what it could to seek alternatives to armed conflict. But these efforts could not restrain those with belligerent intentions.

Chapter 4
The Holy See and the Founding of the League of Nations: 1914–1920
The beginning of the war was accompanied by a new pontificate. Shortly after the German Army entered Brussels, the new pope, Benedict XV labored intensively but quietly to end the conflict. In 1917, he presented a peace plan that included disarmament, compulsory arbitration, freedom of movement, condonation of war damages, and territorial settlements. Thus, the teaching authority of the Church was used to encourage the abandonment of war as the only mechanism for resolving international conflict. The

Holy See was not a participant in the formal proceedings that brought peace and the establishment of the League of Nations in Geneva. This did not, however, prevent it from encouraging efforts to establish the first international organization designed to maintain the peace and security of the world.

The League of Nations was established in 1920 without the Holy See as a member. But the papacy remained active in its efforts to solidify peace in the world. The Holy See strove, through a papal encyclical, to teach what was essential to reinforce and preserve the peace. The pope praised the idea of an organized "league or . . . family of peoples," without naming the League, and called for forgiveness and reconciliation. These writings were also practical by pointing out flaws in the mechanisms, including the League of Nations itself, which had been devised to bring about the reconciliation that should have accompanied the end of war. One important step taken by the Holy See during this period was to plead the cause of the millions of innocent victims of the conflict. With the encouragement of the Holy See, the Catholic intellectual elite of the period also contributed its talents toward the goal of international peace. With the death of Benedict XV in 1922, the world lost a great friend and fellow laborer in the cause of peace.

One issue to which the League of Nations gave much time was the question of Palestine. To the Holy See, it was essential to preserve the international character of the Holy Places so that they could be visited by the faithful from all over the world. While the political interests of the mandatory and other powers often conflicted with those of the Holy See, the latter persisted in supporting an international commission responsible to the League, to regulate the Holy Places. But this was in vain and the Holy See, disappointed in the League, kept working for peace amid mounting tensions.

The death of Benedict XV brought a new pope, Pius XI, to Peter's throne, but the peace endeavors of the Holy See did not falter. Still, the strains on international relations that were manifested in the League itself began to suggest that the peace of 1918 might not be all that secure. The Holy See, through various papal statements and documents, continued to give attention to the crucial issues demanding attention if peace were to be maintained. Like Leo XIII, Pius XI recognized the vital connection between economic and social justice and international peace. Notwithstanding these efforts, the distance between the Holy See and the world's temporal authorities, including the League, grew rather than diminished, although the Holy See followed closely the League's discussion of calendar reform.

While the official relations between the Holy See and the League of Nations remained distant, the Holy See was able to achieve some additional but indirect influence in the international organization. The Catholic intellectual elite in Europe helped bridge the gap. Through the activities of several major Catholic non-governmental organizations, the views of the Holy See on international peace and security could be made known and have some positive impact on the League's work in trying to establish a world order of peace and justice.

The evolution of the Holy See's role in different forms of international organization culminated in its relationships with the League of Nations. These peaked in the late 1920s and developed no further, due mainly to the deteriorating international climate. During this period, the Lateran Treaty of 1929 regained territorial sovereignty for the Holy See. The Italo-Ethiopian conflict was dealt with differently by Pius XI, who worked for peace in a delicate situation, and the League, which failed to prevent aggression. Pius did not place much hope in the League as the war clouds gathered. His death in 1939 marks the end of the present study, which is an introduction to the larger study of relations between the Holy See and the United Nations to be presented in a subsequent volume.

Preface

THE ROLES OF THE HOLY SEE and papal diplomacy vis-à-vis international organizations have a long and intricate story that spans centuries. This present volume will examine the relationship of the Holy See's involvement with the League of Nations. It will conclude with the papacy of Pope Pius XI in 1939.

This inquiry began almost thirty-five years ago when one of the authors, Fr. John Lucal, commenced his study of papal diplomacy and the Holy See's participation in the world of international peace organizations. This book brings to fruition his earlier efforts, which concentrate on the Holy See's interest in the development of the League of Nations and the historical precedents on which this interest rested.

Both authors have had the privilege of working for and representing the Holy See in the environment of international organizations. Consequently, the following investigation has been influenced not only by their academic study of papal diplomacy and its relations with international organizations but also by their participation in the activities of the Holy See within such organizations. One of the authors, Fr. Robert Aruajo, continues to serve the Holy See in its international relations. From his perspective, it is imperative for the Church to continue its engagement with temporal powers and organizations. However, it must be remembered that the Church and these secular establishments nonetheless have distinctive goals and emerge from dissimilar origins. Should this distinction be forgotten, confusion between the transcendent nature of one and the temporal nature of the others may result.

The current volume traces and investigates the ongoing encounter between the Holy See and the international order from its inception but concentrates on the involvement with the League of Nations. While this history sometimes presents an engagement guided by hope for the human family, it will also show the frustrations that have confronted the Holy See in its work as an "expert in humanity." A second volume is underway and continues this investigation. This subsequent book will focus on the post-World War II relationship between the Holy See and the principal international organization of today, the United Nations.

The incentives for writing and publishing this investigation are several in number. First of all, it will introduce the reader to the Holy See and its long relationship with the international order. Second, it will examine the institutional framework within which the Holy See has engaged temporal sovereigns through international organizations. Third, it will analyze the similarities and differences as to how the spiritual and temporal sovereigns conduct themselves in these organizations. Finally, it will present the case for why the Holy See should continue its labor in the venue of international organizations to ensure that all, not just some, human beings are heard. The voice of the Holy See and the message that it brings through the exercise of papal diplomacy is one that is vital for these organizations to hear—not just for the organizations themselves, but for the advancement and welfare of all the people of the world, whom these organizations were established to serve.

The Holy See as International Person and Sovereign: An Overview

THIS STUDY EXAMINES the relationship between the Holy See and the League of Nations. At the foundation of the investigation is their mutual quest for peace in the world. As with any legal relationship in the international order, that between the League and the Holy See has important historical and legal roots. This chapter concentrates on the ancient lineage and legal identity of the Holy See that is pertinent to understanding the relationship with the League. Whilst international organizations are of relatively recent origin, the Holy See, largely through the exercise of papal diplomacy, commenced its participation in the international order much earlier. This most likely occurred shortly after the Roman Empire acknowledged the Church. One might think it peculiar that the Church would enjoy a status under public international law to engage in diplomatic relations. However, when one considers the fact that the Church has sought to achieve world peace for almost two millennia, any perceived peculiarity evaporates in light of the fact the Holy See has engaged temporal authorities in this quest for centuries. But how it has done so necessitates explanation.

To satisfy this, the present chapter investigates the Holy See's juridical personality as an international sovereign. In the context of this examination of the Holy See's relation with international organizations in the quest for peace, the issue of its legal status and

personality are of central importance. After all, its impact and effectiveness in the efforts are formed in large part by the personality it
enjoys under international law. As will be demonstrated, it has a
unique juridical status within the law of nations. Nonetheless, it is a
juridical person in the context of public international and domestic
law notwithstanding its uniqueness.

Within the realm of the international order, the concepts of
statehood, international personality, and sovereignty are generally
well understood. However, when the Holy See is the subject of the
investigation, conventional categories of sovereignty and personality
falter, which raises legitimate concerns about the Holy See's ability
to engage the temporal authorities as a peer in the international
order. A variety of perspectives concerning its sovereignty and personality has surfaced over time.[1] But in fact, the Holy See is a
unique entity vis-à-vis public international law and requires further
explanation.[2] However, its uniqueness does not make the Holy See
an incomprehensible juridical person.

---

[1] See generally Jacques Maritain, *The Things That are not Caesar's,* trans. J. F. Scan-
lan (French ed.) (1930); Carl Conrad Eckhardt, *The Papacy and World Affairs*
(1937); Joseph Bernhart, *The Vatican as a World Power,* trans. George N. Shuster,
(1939); Charles Pichon, *The Vatican and Its Role in World Affairs,* trans. Jean
Misrahi (1950); Robert A. Graham, SJ, *Vatican Diplomacy: A Study of Church
and State on the International Plane* (1959); Hyginus Eugene Cardinale, *The
Holy See and the International Order* (1976); J. Derek Holmes, *The Papacy in the
Modern World* (1981); Eric O. Hanson, *The Catholic Church in World Politics,*
(1987); see *Church and State through the Centuries: A Collection of Historic Documents with Commentaries,* trans. & ed. Sidney Z. Ehler, LL.D. and John B. Morrall, M.A. Ph.D. (1954) [hereinafter *Church and State*], containing an anthology
of documents and commentary on the general themes of this essay. A work not
yet published in English that contains significant insight on the general topic is:
Richard Arès, SJ, *L'Eglise Catholique et L'Organisation de la Société Internationale
Contemporaine* (1949).

[2] The 1917 Code of Canon Law states that: "In the Code, by the term 'Holy' or
'Apostolic See' is meant not only the Roman Pontiff but also, unless a different
meaning appears from the very nature of the matter or the context itself, the
congregations, tribunals and offices which the same Roman Pontiff is accus-
tomed to make use of in affairs concerning the Church as a whole." Canon 7.
The 1983 Code of Canon Law in Canon 361 now states: "In this Code the
term 'Apostolic See' or 'Holy See' applies not only to the Roman Pontiff but
also to the Secretariat of State, the Council for the Public Affairs of the Church
and other institutions of the Roman Curia, unless the nature of the matter or

The term "Holy See" is frequently encountered in the worlds of international law, international relations, and international organizations. The word "see" derives from the Latin word *sedes*[3] and refers to the seat or chair of St. Peter. All subsequent popes, who are successors of Peter, occupy this seat or chair. The Holy See also refers to the residence of the pope along with the Roman Curia and the central administration of the Catholic Church. This term, however, is not synonymous with Rome, the Vatican, or the Vatican City State.[4] Its meaning transcends the restraint of geographic location. Deciphering the nature of the Holy See's personality and the sovereignty it exercises illustrates that the Holy See is a distinctive entity in both regards. It does not, and cannot, fit comfortably within the criteria of conventional state sovereignty and personality.

When studying the Holy See, it is essential to understand and appreciate its historical role in world affairs.[5] History reveals that the Holy See commenced its earliest participation in international affairs and relations when Jesus commissioned his apostles—the predecessors of the college of bishops—to continue His work in the world by bringing the Good News to those whom they met.[6] The men who followed Jesus had a universal mission to teach God's

---

the context of the words makes the contrary evident." 1983 Code c. 361. Canon 100 of the 1917 Code refined the notion of the Holy See by distinguishing between itself and the Church—the two are distinct juridical entities with their own separate juridical personalities. Nonetheless, these two moral persons are united by the Roman pontiff who heads each respectively. Canon 113, §1 of the 1983 Code states that "The Catholic Church and the Apostolic See have the nature of a moral person by the divine law itself." Both of these entities, the Catholic Church and the Apostolic (Holy) See, constitute distinct *juridical* persons.

[3] The original Latin term *Sancta Sedes* is therefore translated as "Holy See." See *Cassell's Latin Dictionary* (5th ed., 1968), 533, 543.

[4] See C. G. Fenwick, "The New City of the Vatican," *American Journal of International Law* (1929): 371, distinguishing between the Holy See and the Vatican City State; Gordon Ireland, "The State of the City of the Vatican," *American Journal of International Law* 27 (1933): 271.

[5] See *The Catholic Church in World Affairs,* eds. Waldemar Gurian and M. A. Fitzsimons (1954), providing an overview of essays focusing on the twentieth century.

[6] Francois Guizot has offered one explanation of this exhortation: "Christianity considered all men, all peoples as bound together by other bonds than force,

commandments throughout the world.[7] Special emphasis must be placed on Jesus's commission of Peter as His principal follower and successor. Peter received the keys of the Kingdom of Heaven (a symbol of the papacy) and primacy among the college of apostles.[8] These origins of the apostolic mission of the Holy See and the Roman pontiff continue to the present day. As shall be seen in the following chapters, the Holy See and the papacy actively participated in international relations throughout their history.[9]

It will become apparent that the Holy See's traditional exercise of sovereignty, while diversified, frequently emphasizes matters concerning international peace, human dignity, human rights, and the common good. The Holy See actively participates with other sovereigns in negotiating and formulating international legal instruments that are the principal means for achieving specific goals relating to global affairs. The Holy See participates in the formation of bilateral and multilateral treaties and concordats, which amply demonstrate its involvement in promoting peace, human dignity, and the common good in international affairs.

It is generally understood that the Holy See's international personality emerges from its religious, moral, and spiritual authority and mission in the world as opposed to a claim over purely temporal matters. This is an incomplete understanding, however,

---

by bonds independent of the diversity of territories and governments. . . . While working to *convert* all nations, Christianity wished also to *unite* them, and to introduce into their relations principles of justice and peace, of law and mutual duties. It was in the name of the Faith, and of the Christina law that the Law of Nations was born in Christendom." John K. Cartwright, "Contributions of the Papacy to International Peace," *Catholic Historic Review* 8 (1928): 157, 159, quoting Francois Guizot.

[7] See *Catechism of the Catholic Church,* §869, explaining that Peter, the remaining apostles, and their successors, the pope and bishops, have continued to preach this message.

[8] See ibid. §553, noting that Peter's succession included the authority to govern the Church, to absolve sins, to pronounce doctrine, and to exercise discipline within the Church.

[9] See generally Philip Hughes, "The International Action of the Papacy," *The Tablet* (November 2, 1940): 345–46; (November 9, 1940): 365–66; (November 16, 1940): 386–87; and (November 23, 1940): 405–7.

of the grounds on which its claim as a subject of international law can be justified. In partial explanation of its status as a subject of the law of nations enjoying international personality, it is said that the Holy See is an "anomaly,"[10] an "atypical organism,"[11] or an entity *sui generis*.[12] Some have questioned the status and international personality of the Holy See during the period from 1870 to 1929 when it held no territorial sovereignty.[13] Yet, such critics concede that,

> [its] international personality is here recognised to be vested in an entity pursuing objects essentially different from those inherent in national States. . . . A way is thus opened for direct representation in the sphere of International Law of spiritual, economic, and other interests lying on a plane different from the political interests of States.[14]

While the Holy See's status may be an anomaly or unique, the statehood-like status of the Holy See cannot be denied.[15] As James Crawford has affirmed, "recognition by other States is of considerable importance especially in marginal or borderline cases."[16] Currently

---

[10] Rebecca Wallace, *International Law* (2d ed., 1992) 76.

[11] See Cardinale, supra note 1 at 80–81. Archbishop Cardinale suggests that "[a]s a subject of international law, the Catholic Church is an atypical organism. That is to say, considering her particular purpose, the social means she employs to further this purpose and her peculiar nature and social structure, the Church cannot be put on exactly the same level as a State, or any other subject of international law. Hence her position is analogous to, but not identical with, that of a national State."

[12] See Ian Brownlie, *Principles of Public International Law* (5th ed., 1998), 64; accord Malcolm Shaw, *International Law* (Cambridge, 4th ed., 1997), 172; Finn Seyersted, "International Personality of Intergovernmental Organizations: Do Their Capacities Really Depend Upon Their Constitutions," *Indian Journal of International Law* 4 (1964):1, 42, 61.

[13] See Oppenheim, *International Law* 1 §§106, 107, ed. Lauterpacht (8th ed., 1955).

[14] Ibid., §107.

[15] See James Crawford, *The Creation of States in International Law* 154 (1979).

[16] Ibid. In the context of the Holy See, Crawford explains that "[t]he chief peculiarity of the international status of the Vatican City is not size or population—or lack of them—but the unique and complex relation between the City itself and its government, the Holy See."

the Holy See is recognized through diplomatic exchange by 173 states, which have applied Crawford's point clearly to the Holy See.[17]

The history of diplomatic relations and international affairs has demonstrated that the Holy See's sovereignty was not adversely affected by the loss of temporal power when the Papal States were confiscated by and absorbed into the Italian unification of 1870.[18] Just prior to the confiscation, the Italian sovereign acknowledged the independence of the Holy See as "outside the imperium of 'any human power.' "[19] A significant number of states maintained diplomatic relations with the Holy See, which was "for various purposes treated as an international person."[20] Notwithstanding the Lateran Treaty's recognition of the Vatican City State,[21] respected authorities contend that states had conceded the non-territorial sovereignty of the papacy.[22] For example, the Czar of Russia asked for papal support and involvement in the 1898 Hague peace initiative.[23]

---

[17] See "Bilateral and Multilateral Relations of the Holy See," <<www.vatican.va/roman_curia/...0010123_holy-see-relations_en.html>>.

[18] See G. LaPiana, *American Journal of International Law* 25 (1931): 405, 406, reviewing Louis LeFur, *Le Saint-Siège et le Droit des Gens* (1929). As this author argued, "The only usefulness of the creation of an independent Vatican City is in meeting the objection of those who deny the possibility of a sovereignty existing without a territory. . . ." See Crawford, supra note 15, at 157. Crawford argues: "Though some writers denied that the Holy See had any international standing at all after 1870, the true position is that it retained after the annexation of the Papal States what it had always had, a degree of international personality, measured by the extent of its existing legal rights and duties, together with its capacity to conclude treaties and to receive and accredit envoys."

[19] Horace F. Cumbo, "The Holy See and International Law," *International Law Quarterly* 2 (1948–49): 603, 607.

[20] William Bishop, Jr., *International Law* (2d ed., 1962), 218; accord Brownlie, supra note 12, at 64.

[21] See Lateran Treaty of 1929, art. 3 & 4.

[22] For example, in a 1935 decision of the Italian Court of Cassation *(Nanni and Others* v. *Pace and the Sovereign Order of Malta)* noted that independence and sovereignty were never denied to the Holy See even prior to the existence of the Lateran Treaty of 1929. See *Law* (1): 42, ed. Whiteman (U.S. Dept. of State, 1963). See Robert Graham, SJ, *Vatican Diplomacy: A Study of Church and State on the International Plane* (1959), 201–2.

[23] See Cardinale, supra note 1, at 88.

After the First World War, Germany asked the Holy See to participate in and become a member of the League of Nations. Italian
opposition, however, may have prevented this participation.[24]

Though the United States temporarily suspended diplomatic
relations with the Holy See after the 1870s, some of its government
organs continued to recognize it as an international personality of
note. In 1908, the United States Supreme Court acknowledged that
the Holy See "still occupies a recognized position in international
law, of which the courts must take judicial notice."[25] Full diplomatic relations between the Holy See and the United States were
not restored until 1984, yet the U.S. Secretary of State observed in
an 1887 dispatch that "[w]hile the probabilities seem to be almost
entirely against the possibility of the restoration of any temporal
power to the Pope, he is still recognized as a sovereign by many
powers of the world. . . . With all such arrangements this Government abstains from interference or criticism."[26] The Supreme Court

---

[24] Ibid.

[25] *Municipality of Ponce* v. *Roman Catholic Apostolic Church in Porto Rico,* 210
U.S. 296, 318 (1908). The Court then stated: "The Pope, though deprived of
the territorial dominion which he formerly enjoyed, holds, as sovereign pontiff
and head of the Roman Catholic Church, an exceptional position. Though, in
default of territory, he is not a temporal sovereign, he is in many respects
treated as such. He has the right of active and passive legation, and his envoys
of the first class, his apostolic nuncios, are specially privileged. . . . His relations
with the Kingdom of Italy are governed, unilaterally, by the Italian law of May
13, 1871, called 'the law of guarantees,' against which Pius IX and Leo XIII
have not ceased to protest." Idem, 318–19.

[26] John Bassett Moore, *A Digest of International Law* 1 (1906): 39, quoting Dispatch of Mr. Bayard, Secretary of State to Mr. Dwyer (November 7, 1887). The
dispatch continued with instruction that should a diplomat of the United States
be at a court in which the Holy See is also represented, it is the "duty" of the
American diplomat to observe those conventions extended to the papal representative due to the 1815 agreements emerging from the Congress of Vienna.
See Idem. See discussion infra Part IV.A.3, discussing the history of past and
present relations between the Holy See and the United States. In 1984, the
Holy See and the United States reestablished full diplomatic relations. Court
challenges based on the First Amendment of the U.S. Constitution to the
reestablishment of diplomatic relations were dismissed. See discussion infra
notes 216–220 and accompanying text. During World War II, presidents Roosevelt and Truman sent Mr. Myron Taylor as a "personal representative" of the
president of the United States to the Holy See from 1939 to 1949. Mr. Taylor

of the Philippines similarly acknowledged the international personality of the Holy See and its status as a foreign sovereign in a 1994
decision.[27] In light of this, the contention that the Holy See had no
international personality from 1870 to 1929 is "wholly untenable in
the light of the practice of states."[28]

In his 1934 lectures at Oxford University, Professor Mario
Falco reached similar conclusions.[29] The crux of his argument concentrated on the relation between the rights of an entity and its status of international personality. As he argued,

> wherever there are rights there is a person or subject of
> rights; hence it follows that, if positive international law
> recognizes in the Holy See one or more international rights,
> then the Holy See is a legal person in international law. The

---

held the title of "Ambassador." See generally *Wartime Correspondence between
President Roosevelt and Pope Pius XIII* (1947); *Correspondence Between President
Truman and Pope Pius XII*. The first collection contains twenty-seven letters
exchanged between President Roosevelt and Pope Pius XII from December
1939 to November 1944. The neutrality of the Holy See during the war did
not preclude this warm exchange between two world leaders who were both in
search of peace in the world. See Marian Lash Leich, "International Status of
States—The Vatican (Holy See)," *American Journal of International Law* 78
(1984): 427. In a widely cited article appearing in 1952 in *The American Journal of International Law*, Josef Kunz commented that "[t]he protests in the
United States against the nomination by the President of an American Ambassador to the Vatican reveal an astonishing lack of knowledge and understanding of the legal problem of the status of the Holy See in international law."
Josef Kunz, "The Status of the Holy See in International Law," *American Journal of International Law* 46 (1952): 308, 311.

27 See *The Holy See v. Starbright Sales Enterprises, Inc.*, 102 I.L.R. 163 (1994). The
Court in an opinion by J. Quiason stated: "Inasmuch as the Pope prefers to
conduct foreign relations and enter into transactions as The Holy See and not
in the name of the Vatican City, one can conclude that the Pope's own view, it
is The Holy See that is the international person. The Republic of the Philippines has accorded The Holy See the status of a foreign sovereign. The Holy
See, through its Ambassador, the Papal Nuncio, has had diplomatic representations with the Philippine Government since 1957. This appears to be the universal practice in international relations." Idem, 169–70 (citation omitted).

28 Kunz, supra note 26, at 309.

29 See generally Mario Falco, "The Legal Position of the Holy See Before and
After the Lateran Agreements: Two Lectures Delivered at the University of
Oxford" (1935).

existence of some such right . . . is necessary, but it is also sufficient; it is sufficient because the holder's status as a subject of rights is not enhanced or diminished according to the quantity of rights held, and so the fact that the Holy See happens to enjoy a lesser quantity of international rights than is enjoyed by states has no importance. Now the international rights which the predominant doctrine recognizes in the Holy See are the active and passive right of legation and the right of concluding concordats.[30]

A recent investigation of the Holy See's status of international personality declared: "Of course, nobody nowadays doubts that the Roman Church is endowed with an international legal personality."[31] After scrutinizing the "constitutional" and "inter-state systems" of international personality over the centuries, Professor Arangio-Ruiz recognized that the Holy See was a part of evolving law since before the creation of strong nation-states. He concluded that, "international personality . . . has thus been maintained by the Holy See without interruption from the time of the inception of the rules governing international relations up to the present time. It has never been seriously contested and it seems very unlikely that it ever would be."[32] Arangio-Ruiz believes that the Holy See's unique or *sui generis* personality is not restricted to purely spiritual or religious matters.[33] Although the Holy See does enjoy roles that are a part of the sovereignty it exercises, there is

---

[30] Ibid., 15. Falco continues: "In reality the attitude of states in general towards the Holy See proves that they have recognized in the person of the Pope the supreme head of the Catholic religion, who as such possesses not only the highest moral authority but also exceedingly great political influence; hence they have recognized in the Pope one who has the capacity of willing and acting not only in the spiritual sphere but also in the sphere of temporal interests and inter-state relations—an international person." Idem, 16.

[31] Gaetano Arangio-Ruiz, "On the Nature of the International Personality of the Holy See," *Revue Belge de Droit International [R.B.D.I.]* 29 (1996): 354. Arangio-Ruiz hastens to add that the relationship amongst the Church, the Holy See, and the Vatican City State creates some ambiguities and doubts.

[32] Ibid., 360.

[33] Ibid., 362–63.

considerably more that makes it a "power" in the world of international relations. As he stated,

> The truth seems to me to be that the Holy See has become a power among the powers: where by power I understand any entity factually existing as a sovereign and independent unit and participating as such in international relations. This concept has nothing to do with any major or superior military, economic, and/or political power. Despite the lack of "divisions" the Roman Church appears to be, as a moral power, far more powerful than many if not most States.[34]

In the exercise of its international personality, the Holy See identifies itself as possessing an "exceptional nature within the community of nations; as a sovereign subject of international law, it has a mission of an essentially religious and moral order, universal in scope, which is based on minimal territorial dimensions guaranteeing a basis of autonomy for the pastoral ministry of the Sovereign Pontiff."[35] Yet, it would be mistaken to conclude that the Holy See does not view itself as having a role in the world of international

---

[34] Ibid., at 364–65. Professor Arangio-Ruiz continues by saying, "It is hardly necessary to add that, just as there is no real foundation for the alleged 'specialty' of the Holy See's personality there is no foundation for the alleged limitations of the Holy See's legal capacity mentioned by some scholars. If the Holy See has ceased, for example, to participate in military operations, it is because of its lofty inspiration, its own constitution and legal order and its choices, not because of any international legal incapacity." Ibid., at 365–66. I suggest that this certainly goes to the heart of sovereignty; each entity having international legal personality, each subject of international law exercises its own identity formed by its self-determination. In the exercise of its rights and obligations under international law, it looks to no other entity for permission or approval in determining who it is and how it operates within the rule of international law. It alone makes that determination and, as the next discussion illustrates, that is what the Holy See has done.

[35] Shaw, supra note 15, at 172, quoting the Joint 11th and 12th Reports to the United Nations Committee on the Elimination of Racial Discrimination, U.N. Doc. CERD/C/226/Add.6 (1993); accord Summary Record of the 991st Meeting of the Committee on the Elimination of Racial Discrimination, U.N. Doc. CERD/C/SR.991 (1993). The Summary Record of the Committee states in part: "As the supreme governing body of the Catholic Church, the Holy See was recognized as a sovereign subject of international

order concerned with issues of peace, the common good, and the general welfare of all men, women, and children.[36]

A similar argument was advanced by the Second Vatican Council that the Church, and therefore the Holy See, is not only concerned with, but also involved in, the affairs of the world as a consequence of its spiritual and religious mission. As the Council noted in the Pastoral Constitution on the Church in the Modern World, the Holy See "does not lodge its hope in privileges conferred by civil authority. Indeed, it stands ready to renounce the exercise of certain legitimately acquired rights if it becomes clear that their use raises doubt about the sincerity of its witness. . . . "[37] Nonetheless, the Council hastened to add that due to its teaching authority and moral vision for all people throughout the world,

> it is always and everywhere legitimate for her to preach the faith with true freedom, to teach her social doctrine, and to discharge her duty among men without hindrance. She also

law. Its territory, the Vatican City State, was very small, its only function being to guarantee its independence and the free exercise of its religious, moral and pastoral mission. Its participation in international organizations, most notably the United Nations, and its accession to international conventions such as the Convention on the Elimination of All Forms of Racial Discrimination differed profoundly from those of States which were communities in the political and temporal sense." Idem, at no. 2. Professor Falco noted, "It may seem paradoxical, but, although the Church has always taught that sovereignty does not belong to states alone and that spiritual sovereignty is superior to temporal sovereignty, yet the Holy See has never abandoned the principle that a basis of territorial sovereignty is absolutely necessary to it in order to make its independence absolute and visible. Moreover, the Holy see has never been willing to admit that its status and the inviolability and immunity of the Popes could rest upon Italian municipal law, that is to say, upon a unilateral act. For these reasons the Holy See never ceased after 1870 to claim restoration of the temporal power and the settlement of its status by means of a convention." See Falco, "The Legal Position of the Holy See," *supra* note 29, at 17–18.

[36] See Kunz, "The Status of the Holy See in International Law," *supra* note 26, at 310, where Mr. Kunz noted, "The Holy See is . . . a *permanent* subject of *general* customary international law vis-à-vis all states, Catholic or not. That does not mean that the Holy See has the same international status as a sovereign state. But the Holy See has, under general international law, the capacity to conclude agreements with states. . . [be they concordats or general international treaties]." Ibid. (citations omitted).

[37] *Gaudium et Spes,* at no. 76.

has the right to pass moral judgments, *even on matters touching the political order,* whenever basic personal rights or the salvation of souls make such judgments necessary. . . . Holding faithfully to the gospel and exercising her mission in the world, the Church consolidates peace among men, to God's glory. For it is her task to uncover, cherish, and ennoble all that is true, good, and beautiful in the human community.[38]

Before concluding this discussion, one should consider the position of the International Law Commission (ILC) regarding the Holy See's status as an international personality competent to negotiate and enter treaties and other agreements with temporal sovereigns. When the Vienna Convention on the Law of Treaties was in its early draft stages in 1959, the ILC made a number of significant observations about the Holy See. First, it stated that,

[i]t has always been a principle of international law that entities other than States might possess international personality and treaty-making capacity. An example is afforded by the Papacy particularly in the period immediately preceding the Lateran Treaty of 1929, when the Papacy exercised no territorial sovereignty. The Holy See was nevertheless

---

38 Ibid. [Emphasis added.] Toward the conclusion of the Pastoral Constitution, the Council stated, "In pursuit of her divine mission, the Church preaches the gospel to all men and dispenses the treasures of grace. Thus, by imparting knowledge of the divine and natural law, she everywhere contributes to strengthening peace and to placing brotherly relations between individuals and peoples on solid ground. Therefore, to encourage and stimulate cooperation among men, *the Church must be thoroughly present in the midst of the community of nations.* She must achieve such a presence both through her public institutions and through the full and sincere collaboration of all Christians. . . ." Ibid., at no. 89. [Emphasis added.] The views of the Council would thus tend to alter the meaning and the impact of Article 24 of the Lateran Treaty which states: "The Holy See, in relation to the sovereignty it possesses also in the international sphere, declares that it wishes to remain and will remain extraneous to all temporal disputes between States and to international congresses held for such objects, unless the contending parties make concordant appeal to its mission of peace; at the same time reserving the right to exercise its moral and spiritual power. in consequence of this declaration, Vatican City will always and in every case be considered neutral and inviolable territory."

regarded as possessing international treaty-making capacity. Even now, although there is a Vatican State . . . under the territorial sovereignty of the Holy See, treaties . . . are . . . entered into not by reason of territorial sovereignty over the Vatican State, but on behalf of the Holy See, which exists separately from that State.[39]

The ILC reexamined the status of the Holy See a few years later as the drafting of the Convention resumed. When deliberations continued, the ILC noted "that"

> [t]he term "treaty" as used in the draft article covers only international agreements made between two or more States or other subjects of international laws. The phrase "other subjects of international law" is designed to provide for treaties concluded by: . . . (b) the Holy See, which enters into treaties *on the same basis as states.* . . .[40]

In its commentary on Article 3 of the Convention on the Law of Treaties, which addresses "other subjects of international law," the ILC hastened to add that "[t]he phrase 'other subjects of international law' is primarily intended to cover international organizations, to remove any doubt about the Holy See and to leave room for more special cases such as an insurgent community to which a measure of recognition had been accorded."[41]

---

[39] See ¶7 commentary to Article 2 of the Vienna Convention on Treaties, 2 ILC Yearbook, 96, U.N. Doc. A/LN.4/SER.A/1959/ADD.1 (1959); see Crawford, supra note 15, at 158–60 (explains the relation between the Holy See and the Vatican City State). As Professor Crawford suggests: "To some extent the desire to particularize or categorize the relationship between the two entities reduces itself to a semantic dispute. . . . The position would appear to be that the relation is one of State and government, but with the peculiarity that the government in question, the Holy See, has an additional non-territorial status, which is in practice more significant than its status qua government of the City of the Vatican." Idem, 159–60.

[40] See ¶8, commentary to Article 1 of the Vienna Convention on Treaties, 2 ILC Yearbook, 162 (1962) (emphasis added).

[41] See ¶2, commentary to Article 3 of the Vienna Convention on Treaties, 2 ILC Yearbook, 164 (1962).

After the Congress of Vienna in 1815, several important multilateral treaties specifically acknowledged the role and status of the
Holy See as a subject of international law. Treaty references are
compelling evidence demonstrating that the state members of the
international community did not question the status of the Holy
See as a subject of international law but openly accepted this status
as a fact of international law.

At the conclusion of the Congress of Vienna, the eight participating states[42] agreed upon a regulation concerning the precedence
of Diplomatic Agents.[43] These regulations of March 19, 1815,
while brief, revealed several critical points acknowledging the legal
status of the Holy See. The first point is found in Article 1, which
declared that there are three classes of diplomatic agents, and the
first or highest level include "ambassadors, legates or nuncios."[44]
Nuncios are those representatives of the Holy See who are permanent representatives of the pope vested with both political and
ecclesiastical authority and accredited to the court or government of
a sovereign State.[45] The second point is taken from Article 2, which
equates the status of nuncios with ambassadors. The third point
comes from Article 4, which states that the precedence or rank
given to diplomats based on the date of assuming official duties
(usually involving the presentation of credentials) would not in any
way prejudice the precedence accorded to papal representatives.[46]

---

[42] The eight states were Great Britain, Austria, France, Portugal, Prussia, Russia,
Spain, and Sweden. See *Major Peace Treaties of Modern History: 1648–1967*,
ed. Fred L. Israel (1967), vol. 1, 519.

[43] See ibid., 570. Annex VII of the Congress of Vienna refers to these regulations
of March 19, 1815. Ibid., 575. Interestingly, the Congress in Article 103
restored the Papal States, which had briefly been confiscated by Napoleon.
Ibid., 565.

[44] See *The Consolidated Treaty Series 1*, ed. Clive Parry (1815), 64. Article 1,
"Réglement sur le Rang entre les Agents Diplomatiques," which states in pertinent part, "Les Employés Diplomatiques sont partagés en trois Classes. Celle
des Ambassadeurs, Legats ou Nonces." Idem, at 2.

[45] See *The Catholic Encyclopedia Dictionary* (1941), 687; see *Sollicitudo Omnium
Ecclesiarum*, Apostolic Letter of Pope Paul VI, promulgated 24 June 1969, at
no. 10.

[46] Ibid. The original text of Article 4 reads, "Les Employés Diplomatiques pren-
dront Rang entre eux dans chaque Classe, d'après la Date de la Notification

The significance and effect of these regulations concerning diplomatic relations continue to this day. The categories of diplomats, and the precedence that could be given to papal representatives were largely incorporated into the Vienna Convention on Diplomatic Relations of April 14, 1961, and entered into force on April 24, 1964.[47] As with the 1815 Regulations from the Congress of Vienna, the Vienna Convention on Diplomatic Relations divides diplomatic missions into three classifications, the first of which includes ambassadors or nuncios.[48] Like the 1815 Regulations just mentioned, the 1961 Vienna Convention also specifies that precedence (given in the respective classes) is based on the order in which representatives assumed their posts and presented their credentials.[49] However, as with the 1815 Regulations, the 1961 Convention does not discriminate against or interfere with "any practice accepted by the receiving State regarding the precedence of the representative of the Holy See."[50]

---

officielle de leur Arrivé. Le présent Réglement n'apportera aucune innovation relativement aux Représentants du Pape."

[47] Over 170 states are parties to this convention. The Holy See is a part and ratified the convention on April 17, 1964. The convention entered into force on April 24, 1964.

[48] Vienna Convention on Diplomatic Relations, Article 14.1(a). The second class includes envoys, ministers, and internuncios. Article 14.1(b). Internuncios are in the order of pontifical diplomats who are equivalent to the ministers of the second class. See Legates, *The Catholic Encyclopedia* (1910) at <<www.newadvent.org/cathen/09118a.htm>>. Eileen Denza has noted that "Articles 14 to 16 and Article 18 of the Vienna Convention are a restatement in modern terms of the rules enunciated in 1815 by the eight signatories of the Regulation of Vienna: Austria, Spain, France, Great Britain, Portugal, Prussia, Russia, and Sweden." See Eileen Denza, *Diplomatic Law: Commentary on the Vienna Convention on Diplomatic Relations* (1976), 58.

[49] Vienna Convention on Diplomatic Relations, Article 16.1.

[50] Vienna Convention on Diplomatic Relations, Article 16.3. As Eileen Denza points out, "At the Vienna Conference an amendment introduced by the Holy See replaced the word 'existing' by 'accepted', so making clear that States were entitled if they wished to adopt in the future the practice of giving precedence to the representative of the Holy See. This was opposed . . . only by representatives of the Communist states," who abstained in the voting in Committee on this amendment. See Denza, supra note 48, at 97. The amendment of the Holy See was accepted as the final text indicates; moreover, the concerns of "Communist delegations" after 1990 would have begun to disappear.

The consequence of these diplomatic practices, which have spanned almost two hundred years, is this: notwithstanding its status as a unique person in international law, the Holy See deals with virtually all other sovereign states in the world today as a co-equal. The Holy See is respected by the international community of sovereign States and treated as a subject of international law having the capacity to engage in diplomatic relations and to enter into binding agreements with one, several, or many states under international law that are largely geared to establishing and preserving peace in the world. It is unequivocal that the sovereign states of the world acknowledge no impediment in the Holy See's unique status that would deprive it of the ability to exercise fully its membership in the community of sovereigns who are subjects of the law of nations. Its voice in this realm speaks not just for some, but for all of humanity in its quest for peace.

With this understanding of the Holy See's juridical personality and sovereignty in mind, we can proceed to examine in greater detail how it has worked with international organizations in addition to states in the world's efforts to achieve peace and avoid armed conflict. To do this, we must examine the historical development in which the Holy See as an international person exercised its sovereignty to further the cause of peace.

The Holy See and the Ages of Christendom, Absolutism, and the Nation-State

W HILE NEITHER the New Testament nor the earliest Christian tradition contains any systematic teaching on international organizations, both Christianity and many modern international organizations are imbued with the indispensable concept of establishing and maintaining a universal realm of justice and peace. Needless to say, the early Church did not inherit from its Founder a body of doctrine on international relations. But the Church's relevant teaching on this matter contains a concept fundamental to Christianity, namely, that the Church was to unite all humankind in a universal family under the fatherhood of God. The mission of the Church to introduce Christianity to all peoples advanced this concept. Emergent in this idea was a vision of humanity enjoying the reign of *Pax Christi*, in which there would be no hatred, no warfare, no injustice.[1]

At the same time, membership in the Church did not preclude respect for and obedience to civil authority whenever it commanded nothing contrary to the law of God. As St. Paul once stated, "You must obey the governing authorities. Since all government comes

---

[1] John Eppstein, *The Catholic Tradition of the Law of Nations* (London: Burns, Oates, and Washbourne, 1935), Chapter 1 generally.

from god, the civil authorities were appointed by God. . . . The state is there to serve God for your benefit."[2]

The recognition of Christianity by Constantine enabled the Church to encounter and engage without fear of persecution the temporal authorities in a discussion of the use of force and the quest for peace. The nature of a Christian society, the relation of the earthly to the heavenly kingdom, and the legitimacy of the use of armed force by the state were important questions that began to emerge. Though the obligation to strive for peace was paramount, the duty to help those unjustly attacked was stressed, and the just use of force emerged as a social virtue when necessary to defend others in the cause of righteousness.[3]

The development of a just war theory surfaced in the work of St. Augustine a most important thinker on war and peace. His influence is reflected in today's views on the justification of armed conflict.[4] Augustine looked for the criterion not in the citizen but in the individual and in his conscience as open to the will of God, the final arbiter of justice. Augustine's condemnation of wars of conquest and ambition advanced international law.[5] Augustine's authentic emphasis was on amity. In his praise of efforts to settle disputes by reason, he singled out peace as the greatest good of this life by promoting man's natural sociability and cooperation. In his definition of peace as the serenity of order, he linked human tranquillity to the peace of the

---

[2] Romans 13:1, 4a.

[3] Eppstein, supra note 1, at 49–62. Mr. Eppstein's narrative and the original texts he cites in this chapter concern the civic duties of Christians as they began to evolve from the time they were accepted into mainstream society.

[4] See James Brown Scott, *Law, the State, and the International Community* (New York: Columbia University Press, 1939), 184–95; Eppstein, supra note 1, at 65–96, and René Coste, *Le Probléme du Droit de Guerre dans la Pensée de Pie XII* (Paris: Aubier, 1962), 19–60. See generally Jean Bethke Elshtain, *Just War Theory* (New York: New York University Press, 1992); and John Finnis, Joseph Boyle, and Germain Grisez, *Nuclear Deterrence, Morality, and Realism* (London: Oxford University Press, 1987).

[5] Paul Manceaux, *L'Eglise et le Droit de Guerre,* reprinted in Eppstein, supra note 1, at 80.

Heavenly City.[6] *The City of God (De Civitate Dei)* has fittingly been called the "chief source" of the Christian attitude toward peace.[7]

The first centuries of Christianity produced a worldview firmly committed to gentleness, peaceful reconciliation of disputes, the brotherhood of all peoples, and a fundamental yearning for universal community. Yet it was also marked by unresolved ambiguities that allowed war as an instrument to achieve that degree of justice essential to world community without proposing any new institutions for the peaceful settlement of conflict. It was universalist in both sacred and secular spheres without really integrating the two traditions, Christian and pagan, from which this universalism was derived. The result contained the seeds of future tension between just war and the search for peaceful resolution of disputes.

The rise of the papacy as a most important and, perhaps, central agent of pacification and order in feudal Europe had been preceded and was assisted by other elements in the Church. These elements attempted in various ways to mitigate the violence and lawlessness endemic to a society still emerging from its barbarian past. For example, in tenth-century France, local Church councils decreed spiritual penalties for brigandage, while in the eleventh century the *Treuga Dei* (Truce of God) restricted the times when fighting was permitted and the *Pax Dei* (Peace of God) protected non-combatants. Churchmen condemned tournaments and proscribed the crossbow as too deadly a weapon—an early step to ban the use of certain armaments.[8] The ideal of the Christian warrior-hero was counterbalanced by the spread of voluntary pacifism among the growing religious element in society. Precepts of canon law, as codified by Gratian, forbidding clerics from fighting or bearing arms were more strictly enforced. Associations of laymen affiliated with religious orders adopted the same vocation to

---

[6] Ibid., Book XIX, Chapter 11: "The bliss of everlasting peace, which is the fulfillment of the saints"; and Chapter 12: "Peace is the instinctive aim of all creatures, and is even the ultimate purpose of war."

[7] Herbert F. Wright, "St. Augustine on International Peace," *The Catholic World* CV (September 1917): 745.

[8] Georges Goyau, "L'Eglise Catholique et le Droit des Gens," *Recueil des Cours* 6 (1925): 150–57.

non-violence. While such efforts were only partially successful in their goals, this medieval "peace movement" established an important foundation by promoting belief in the abnormality of violence, the superiority of moral over physical power, and the social necessity of peaceful settlement of disputes.

Popes had encouraged these pacific activities and had made concrete these exhortations by mediating conflicts. "The Holy See could not suffer two Christians to draw the sword against one another," wrote William of Malmesbury concerning a papal arbitration of the tenth century.[9] This was an affront to the Church and its Founder. But the papacy also acknowledged that diversion of the military urge to a common defense against Islam would bring both internal peace and external security. As Eppstein has noted:

> But the constant purpose of the Popes from the tenth to the seventeenth century was undoubtedly to stop war and remove the causes of war between Christian princes, in order that Christendom might be saved from the aggressions of the infidel.[10]

At a time when the concept of the state was rudimentary, the unity of the Church provided a concord within society that gave meaning to the *respublica christiana*. As the head of the Church, the pope was the most influential figure in this organic community. He was thus able to fill any political vacuum—a task made necessary by the failure of the Holy Roman Emperor, who was frequently opposed by popes as well as the rulers of the emerging nation-states of Europe.[11]

The authority of the Holy See as supreme mediator in Christendom was generally acknowledged by all classes of society, although particular decisions were resisted and the extreme claims to papal power made by certain curialist writers were often rebutted by imperial or royal counter propaganda. Theory and controversies

---

[9] Quoted in Eppstein, supra note 1, at 156.

[10] Eppstein, supra note 1, at 156.

[11] Gerald F. Benkert, *The Thomistic Conception of International Society* (Washington, D.C.: Catholic University of America Press, 1942), 23–25.

apart, popes claimed and effectively exercised both temporal and spiritual power.

The Holy See exercised the right to supervise the conduct of international relations. Many treaties were concluded under papal mediation and signed in a consecrated place because churchmen had tremendous influence in the negotiations. The bond of religion was invoked as the guaranty of treaty obligations, and so they were subject to papal annulment. The Holy See was the judge of the legal relations between sovereigns and gave orders to terminate wars and submit the disputes to papal decision. Innocent III ordered Philip Augustus and Richard the Lion-Hearted to stop their wars and submit their differences to him.[12] Examples of papal intervention could be multiplied, lending some support to the widely shared opinions that by the time of Innocent III the pope had become "a sort of spiritual emperor of the world,"[13] while the Church in Europe had become an "international state," for it could do anything a state could do.[14]

Still, the duty to prevent war by peaceful settlement was the dominant Christian tradition, pervasive in the Gospels and the conclusion of Augustine himself, who said that it is more glorious to kill war with words than men with the sword *(magis est gloriae ipsa bella occidere verbo quam homines ferro)*.[15] Yet this obligation was neglected by some. Despite the authority of the Holy See, the medieval papal system did not succeed in preventing all war, and so various remedies were proposed for the organization of Christendom on a more rational and legally explicit basis. These were essentially efforts to implement the just war theory by designating an authority empowered to make the final decision as to when the use of arms was licit and to enforce the decision with sanctions.

An early illustration of these plans for abolishing war was proposed during the twelfth century by Gerhohus of Reichersberg and

[12] Ibid., 11–13.
[13] Ibid., 5.
[14] August C. Krey, "The International State of the Middle Ages: Some Reasons for Its Failure," *American Historical Review* XXVIII (October 1922): 7.
[15] Eppstein, supra note 1, at 149.

made the pope the sole arbiter. Assuming the existence of a united Christendom, Gerhohus proposed that the pope should forbid all war, that all differences between princes should be submitted to him, that any party rejecting his decision should be excommunicated and deposed, and that priests should accelerate the deposition by stirring up popular sentiment. The idea was not an isolated bit of extravagance for similar plans were being circulated in France and Germany.[16] This would not be the last scheme to institutionalize the papal role in the arbitration process. Obviously, none of these plans were put into effect, but they indicated the continuing effort to bestow moral authority on a tribunal superior to the temporal authorities.

An early secular international organization was proposed by Pierre Dubois, adviser and supporter of Philip the Fair against Boniface VIII, in his *De Recuperatione Terre Sancte*, written between 1305 and 1307.[17] He advocated a federation of Christian states called the *respublica christiana*, with a council of nations to settle disputes. But here, too, the papacy had a role. The council was to be summoned by the pope at the request of the king of France; the pope was to hold primary rank and could introduce in the first instance proposals to the council; if the council could not settle a dispute, nine judges were to be appointed, with final appeal from this panel to the Holy See.[18] The plan was not attractive, however, except to the French, for the papacy was then in Avignon under French influence.

When Constantinople fell to the Turks in 1453, Christian Europe was threatened. To meet this danger, Georg Podiebrad, king of Bohemia, proposed the organization of the Christian rulers of Europe into a federation or league possessing considerable powers. The first version of this plan placed great emphasis on a crusade in

---

[16] See A. C. F. Beales, *The History of Peace: A Short Account of the Organized Movements for International Peace* (New York: Dial Press, 1931), 22; Goyau, supra note 8, at 162.

[17] Sylvester John Hemleben, *Plans for World Peace through Six Centuries* (Chicago: University of Chicago Press, 1943), 1.

[18] Ibid., 3, and note 12.

which the papacy would assume a leading role. Later versions, however, excluded the pope from the league even though his cooperation was expected.[19] The pope was not numbered among the representatives of the Italian nation, despite the size and influence of the Papal States at the time. However, he was expected to maintain peace among non-members of the league and punish offenders with spiritual penalties. Podiebrad was a Hussite, not a Catholic, which might explain his attitude toward the papacy, but his scheme also expressed the rising power of nationalism. The Holy Roman Emperor, for example, was to be included in the league only as a German king.[20] As Walther Schücking has argued, the exclusion of pope and emperor constituted the essential weakness of the project, for the Empire was experiencing a resurgence of power under Sigismund and the influence of the papacy was still strong in a Europe not yet divided by the Reformation.[21]

By the end of the fifteenth century, nationalism and the secular state were on the rise. Yet the Holy See, which had been the first Western power to make a systematic use of diplomacy designed to promote international peace, adapted to the new situation. Papal diplomacy entered a new phase, and Rome had the first and only organized diplomatic corps during the Renaissance period.[22] Mattingly described this function in the following manner: "From the 1460s on, then, Rome became what it was long to remain, the chief training school and jousting field of diplomacy, the listening post of Italy, the center, above all others, of high political intrigue."[23]

The last international act of the Holy See on the grand medieval scale resulted from the new problem of colonialism in the age of discovery. It was performed by a more than typical Renaissance pope, Alexander VI (1492–1503). At the request of Spain and Portugal, whose colonial competition was leading them to war, Alexander arbitrated their differences over territorial dominion. On

---

[19] Hemleben, supra note 17, 14–15.
[20] Benkert, supra note 11, at 44.
[21] Ibid.
[22] Ibid., 105–6.
[23] Ibid., 106.

May 4, 1493, he issued the bull *Inter Cetera Divinae*, which drew
the famous line around the globe that assigned each nation separate
hemispheres for exploitation, evangelization, and colonization.[24]
His bull foreshadowed the mandate system. It also condemned slavery and other violations of the human rights of the inhabitants, provided for their conversion by preaching and good example, and
prepared for automatic excommunication for offenders of the pope's
instructions.[25] In the Treaty of Tordesillas, signed the following
year, the parties formally agreed to this line of demarcation with
only minor changes. Alexander's arbitration was thus a great success.
But in a changing age, it was like a signpost pointing in two direc-
tions: backward to the Middle Ages where papal power was unsur-
passed, and forward to a new age of conflict in which Europe, the
Church, and the whole international system would experience the
growing power of the emerging nation-states.

The Peace of Augsburg in 1555, with its principle of *cuius regio
eius religio*, marked the end of the medieval community of Christendom as an organic whole. Still, papal emissaries continued to
mediate disputes between Catholic sovereigns, and the unifying role
of the Holy See earned respect even beyond Catholicism. However,
the role of the papacy as leader of a single Christian commonwealth,
the *respublica christiana*, was ending. That commonwealth, and the
papal system which governed it, had demonstrated the importance
of non-material power based on supranational allegiance that tempered state sovereignty. It may have also been that the medieval
experience, precisely because the Church with the Holy See at its
head exercised the functions of an international organization, may
have hindered the development of a secular international organization based on religious pluralism. Still, even with the rise of nationalism and the nationalist state, the Holy See did not abandon the

---

[24] See Sidney Ehler and John Morrall, *Church and State Through the Centuries: A Collection of Historic Documents with Commentaries* (London: Burns and Oates, 1954), 153–59.

[25] Liam Brophy, "The Popes as International Arbitrators," *Social Justice Review* LIX (April 1966): 11–12.

world of diplomacy and international relations. Whilst its role may have been altered, its presence was not.

The political significance of the Protestant Reformation begun at the Peace of Augsburg in 1555, and completed a century later at the Peace of Westphalia in 1648, signaled the gradual weakening of the community of Christendom. The Reformation eroded a Christendom that was unified by a single religion and shared cultural tradition. As a result, the Law of Nations began to change. What happened between Augsburg and Westphalia was that the ideal of an organized Christendom was surrendered to the reality of religious division, and the organic unity based on a common faith dissipated.

The remnant of the community of Christendom was torn by the most profound divisions. The force capable of grounding an institution of political unity was no longer the Church. The once common religious base no longer existed. The former single power to command allegiance was fragmented, and the members were picked up by a multiplicity of independent sovereign states. They were in no mood to surrender their new power, especially their increasing power over the Church and religious institutions within their territorial jurisdictions. In the name of the preservation of their beliefs, many churchmen turned to the recipients of this new power to fight their holy wars for them. Those who did found themselves in danger of accepting implicitly a new doctrine alien to the old notion of an organic community—the doctrine of absolute national sovereignty.

The effect of the political evolution on the relations between Church and state, and thus between the Holy See and the courts of Europe, has been succinctly summarized by Paul Reuter:

> The State was strengthened by the decline of the international role of the Church and by the threat of anarchy which hung over Europe with the religious crisis of Protestantism. The Protestants appealed to the princes, the Catholic Church did the same. It was not only the religious schism which diminished the part played by the Church, but the fact that even in Catholic countries the services rendered to the Church by the State made the former into an ally of the

civil authorities. The Catholic Church did not theoretically abandon its ecumenical position, but its temporal influence diminished, although it still maintained some debatable political positions.[26]

In this new environment, the Church was weakened by the rising spirit of nationalism—not merely by the external threat to its supra-national role coming from royal assertions of power, but even more by the internal threat of the substitution of national loyalty for the spiritual loyalty to Christendom. By eliminating the internal unity of the Church, nationalism diminished Christendom's external role as a force for unity in political life.

The loss of a sense of Christendom and the appearance of new centers of temporal power and loyalty had annihilating intellectual and cultural effects. Garrett Mattingly describes the developing situation and the resulting challenge which confronted the legal theorists who were attempting to grapple with the problem of international organization:

> A chasm was opening in the European tradition. The public law of Christendom was crumbling and sliding into the gap. The theorists . . . had to reshape the familiar concept of a law of nations, a *jus gentium*, governing the relations of individuals and public authorities within the commonwealth of Christendom, into the notion of a law for sovereign states, a law, that is, not of but among nations, a *jus inter gentes*. Although there was never a time when relations within Christendom had not been regarded as under the rule of law, it is literally true that "international law" was something which the publicists of the later Renaissance were obliged to invent.[27]

---

[26] Paul Reuter, *International Institutions* (New York: Rinehart, 1958), 42. While nation-states did reduce the temporal authority of the Holy See, many of these states have come and gone, but the Holy See has persevered.

[27] Garrett Mattingly, *Renaissance Diplomacy* (London: Jonathan Cape, 1955), 284–85.

The *jus gentium* had rested on a foundation of Natural Law (reason), Divine Law (Revelation), and human law (code and custom) collaborating within an integral view of the universe shared by theologians, philosophers, and lawyers alike. In the sixteenth century this collaboration broke down. The enthusiasm of the Renaissance humanists for the glories of Greece and Rome eroded respect for medieval tradition. At the same time, the support of Divine Law fell away because Revelation, instead of unifying western culture, as it once had, was now dividing it. The literal-mindedness and demand for a return to original sources also undermined the authority of the common law. As Mattingly further argues:

> It became useless for publicists to appeal to sanctions of the Church to guarantee treaties or protect ambassadors, or to mitigate the horrors of war. Most Protestants indignantly rejected the suggestion of any earthly sanctions superior to the conscience of their rulers. At the same time Catholics began to contend that restraints once applied universally should not be invoked to protect heretics and rebels. Europe was losing its sense of moral unity. The levers which had moved Western public opinion no longer had a solid fulcrum.[28]

In response, the Council of Trent reasserted the authority of tradition, canon law, and the pope. But "Protestant Europe mocked the Tridentine decrees, and Catholic monarchies received them only tardily and coldly."[29] Meanwhile, the religious ground of the argument had shifted. Catholics and Protestants were compelled by the temper of their time to buttress their theories by quoting the Bible. Since legal publicists were looking for concrete examples of state behavior they excluded consideration of the New Testament, which contains little political history, though much of relevance to peace and genuine international community. Instead they employed the historical parts of the Old Testament, which they accepted,

---

[28] Ibid., 289.
[29] Ibid.

. . . as the record of states like their own and men like
themselves, only more heroic and admirable, having, in the
case of the ancient Jews, so direct a relation to God as to lift
them altogether above criticism. The most potent precedents in international law were drawn, then, from the leg-
ends of a society more savage and barbarous than historic
Greece and Rome.[30]

Old Testament history is marked by fierce tribal exclusiveness and a
self-righteous national egotism. "As the Bible became the common
property of the people of Europe, it was open to any group of them,
national or religious, to imagine themselves, like the ancient Jews,
divinely authorized to any lengths of guile or violence in the pursuit
of their peculiar ends."[31] Nations, churches, and sects (especially
the Puritans) were quite willing to regard themselves as the Chosen
People of God, and the concept of Holy War that would further
divide people received an invigorated momentum.

Since classical and biblical precedents were poor substitutes for
living traditions, influential legal theorists were driven to base their
arguments chiefly on Natural Law. Again, Mattingly states:

The assumption that natural reason induces universal agreement on basic principles of conduct, and the further
assumption that the agreement of all (or most) peoples has
legislative force enabled writers from Vittoria to Grotius to
reestablish the existing rules of *jus gentium* on what they
thought was a Natural Law basis. But the logic of their
arguments depended, really, on the inner coherence of the
Western tradition, just as their eloquence derived its force
from the persistent sentiments of Christendom.[32]

It was here that the Church as an intellectual and social force, rather
than as an actor in politics, continued to contribute to international

---

[30] Ibid., 290.
[31] Ibid.
[32] Ibid., 291.

order by developing the Catholic tradition to meet the challenge of the times.[33] Those who accepted this challenge were given the name of Neo-Scholastic moral theologians, and most were Spanish. The outstanding members of this school were the Dominican Francisco de Vitoria (1480–1546) and the Jesuit Francisco Suárez (1548–1617). The former responded to the egotism of the state—including Catholic temporal sovereigns—with the voice of Christendom. The latter, who lived almost to the Thirty Years War, conceded to the state as much sovereignty as was compatible with the Catholic tradition. Yet one can say—without detracting from the acknowledged role of the Protestant Hugo Grotius (1583–1645)—that both helped to lay the foundations of modern international public law.

Vitoria's entire thought is predicated on the existence of a natural, organic community of mankind governed by a single law, the *jus gentium*, or Law of Nations. While this was a traditional Scholastic position, he developed its implications in his sophisticated writings. In this regard, the following passage captures the essence of his work:

> The Law of Nations does not only derive its force from human contract but also has the force of law. For the whole world which is, in a way a single commonwealth, has the power to make laws which are equitable and applicable to all alike; and such are the precepts to be found in the Law of Nations. . . . Any one kingdom has not the right to refuse to be bound by the Law of Nations: for it has been established by the authority of the whole world.[34]

In his search for the basis of the *jus gentium*, Vitoria elucidated a basic principle of international organization. Reuter describes his contribution in this way:

---

[33] See, e.g., James Brown Scott, *The Spanish Origin of International Law* (Washington, D.C.: Georgetown University School of Foreign Service, 1928).

[34] Francis de Vitoria, "On Civil Power, §21, Question 3, Article 4: Civil laws are binding on legislator," sometimes known as the corollary concerning the binding force of international law, in Eppstein, supra note 1, at 261.

The author held that universal sociability was the fundamental principle of law. All men, by virtue of the *jus com-
municationis*, have the right to enter into relations with each
other. The result is an international community based on
the quality of men. This community is not organised but it
recognizes common interests; for the defence of these interests the princes are in duty bound to undertake just wars.
These are concepts which, despite their origin, remind us of
the principles underlying the modern social sciences. A general system of international relations emerges quite naturally
from these principles, and the author elaborates from them
a precise and vigorous theory of the duties of the colonisers.
The Church preached them without success. Only in the
present day have they found formal expression in the League
of Nations and the United Nations.[35]

On the basis of these principles, Vitoria made an important contribution to the controversy that divided sixteenth-century Spain on
subjecting the Indians of the New World to slavery. Taking up the
protests of Bartolomé de Las Casas (1474–1566) and others against
the practice, he developed a colonial doctrine based on universal
human rights.[36] For Vitoria, colonial conquest was a moral question
and subject to Church authority. He argued that native peoples were
not irrational and were the true owners of the territory they inhabited
regardless of whether they were in the state of grace. Neither the pope
nor the emperor was the civil lord of the world with temporal power
over the Indians. Even if they refused to listen to or accept Christianity, there was no legal or moral justification for attacking, then,
despoiling their property, and converting them by force. It was argued
that the Spaniards had a right to travel and trade in the New World
according to the principle of sociability; furthermore, they had the
right to defend themselves, but they could not enslave the Indians as
a punishment. The only possible justification for their conquest

---

[35] Reuter, supra note 26, at 44.
[36] Scott, *The Spanish Origin of International Law,* supra note 33, at 19–20.

would be as a last resort of self-defense. Such grounds permitting conquest would arise in those situations where the Indians forcibly hindered the peaceful preaching of the Gospel or mistreated Christian converts; to save the Indians from tyranny or nefarious laws and customs, such as human sacrifice; or a voluntary invitation by the Indians to rule over them.[37]

Vitoria hesitated to affirm the principle of mandate, perhaps fearing that it might serve as a pretext for Spanish self-interest. Still, he acknowledged that some right to temporary subjection, but not enslavement, could be deduced from this principle. Since the Indians had no proper laws, magistrates, literature, arts, and other necessities of life, Spain might undertake the administration of their country, so long as this was clearly for the benefit of the indigenous people. Ultimately, however, Vitoria found a secure title for Spanish presence in the New World, since "there are already so many native converts, that it would be neither expedient nor lawful for our sovereign to wash his hands entirely of the administration of the lands in question."[38]

Both Vitoria and Suárez held that it was unlawful to make war "by diversity of religion," and that the only just cause of war was violation of a natural right. The view of Gratian that enemies of the Church could be coerced by war was rejected by the Spanish Neo-Scholastics.[39] In general, the Spanish school developed and tightened up the just war theory without departing from its basic principles. War is odious, though it may be necessary; however, offensive war is a penal act justified by only the gravest injury. Arbitration is required if a competent tribunal exists; the certitude of a just cause is required (except by Suárez) and if it is lacking then arbitrators or mediators must be the source of resolution of disputes.[40]

The distinctive contribution of the Neo-Scholastics was the clarification of the rights of a third party—the general society of

---

[37] John Eppstein has brought together the core principles developed by de Vitoria in his *De Indis*. See, Eppstein, supra note 1, at 432–56.

[38] Ibid., 450–52.

[39] See Eppstein's analysis of the Neo-Scholastic departure from Gratian and his work. Eppstein, supra note 1, at 82–83.

[40] Ibid., 97–123.

peoples. In their view, the only justification of war was that it was for the benefit of natural society and the human race.[41] Thus when Vitoria wrote that if a war is injurious to the world or to Christendom that war is unjust.[42] Thus, he added a new criterion for a just war, namely, the common good of the world. But after Vitoria, this conception escaped almost entirely the thought of the moralists. Cajetan (1469–1534) found the formal justice of war in sovereignty. Suárez provided a theory of jurisdiction of the victim over the aggressor, *ratione delicti,* in which the offender is accountable to no one except the offended.[43]

Vitoria upheld the right of the pope to judge between claims of Christian princes in order to prevent the spiritual evils that are the inevitable result of such wars.[44] Suárez admitted to the same principle, holding that there is rarely a just war between Christian rulers since papal arbitration would generally be available. In his elaboration he stated that "the pontiff sometimes refrains from interposing his authority, lest greater evil should follow." Rulers may then fight for their rights, but "they should be careful, however, that they themselves are not the cause whereby the Pontiff dare not intervene: for then they are not excused from blame."[45]

---

[41] Ibid., 114.

[42] Ibid., 107, 120.

[43] Francisco Suárez, *De Caritate, Disp. XIII* §iv, no. 3, in *Classics of International Law,* Suárez, ed. James Brown Scott (London: Oxford University Press, 1944), 817, where Suárez states, "[A] wrong done to another does not give me the right to avenge him, unless he would be justified in avenging himself and actually proposed to do so. Assuming, however, that these conditions exist, my aid to him is an act of co-operation in a good and just deed; but if [the injured party] does not entertain such a wish, no one else may intervene, since he who committed the wrong has made himself subject not to every one indiscriminately, but only to the person who has been wronged. Wherefore, the assertion made by some writers, that sovereign kings have the power of avenging injuries done in any part of the world, is entirely false, and throws into confusion all the orderly distinctions of jurisdiction; for such power was not [expressly] granted by God and its existence is not to be inferred by any process of reasoning."

[44] See Eppstein, supra note 1, at 164, quoting from *De Indis II,* 16 and *De Potestate Ecclesiae V,* 13.

[45] See Eppstein, supra note 1, at 165, quoting from *De Caritate: De Bello, Sect. II, 5: The arbitral power of the Holy See: guilt of princes who prevent the exercise of it.*

The basic problem facing the Neo-Scholastics, which they never solved, was the reconciliation of the concept of the state as a perfect (independent and self-sufficient) society, and the concept of a single community of mankind, implicit in much of Scholastic philosophy. The tension between the independence and interdependence expressed by these two concepts is evident in the following well-known passage from the *De Legibus* of Suárez, the first sentence of which is inscribed on the wall of the former Council Hall in the Palais des Nations in Geneva:

> The reason for the Law of Nations, under this aspect, is, that the human race, though divided into no matter how many different peoples and nations, has for all that a certain unity, a unity not merely physical, but also in a sense political and moral. This is shown by the natural precept of mutual love and mercy, which extends to all men, including foreigners of every way of thinking. Wherefore, though any one state, republic or kingdom be in itself a perfect community and constant in its members, nevertheless each of the states is also a member, in a certain manner, of the world, so far as the human race is concerned. For none of these communities are ever sufficient unto themselves to such a degree that they do not require some mutual help, society or communication, either to their greater advantage or from moral necessity and need, as is evident from custom. For this reason therefore they need some law whereby they may be directed and rightly ruled in this kind of communication and society.[46]

For all of their insight into sociability and interdependence among states, none of the Neo-Scholastics proposed the creation of an international institution or organization with authority to settle international disputes and keep the peace. Perhaps concerned with the need to preserve the traditional papal prerogative as arbiter, they

---

[46] See Eppstein, supra note 1, at 265, quoting from *De Legibus ac de Deo Legislatore,* Lib. II, Cap. XIX, Par. 9.

seemed content with an unorganized, natural community of states governed by a universally respected Law of Nations, a just war theory, and an accepted obligation to seek papal arbitration of all disputes. The notion of the state as a perfect society held by many at the time had led them to make considerable concessions to the increasing claims of national sovereignty. They preferred to let sovereigns settle disputes and police the world freely, leaving supreme judicial power in the sphere of spiritual and moral persuasion—that is, with the pope—rather than vesting it in an institution of the temporal legal order.

Suárez, who was born two years after Vitoria's death, reflected the trend in the Spanish school by making the greater concession to state sovereignty, firmly supporting each nation's right to declare war to protect justice. This is not to suggest that in his view the state was perfect, for it was not. He argued that a world state or organization having a universal legislative authority to bind all people in the world would be difficult to achieve. It was not necessary because no good of human nature demanded it; it was not expedient because if Aristotle found the government of too large a state difficult, the government of a world state would obviously be impossible.[47] The success of such an institution was contingent on the ability of sovereign states to reach agreement on the existence and rule of a unifying international organization, which may be logical, but which would be difficult to implement. As a result of this position, Suárez had the most dominant and lasting influence of all the Neo-Scholastics over thinkers of the Catholic tradition. Thus, Catholic intellectuals were for three hundred years opposed to or skeptical about projects for world organization. Not until the twentieth century was it generally accepted that the state was no longer self-sufficient enough to constitute a "perfect" society in the traditional sense. Johannes Messner of the University of Vienna, whose *Social Ethics* has had a great influence on modern Catholic thought, suggested that in today's world of nuclear weapons Suárez would insist on the need for an international authority with definite pow-

---

[47] Eppstein, supra note 1, at 290.

ers to prevent war and control armaments. But this authority would by no means constitute a unitary world state.[48]

On the other hand, Mattingly criticizes Vitoria for not facing squarely the problem of national sovereignty. In appealing to a *jus gentium* established by the authority of the whole world and to the common good of that world, Vitoria was "speaking rather to the thirteenth century or the twentieth rather than to his own time."[49] According to Mattingly, Vitoria did not seem to realize that he could not command princes by appealing to accepted ethical principles at a time when the moral consensus of Europe was breaking down. As Mattingly contended:

> The dilemma gives the friar's flights of idealism a more than medieval unreality, and his returns to practicality an almost cynical air. Though he demolished the customary claims of Castile to its American empire with ruthless logic, and spoke up for the natural rights of the Indians as eloquently as Las Casas, in the end he conceded enough rights to the Spanish crown to enable it to do about what it was doing. Though he marshaled all the old pleas against aggressive war with unsurpassed cogency, he still saw war as part of the eternal scheme of things. He never pressed his argument about the moral duty of subjects to refuse to fight in an unjust war and of third party states to help repress it to the point of saying that since no war can be "just" on both sides, then, if men would do their moral duty, there would be no wars at all. And, though Vittoria restated the medieval rejection of an omnicompetent parochial state with a sharpness born of Europe's new experience, his remedies are less practical than Dante's. For the civil power which so much concerned him, his logic never devised a workable bridle.[50]

---

[48] Johannes Messner, *Social Ethics: Natural Law in the Modern World* (St. Louis: B. Herder, 1949), supra note 47, at 517, n. 4.

[49] Mattingly, supra note 27, at 292.

[50] Ibid.

In another of his many insights into the period, Mattingly indicates that the crux of the problem was how the European community was to escape anarchy if no check could be imposed on the absolute monarch and the absolute state.

> In the heat of the religious wars, the two religions which thought of themselves in ecumenical terms both offered solutions which were reformulations of the medieval answer. Both Rome and Geneva invoked against the claim of the State to the final and unquestioning allegiance of its subjects the claim of the Church to a higher allegiance. But the Calvinist solution could be applied only by internal rebellion, and the Catholic one only by the intervention of what many Europeans had come to think of as a foreign power. Each threatened civil war, and the rivalry between them widened the schism in Christendom.[51]

Unfortunately, the Church was unable to render the assistance needed to overcome the dilemma. The problem was no longer the medieval tyrant prince but the new monster that men had created to rule over them, the Leviathan of Hobbes. As Mattingly has suggested, "The real problem of the founders of international law was the one which mocked Job: by a slender line of logic to draw up Leviathan with a fishhook."[52]

In Mattingly's view, Grotius saw the problem more clearly than the Neo-Scholastics. By accepting the concept of absolute sovereignty he was able to argue that it is always in the best interest of the state to accept the rule of law, since to preserve its own existence there must be some set of principles that bind the community of nations. He was adapting his theory to contemporary reality, and Mattingly is proper in pointing out that Grotius cannot be blamed for the breakup of Christendom. Still, the Spanish school also accepted the assumption of an unorganized community of states, dependent for peace and security upon the conscience and goodwill of princes:

---

[51] Ibid., 292–93.
[52] Ibid., 293.

If it is a mistake to believe that in any dynamic society a dependable structure of law can be maintained for long without judges to administer it and police power to enforce it, the error does not begin with Grotius. After the failure of papacy and empire, the law schools had already embraced it. Grotius did no more than adapt and make explicit for his generation the reliance on persuasion which is clear enough in Bartolus. In a world in which the Leviathans were loose, clearly the terms of persuasion had to be altered.[53]

At any rate, the Spanish school could not in conscience go so far as Grotius in altering the terms of persuasion. Their own tradition prevented them from sacrificing the more basic concepts of spiritual freedom, the rights of the Church, the resulting need for limited government, the imperative of a *jus gentium* binding independently of state consent, the primacy of the world common good over particular national interest, and the most basic of all goals, the drawing together of the universal community of mankind. That Grotius became accepted as the father of modern international law disregards the contributions made by the earlier Catholic tradition.

Still, there was a continuity of thought within a larger European tradition. Mattingly acknowledges that Grotius, by abandoning Scholastic arguments unacceptable to Protestant Europe "extended the path marked by St. Thomas and Vittoria toward a more inclusive world community."[54] The tendency of Grotius to secularize the form while retaining the substance of ideas taken from the Neo-Scholastics is illustrated in his most famous work *De Jure Belli ac Pacis* (1625). In it he quoted Luis Molina, a Jesuit priest, who had written a book in 1614 recommending the pope as an international arbitrator. Grotius, however, replaced the pope with a conference of princes to settle disputes.[55] His contribution must be understood in its complete context. While the Spanish school did not save the unity of

---

[53] Ibid., 295.

[54] Mattingly, supra note 27, at 295.

[55] Hugo Grotius, *De Juri Belli ac Pacis,* ed. James Brown Scott (London: Oxford University Press, 1925), Book II, Ch. XXIII, §VIII, 561–63.

Christendom, the peace of Europe, or the freedom of the Indians, neither did Grotius or the Protestant reformers. The Neo-Scholastics exercised a restraining influence on human violence and greed through their contribution to moral theology and international law. In fact, there has been a great renewal of interest in their writings in recent times. When Mattingly wrote that Vitoria spoke more to the twentieth century than to his own, he was himself proof that some in the twentieth century would be listening.[56]

But during the centuries after the Spanish Neo-Scholastics, Catholic teaching on international questions languished. The just war theory, which had arisen from the absence of a supranational authority, was abused. Each state became the judge in its own case and invariably judged itself in the right. The scandal of Christian states warring against each other with the spiritual support of their clergy became tolerated in a comparatively short time and led to a laxity of conscience. What began as a mere conditional right was elevated into a venerated norm. This abuse led to the subordination of the Church to the interest of the nation-state. In post-Reformation times, the Holy See intervened less frequently in international disputes. One justification for this might be that the unity of the Church would be preserved, even at the price of disorder among Christian states. As Robert Bosc has noted, the absence of the Holy See during this period may have also contributed to a stagnation of doctrine on international relations and issues.[57]

There is general agreement that the peace of Westphalia in 1648 virtually ended the old religious Europe and eclipsed the traditional international role of the papacy. The successor of Peter moved from the headship of Christendom to a moral authority, greater neutrality, and more pacifism.[58] Conrad Eckhardt goes so far as to suggest that 1648 marked the "secularization of politics," which

> may be said to have taken place when at the Congress of Westphalia the Catholic and Protestant princes agreed to dis-

---

[56] See supra note 49, and accompanying text.
[57] Robert Bosc, *La Société et l'Eglise* (Paris: Spes, 1968), Tome II, 60.
[58] Herder correspondence, IV (October 1967), 295.

regard the protest of the Pope against the treaties of Münster and Osnabrück, which were, after a long period of turmoil and confusion, to become the fundamental law of Europe.[59]

By way of contrast, Robert Graham contends "The Protestant revolt in the sixteenth century and the treaties of Westphalia in the seventeenth century failed to alter notably the international importance of the Holy See."[60] In Graham's view, various factors were responsible for this: "One of the most important was the intense competition between the rival Catholic houses of Bourbon and Habsburg. The religious stake in the wars of the period was another. . . ." The papacy was still strong in Catholic Europe, and the great monarchs of Europe were Catholic. "There were only a few Protestant rulers enjoying royal rank and thereby entitled to send ambassadors to the major courts."[61]

The contrasting theses of Eckhardt and Graham are not necessarily contradictory. Politics was indeed becoming secularized in the sense of freedom of policy from moral restraint and legitimate criticism from a supranational religious body. However, conscience had not disappeared and religious issues were often pivotal to secular policy. In addition, the Holy See still considered its obligation to act as peacemaker, despite its declining influence, and its efforts were sometimes successful. In illustrating this point, Joseph Müller, author of *Das Friedenswerk der Kirche in den letzten drei Jahrhunderten*, lists seven arbitrations by popes or papal nuncios between 1659 and 1713.[62] The Turkish question kept papal activity alive on the international plane, and gave it some consistency and dignity. Pope Clement XI (1700–1721) attempted peacemaking during the War of the Spanish Succession, but the states still thought of the papacy as another European power. Consequently, the pope was pressured by rival Catholic powers during the war, and since he appeared to

---

[59] Conrad Eckhardt, *The Papacy and World Affairs* (Chicago: University of Chicago Press, 1937), vii.

[60] Robert A. Graham, SJ, *Vatican Diplomacy: A Study of Church and State on the International Plane* (Princeton, NJ: Princeton University Press, 1959), 105.

[61] Ibid., 105–6.

[62] See Eppstein, supra note 1, at 470–74 for a summary in English.

the Protestant-dominated peace congress as having failed in neutrality, he found his claims ignored.

One reason the Holy See was less active internationally during the Age of Absolutism is that it was preoccupied in defending the Church against the claims of absolutist Catholic monarchs. In France, the Bourbons and subservient bishops evolved the theory of Gallicanism, which propounded a quasi-national Church. In Austria, Joseph II attempted to keep the Church in the sacristy, apart from any influence on public affairs, and manipulated it as part of his domestic policy. Also disturbing to Rome was the heresy of Jansenism, a rigorous and ascetical doctrine which attempted to turn Christians from the world. This movement split the Catholic community and challenged papal authority. Catholic monarchs were not necessarily anti-Church, for they wanted and often needed its blessing. In addition, it was important not to alienate the Church because monarchs were anointed by bishops at their coronation, supported the clergy, had royal confessors, and even employed clerics as diplomats. Jesuits were especially prominent in the last two roles, and they acquired a reputation for diplomacy such that even non-Catholic monarchs called on their services. For example, Peter the Great employed Jean-Francois Gerbillon, SJ, to negotiate the Treaty of Nerchinsk in 1689 with K'ang Hsi, the Manchu Emperor of China.[63] But in all this the state was capturing the Church and absolute sovereignty in a practice that undermined the role of the Holy See as peacemaker, challenged its internal ecclesiastical authority, and threatened the existence of the Church as a supranational community.

Yet this was not a period of total decline for the Holy See. Although Rome was losing its universal role in Europe, it was laying the foundation for a new type of papal authority more far-reaching than before. In the sixteenth century, the Church encountered for the first time the peoples of Africa, Asia, and America, and the mis-

---

[63] See Mme. Yves de Thomas de Bossierre, "Le Traité Sino-Russe de Nerchinsk," *Jean-Francois Gerbillon, SJ* (1654–1707) (Leuven: Ferdinand Verbiert Foundation, 1994), 29–42.

sionary movement flourished. Its earliest efforts were cast in a Euro-
centric mold and predicated on the assumption of European cultural superiority and the identification of Christianity with Western
culture. But the Jesuit Alexander Valignano, one of the great successors to St. Francis Xavier, perceived the error of this method and set
about to correct it. In Japan he saw clearly that the missions could
not be established by the force and prestige of the mother country,
but had to be built on love of the people, a local clergy, and forms
of worship that reflected the indigenous culture. This was the famous
method of "adaptation" pursued in China by Matteo Ricci and his
successors, and in India by Robert De Nobili.[64]

In 1622 during the Thirty Years War, there was founded the
Congregation *De Propaganda Fide* (For the Propagation of the
Faith), which supported the new approach of inculturation. Ricci
not only learned Chinese to perfection but mastered the Oriental
classics and gained entry to the circles of scholars and nobles. He
also studied the writings of Confucius and harmonized their ethical
teaching with Christianity. De Nobili did much the same thing in
India, studying Sanskrit, Tamil, and Telugu, learning the religious
thought of Hinduism, and putting on the dress of the Hindu ascetic. He secured papal approval of his methods in 1623.[65] Some
efforts at adaptation of missionary techniques were also made in
Latin America. Especially noteworthy were the Jesuit reductions in
Paraguay, begun in 1609, that became a kind of community development program centuries before western concerns attempted such
enterprises in their own countries.

But these efforts would not survive the eighteenth century. The
policy of adaptation was denounced by other missionaries who considered the Jesuits dangerous innovators, and was finally discontinued by the condemnation of the Chinese and Malabar rites. The
opponents of adaptation had powerful and influential friends in
Rome.[66] European pride resented the honor given alien cultures.

---

[64] Jerome D'Souza, SJ. *The Church and Civilization* (Garden City, NJ: Doubleday, 1967), 73–90.
[65] Ibid., 79–81.
[66] Ibid., 91–104.

Ironically, the Church in Europe was in a crisis of stagnation caused by the growth of disbelief during the Enlightenment. So the Baroque burst of vitality in world missionary activity did not last. Like the international teaching of Vitoria and the Jesuits, it would have to pass on in order to bear fruit. Nonetheless, this first creative contact with what is now called the Third World would not be forgotten, and would generally serve the Church well during the renewed interest in international development of the twentieth century.

Meanwhile, the growth of absolute sovereignty as the basis of European public law did not put a stop to the recurrent proposals for world organization produced by western civilization. Nor was the Holy See eliminated from many such plans. In a work titled *Le Nouveau Cynée* (1623), the French monk Emeric Crucé initiated some ideas about early international organizations and proposed an assembly of permanent representatives to decide disputes among nations.[67] On the delicate question of primacy within diplomatic relations, Crucé decided to accord it to the pope, who should also initiate the movement for the abolition of war.[68] This was the earliest completed plan for a worldwide organization that embraced both Christian and non-Christian nations.[69] It is better known as the Grand Design of Henry IV of France, attributed by many to his chief minister, Sully. It appeared in two volumes revised in 1638 with two more published in 1662. The Grand Design proposed the reorganization of Europe with a general council to resolve disputes. The papacy was included as one of the five elective monarchies (there were also six hereditary monarchies and four republics). Significantly, the plan assigned the pope no particular spiritual role. Europe was to be divided into three religious zones, Catholic, Protestant, and Reformed (Calvinist), and these faiths were to be securely

[67] *The New Cynée of Emeric Crucé,* ed. Thomas Willing Balch (Philadelphia: Allen Lane & Scott, 1909), 102, 104.
[68] Ibid., 106. It is interesting to note that the primacy of papal legates in some contexts was recognized by the Congress of Vienna and the 1963 Vienna Convention on Diplomatic Relations.
[69] Sylvester John Hemleben, *Plans for World Peace through Six Centuries* (Chicago: University of Chicago Press, 1943), 21–31; Eppstein, supra note 1, at 294–98.

established in each area. The ulterior purpose of the Grand Design would seem to have been to destroy the power of the Habsburgs so that France would be sure of her place in Europe.[70]

Of the many peace plans originating outside the Catholic tradition, that of William Penn is perhaps most in harmony with its spirit.[71] But the plan of the Protestant Leibnitz provided a role for the Holy See. In a pseudonymous Latin work of 1678, *Caesrinus Furstenerius,*[72] Leibnitz advocated a permanent council of the Christian community and a public authority issuing from the pope and the emperor to direct the temporal and spiritual affairs of Europe. The proposal was essentially for a restoration of medieval Christendom, despite the Reformation, against the common enemy, the Turk.[73] Leibnitz wrote later in 1693 that the pope's concern for Christian discipline shown in interventions with princes had prevented numerous evils. Admitting that like all human things this international power of the papacy had been corrupted by certain abuses, he still saw much good in the body of Christendom.[74] However, he later wrote to a friend that his proposal had little chance of being adopted unless the pope could get everyone to accept papal authority.[75] That Leibnitz should suggest such a plan is interesting in itself for it illustrates the continuing appreciation of the international role of the Holy See in influential Protestant circles.

One of the better known peace plans of the eighteenth century was that of the Abbe de Saint-Pierre, whose *Projet de Paix Perpetuelle* appeared in several editions between 1713 and 1738. Based on the Grand Design, the plan proposed a senate of Europe in which the pope would be represented, but only as sovereign of the Papal States.[76] Though a priest, the Abbe de Saint-Pierre was not a typical Catholic thinker, showing the influence of the Enlightenment's

---

[70] Hemleben, supra note 69, at 34–39.
[71] Eppstein, supra note 1, at 291–93.
[72] Georges Goyau, "L'Eglise Catholique et le Droit des Gens" *Recueil Des Cours* 6 (1925): 211.
[73] Hemleben, supra note 69, at 66 n. 94.
[74] Goyau, supra note 72, at 211–12.
[75] Ibid.
[76] Hemleben, supra note 69, at 62 n. 74.

complacent belief in human progress.[77] His work anticipated many liberal aspirations of the next two centuries, and heavily influenced Rousseau, who himself proposed a commonwealth of Europe in which nineteen sovereigns, including the pope, would each have an equal voice.[78] These plans interestingly included the pope solely as a temporal monarch. Ironically, it was Voltaire who reminded Europe of the spiritual role of the papacy in international politics when he said,

> The interest of the human race requires a power to restrain sovereigns and to watch over the life of nations. That restraining power of religion could be, by general consent, placed in the hands of the Popes, who, reminding kings and people of their duties and condemning their crimes, would be regarded as images of God on earth.[79]

Coming from the outstanding representative of the Enlightenment's hatred for the Church and the whole supernatural order—as reflected by Deism, rationalism, Freemasonry, and the Encyclopedists—Voltaire's remarks constitute an effective testimonial to the hardiness of the notion, perennial in Western civilization, that the pope should act as the conscience and judge of nations.

The eighteenth century saw the Church suffer a loss of influence on society, and the international role of the Holy See reached a low point. Rome found itself exhausted in its efforts to preserve neutrality between Habsburgs and Bourbons, and it struggled to preserve its supranational authority against movements like Josephism in Austria and Febronianism in Germany toward quasi-national churches that were confined to the sacristy and run from the court. In addition, the papacy lost one of its strongest supports when it was forced by

---

[77] Jacques Hodé, *L'Idée de Fédération International dans l'Histoire: Les Précurseurs de la Société des Nations* (Paris: Editions de la Vie Universitaire, 1921), 66–67, n. 94.

[78] Hemleben, supra note 69, at 76, n. 136; Georges Goyau, *L'Eglise Libre dans l'Europe Libre* (Paris: Perrin, 1920), 211.

[79] Quoted in Liam Brophy, "The Popes as International Arbitrators," *Social Justice Review* 59, no. 1 (April 1966): 10.

pressures from the Bourbon courts of Europe to suppress the Society of Jesus. Further illustrative of the problem was the ineffectiveness of the Holy See at the first partition of Poland in 1772. After offering public prayers and pleading with the powers to respect the religious freedom of their new subjects, the pope obtained a promise from Maria Theresa that Austria would give up her share of Poland if Prussia and Russia did likewise. When this commitment was conveniently forgotten, all that Cardinal Secretary of State Pallavicini could do was instruct the nuncio in Vienna to raise the matter "in such a manner as not in any way to excite the susceptibilities attached to such a delicate question."[80] The Church was to face even greater problems in France.

The French Revolution attacked the Church as upholder of the *ancien regime* and enemy of the rights of man. Ironically, many who manned the barricades to secure those rights were actually drawing inspiration from a Christian tradition long forgotten. But the Church's difficulties and sufferings in the French context were vastly outweighed by the ideological and political excesses of the Revolution as a whole, which shocked even advocates of reform by its virulent attempt to destroy not only absolutism, but the fabric of Western civilization. As the Revolution was exported and the peace of Europe threatened, there was a new appreciation of the established role of the papacy as protector of traditional values and mobilizer of Christendom. A common bond was needed to hold Europe together, said William Pitt to the Bishop of Arras in 1794, and only the papacy could play this central role. If its authority could recover its lost prestige, the Holy See alone among the powers would be able to speak out with impartial effectiveness.[81]

But Pope Pius VI (1775–1799) would be in no position to fulfill this role. France invaded the Papal States in 1796 and two years later set up a revolutionary Roman republic. The pope was carried off to Valence where he died in exile, but Napoleon restored a portion of the Papal States to his successor, Pius VII (1800–1823).

---

[80] Goyau, supra note 72, at 214–15.
[81] Eppstein, supra note 1, at 192.

Under the Concordat of 1801, the secular government was to have a role in the nomination of bishops. The Holy See would surrender all claims to confiscated Church property already sold, and the liberties (from Rome) claimed by the Gallican Church were reinforced.[82] Friction developed over the working of the Concordat and with the further reduction of the papal territories. The pope's refusal to support the continental system of blockade against Britain intensified the deterioration of relations with France. With this papal rejection of the anti-British strategy, France invaded Rome and annexed the Papal States entirely. Pius retaliated by excommunicating Napoleon, who then had the pope arrested and removed to France. But Pius VII gained prestige for the papacy through all of this by his patience and dignity in suffering and his refusal to support Napoleon's appetite for conquest. The Concordat, furthermore, made evident Napoleon's conviction that he could not do without the support of the Church in France, for which Rome's cooperation was essential. This need was reinforced by Article 6 of the Concordat that required some holders of ecclesiastical office to profess an oath of fidelity to the secular government. Fortunately for the Church, this pope would outlive the threats of both the Revolution and Napoleonic Caesarism.

The regenerated prestige of the papacy was evident at the Congress of Vienna in 1815. Through the change of climate and the skill of Cardinal Consalvi, there was brought about the restoration of the Papal States and a confirmation of the long-standing custom that the apostolic nuncio, regardless of his personal seniority, should take precedence and be dean of the diplomatic corps. This provision would survive and find its way into the 1963 Vienna Convention on Diplomatic Relations. The Congress of Vienna was the last great international political assembly to which the Holy See would be invited until the twentieth century.

The pope was not asked to join the Holy Alliance proposed by Alexander I of Russia in which the reciprocal relations of the powers

---

[82] See *The Controversial Concordats: The Vatican's Relations with Napoleon, Mussolini, and Hitler,* ed. Frank Coppa (The Catholic University of America Press, 1999), 191–93.

were to be guided by "the sublime truths which the holy religion of our Savior teaches."[83] But Pius VII presumably did not need the Czar to explain Christian principles of government and may have refused an invitation had one been offered. At any rate, he joined the British King and the Ottoman Sultan as one of the three European sovereigns who remained aloof.[84] Without passing judgment on the sincerity of Alexander's religiously oriented proposal, and despite the insincerity which it occasioned, one can still see in it a recurrence of the theme of Christendom in international politics. However, due to the fact that the origin of this initiative was rooted in Orthodox inspiration, one may fairly presume that Moscow desired to exercise its influence as another "Rome." The first Rome was thus not a potential ally in this enterprise.[85]

The Holy See would clearly not be a participant in the Concert of Europe. However, at the Congress of Troppau in 1820, Metternich and the Russian minister both advocated the intervention of the Holy See with the King of Naples, after revolution had broken out.[86] The incident demonstrated that in the eyes of some European powers the Holy See could provide useful assistance, but only when necessary. The pope would not be invited to the Congress of Paris in 1856 or the Conference of Berlin in 1878, although both of these conferences discussed the means of persuading Turkey to respect the rights of its Christian subjects, which was clearly a religious issue of concern to the Holy See.[87] In fact, the Holy See would have to defend strenuously the right of religious freedom even in the so-called Catholic countries against attacks from the remnants of absolutism during the nineteenth century. Pius VII entered this struggle at the international level by expanding the policy begun with Napoleon of signing concordats to specify and guarantee as much freedom for the Church as possible. Even then, this period would be characterized by dangerous Church–state tensions.

---

[83] Hemleben, supra note 69, at 98.

[84] Ibid., 99.

[85] Ibid., 100.

[86] Goyau, supra note 72, at 218–20.

[87] Eckhardt, supra note 59, at 237.

After the defeat of Napoleon, amid a general reaction to revolutionary violence and war, there was a "remarkable return among political philosophers to a respect for medieval unity and the specific power of the Papacy."[88] Early Romanticism initiated a Gothic revival that had more respect for Christianity than had the Age of Reason. St. Simon revived esteem for medieval unity and opposed the balance of power system. Joseph de Maistre went so far as to propose in *Du Pape* (1819) and *Les Soirees de Saint-Petersbourg* (1821) that the world should be ruled by the pope absolutely as spiritual sovereign, and that no temporal ruler have an independent authority.[89] The nostalgia for reestablishment of papal power in such proposals should not obscure their importance. They offered signs of intelligent opinion reevaluating the Church's medieval heritage. Thus began a long journey through a century of nationalism toward a new esteem for international organization built upon the contributions of the medieval Church.

The transition, however, would prove not to be an easy or painless one. The Church and much of the secular world were not well prepared by their traditions, and certainly not by medieval nostalgia, to face the emerging problems of international life. With the mass conscription begun by France in 1792 and the steady rise of the politics of nationalism, the very nature of war had changed. There were no longer dynastic or territorial quarrels involving professional armies taking casualties in the hundreds. They became mass slaughter consuming entire peoples. The politics of nationalism was, furthermore, endowed with a kind of mystical fervor that made it impervious to the limitations on war previously imposed by the Church. The Catholic tradition had yet to incorporate into its universalism a coherent theory of nationality. Meanwhile, the captivating fervor of nationalism had carried away many Christians to the point where their religion became more an ethnic heritage of reverence for a *patria* than a fidelity to the universal Kingdom of

---

[88] Eppstein, supra note 1, at 192.
[89] Goyau, supra note 72, at 218. See Joseph Burnhart, *The Vatican as a World Power* (London: Longmans, 1939), 347.

Christ. In addition, the increasing power of the nation-state in the realm of belief was coveted by liberal and conservative elements as the most potent weapon available in the ideological struggles that racked the Church and society.

Despite the restoration of a French monarchy in 1815, the ideological forces emerging from the Enlightenment and the French Revolution were still strong. They have been summed up by many historians under the rubric of "Liberalism." This was not the progressive and tolerant liberalism of a later age, but a political philosophy that was antireligious, ferociously anticlerical, morally libertarian, and ready to suppress religious freedom in the name of its aggressively held ideals of liberty and democracy. With the universities taken over by the state and the religious teaching orders at their lowest concentration ever, the Church had lost the intellectual resources needed to meet this challenge either in disputation or dialogue. Although a kind of Catholic restoration soon began—the Jesuits were restored in 1814, the Catholic University of Louvain in 1834—its fruits would not come until later. The ideological struggle only increased the firmness of Catholic thought during the pontificate of Pius IX.

However, that century did produce one outstanding and creative theorist of international relations in the Catholic tradition who was strangely overlooked by historians as well as the general public. The Italian Jesuit Luigi Taparelli d'Azeglio (1793–1862) developed a complete theory of international organization in his most important work, the *Saggio teoretico di diritto naturale appogiato sul fatto (Theoretical Essay on Natural Law Based on the Facts)*. This important achievement first appeared in Palermo in the early 1840s and constituted a significant if unheralded contribution to modern political philosophy. Taparelli was familiar with both secular authors, such as Grotius, Machiavelli, and Montesquieu, and the Scholastic and Neo-Scholastic authors.

The sixth book of the *Saggio* is devoted to the principles of international law and established a foundation for all international relations as based on the principle of benevolent sociability among peoples postulated by the community of human nature. Taparelli made an explicit connection between the just war theory, which he updated and made more humane, and the current states of organization in international society of the era. As long as international society remained unorganized, each state possessed the right of war. But once an established and recognized international authority existed, it has the power to impose its will against the unfettered sovereignty of the state. The state would then cede its right to the authority, and war would be restricted to international police operations.[90]

Taparelli's most original contribution was the affirmation of the existence of a social community among nations with a common good that must be safeguarded. This community was necessarily endowed with the authority to survive. In order that this authority be exercised for the common good, nations had to create an organ armed with the necessary powers, which he called an ethnarchy. It would possess and exercise power over peoples, but it would also be a polyarchy because it would govern a collectivity of powers. This organ of administration would have a number of responsibilities. It would protect the peace, exercise guardianship of the rights of all, procure peaceful settlement of disputes, proceed if necessary to coercive measures with authority of justice against transgressors of law, and favor general reduction of armaments and military expenditures by collective guarantees of common security. In Taparelli's view such an organization would be in the interest of the greatest number. Consequently, by combining self-interest with right, this organization could determine the forms of order which are most in harmony with the needs of society. In time, there would be established a universal, international, federal tribunal which would replace the alliances, congresses, and treaties of the time, just as the political initiatives of the modern era replaced the supreme authority of the emperors and the patriarchal government of the popes.[91]

---

[90] See Eppstein, supra note 1, at 133–37, for the relevant excerpts from Taparelli in English. Unfortunately, Taparelli's important work, while appearing in other languages, has not been translated into English.

[91] Ibid., 135–36.

Taparelli's ethnarchy was neither a state nor a super-state. Under his scheme, the proper independence of nations would be respected. Anticipating the principle of subsidiarity, he wrote,

> To avoid all ambiguity, we will recall only that the word *govern* does not mean *do a thing oneself*, but signifies especially to act so that others act according to their nature and their qualities. *To govern a society of nations* will be, then, *to act so that* these nations, through the intermediary of their legitimate authorities and in the threefold order of *knowledge*, *volition* and *execution*, develop for themselves the *forms* which can best contribute to the common good.[92]

Taparelli also discussed the legislative, judicial, and coercive powers of the ethnarchic authority, the codification of international law, and developed sanctions to guarantee respect for both. He was under no illusion that such an organization would be soon realized, but he retained his conviction that "a day will come when humanity will accomplish this magnificent unity of the universal society which is in the designs of providence and the deepest tendencies of our nature."[93]

The *Saggio* drew little attention when it first appeared, and it did not modify the traditional moral teaching on the just war. But Taparelli nevertheless supplied an exceptional advancement in just war theory. While he is little known, even to Catholics, he inspired many of the positions taken by popes Leo XIII, Benedict XV, Pius XI, and Pius XII in favor of an international organization of states,

[92] Luigi Taparelli d'Azelio, *Essai Théorique de Droit Naturel* (Paris: Libraire Internationale-Catholique, 1875), no. 1389, at 72, which reads in part, "Nous rappellerons seulement pour éviter toute ambiguité, que le mot *gouverner* ne signifie pas *exécuter une chose par soi-même*, mais signifie surtout *faire en sorte* que les autres agissent d'après leur nature et leurs qualités . . . ; *gouverner une société de nations* sera donc faire en sorte que ces nations se donnent à elles-mêmes, par l'intermédiaire de leurs autorités légitimes, et dans le triple ordre de la *connaissance* de la *volonté* et de *l'exécution*, les *formes* qui peuvent le mieux contribuer au bien commun." [Italics in the original.]

[93] Ibid., no. 1401, at 81, which states in part, "un jour viendra où l'humanité réalisera cette magnifique unité de la société universelle, qui est dans les desseins de la Providence et dans les plus intimes tendances de notre nature. . . ."

arbitration, and the reduction of armaments.[94] The concepts contained in the *Saggio* moved imperceptibly from the realm of pure theory to that of policymaking, and they became the basis of papal attitudes toward international organization for over a century.

There is little evidence that Pope Pius IX (1846–1878) was influenced by the thought of Taparelli. But Pius IX was necessarily preoccupied with Italian affairs and the loss of the Papal States in 1870. He was initially greeted as a progressive upon his accession, and he substantively sought to reform the autocratic administration of the Papal States by granting a more liberal constitution in 1848. But in that year the tide of revolution swept over Europe, and the first war of liberation of the Italian provinces under alien domination broke out. Maurice Vaussard wrote that "Pius IX as an Italian patriot was inclined to favor unification and promised that pontifical troops would join those of Piedmont to liberate Lombardy-Venetia from Austria, but that as pope his duty was something else: after having committed his army, Pius reversed his decision. . . ."[95] It was a fateful decision made under tremendous pressures. That he needed the Papal States to be fully pope would not be borne out by history, as Paul VI acknowledged in his October 1965 address before the United Nations.

Despite the turmoil in Italy, the long reign of Pius IX was a time of spiritual growth in the Church. There was also a growth in the power of the Holy See as central ecclesiastical authority. Pius used the reaction against the revolutions of 1848 to obtain several concordats favorable to Rome. In addition, he reestablished the hierarchies of England and Holland. Still, the temporal power remained under challenge from the Risorgimento.

It has been suggested that the First Vatican Council was convened in 1869 to promote papal infallibility.[96] While this may be

---

[94] René Coste, *Morale Internationale, L'Humanité à la recherche de Son âme* (Paris: Desclée, 1964), 69–70.

[95] Maurice Vaussard, "L'Eglise Catholique, La Guerre et la Paix" in *Guerre et Paix* (Lyon: Chronique Social de France, 1953), 123.

[96] For an in-depth examination of this issue, see Cuthbert Butler, OSB, *The Vatican Council: The Story Told From Inside in Bishop Ullathorne's Letters,* 2 volumes (London: Longmans Green & Co., 1930).

debated, there is another issue that came before the Council that had major international significance and enhanced the Holy See in world politics. The Council began to review the Church's teaching on war and peace. The proposal under examination would put the authority of the Church behind a strengthened Law of Nations. This attempt was due largely to the efforts of an extraordinary English Protestant, David Urquhart (1805–1877), a firm believer in the Church as a juridical bulwark of peace. In September, 1868, a group of English Catholics had asked for the creation in Rome of a college to teach and disseminate the Law of Nations and on occasion act as an arbiter of international disputes. Urquhart was behind this move, and in the following year he appealed to Pius IX to use the authority of the Catholic Church to restore the Law of Nations through a proclamation by the forthcoming Council, for no other authority could achieve this goal.[97]

With the help of his many Catholic friends, Urquhart persuaded the Armenian Patriarchal Synod to pass a petition to the Council supporting the declaration of the Law of Nations, which became the basis for two *postulata*, one in Arabic and another in Latin.[98] The latter, *De re Militari et Bello,* was signed by forty bishops under the leadership of Cardinal Manning, and proposed to the Council on February 10, 1870. It is strong evidence that the Church, rather than temporal authorities, was awakening to the desperate need to resolve international conflict through due process of law rather than through the carnage of armed conflict. It stated in part:

> The present condition of the world has assuredly become intolerable on account of huge standing and conscript armies. The nations groan under the burden of the expense of maintaining them. The spirit of irreligion and the forgetfulness of law in international affairs open an altogether readier way for the beginning of illegal and unjust wars, or rather hideous massacres spreading far and wide. On the one hand, help for

---

[97] See David Urquhart, *Appel d'Un Protestant au Pape pour le Retablissement du Droit Public des Nations* (Paris: Charles Douniol, 1869).

[98] Eppstein, supra note 1, at 130.

the poor has been curtailed and trade cannot pursue its course; on the other, man's conscience has become distorted or perverted or grievously weakened and numbers of souls indeed are going to eternal ruin. Now the Church alone can heal evils so serious. Even though not everyone may listen to her voice, yet she will always stand out as a leader to number-less thousands and sooner or later gain a hearing. Moreover, the assertion of divine principles in itself is a vindication of the Divine Majesty and must gain its own reward. Of this function of the Church in the world, as far as these truths are concerned, serious men experienced in public affairs are of the same opinion as not a few others who are noted for their sanctity and are animated by zeal for religion. They are per-suaded that there is an extreme need for a pronouncement in which those parts of the Canon Law, which concern the rights of nations and all those principles which determine whether war is a duty or a crime, should be authoritatively promulgated. When by this act the moral conscience of man has been revived, then shall we see perils already most immi-nent removed, a consummation impossible to expect from mere earthly wisdom and political action.[99]

This petition requested a declaration about traditional just war theory as viewed and understood through the lens of canon law that was, at the time, still uncodified. Eppstein noted that the *postulatum* belonged to a school of thought less developed than that of Taparelli, for it had not yet integrated the problem of war into the problem of an effective society of nations.[100] The *De re Militari et Bello* consti-tuted a notable effort to involve the Council and the pope in a forth-right statement on the problem of war. It marked a distinct advance in Catholic consciousness of the Church's responsibility to protest war and declare the moral law in international affairs.

As far as the Council was concerned, the *postulatum* gained adherents steadily with the help of the Eastern bishops, despite

---

[99] Ibid., 132.
[100] Ibid., 130.

opposition from the Gallican faction. Urquhart, soon known as its promoter and editor, was favorably received by Pius IX at an audience in February, 1870. Petitions were solicited from all over the world asking the pope to declare the Law of Nations, and the *postulatum* was accepted by the appropriate commission.[101] But it would never be acted upon. On 15 July, 1870 the Franco-Prussian War broke out. Three days later the dogma of papal infallibility was speedily proclaimed, having been given urgent priority over all other matters. Four days later the pope offered to mediate between Prussia and France, but his proposal was refused. On August 19 French troops were withdrawn from Rome, and on September 20 Victor Emmanuel entered the Eternal City.[102] After a plebiscite, the king annexed Rome as the capital of Italy. On October 20 the Council was prorogued indefinitely by Pope Pius IX and further action on the *postulatum* was impossible. There is an irony in the events surrounding the conclusion of the Council. Being unable to present a final document on the morality of war, the Council was itself prematurely and abruptly dissolved because of war.

The events of 1870 marked a turning point in Catholic history, spiritual and temporal. They presented new or renewed conflicts with the papacy. Austria annulled its concordat even before the Council was over, and the *Kulturkampf* was unleashed in Germany. The loss of the Papal States was mourned as a victory for anticlerical liberalism and a threat to the sovereignty of the pope and the international role of the Church. However, the loss of temporal power by the pope and his self-imposed imprisonment in the Vatican won him sympathy and new respect as a purely spiritual leader, freed from the unnecessary secular burden and religious liability of acting as a temporal sovereign in the European state system. These events, the culmination of centuries of uncertainty, finally provoked a fundamental rethinking of the structure of the Church and its function in the world, particularly the international position of the Holy See.

---

[101] See J. B. Bury, *History of the Papacy in the Nineteenth Century* (New York: Schocken Books, 1964), 72–73.

[102] Butler, supra note 96, at 166–67.

But the departure of its extensive temporal sovereignty did not, as we shall see, deprive the Holy See of its far-reaching role as a unique international personality exercising an equally distinctive sovereignty. As the next chapter demonstrates, the papacy of Leo XIII, Pius IX's successor, would demonstrate that the Holy See retained and exercised its broad moral authority—an effective tool in the international quest for peace.

The Holy See in an Age of Transition: 1870–1914

THE LOSS of its temporal sovereignty in 1870 posed a great challenge to the international position of the Holy See. Despite the past efforts of popes to assert their spiritual role, much of their influence had been exercised as a temporal sovereign among sovereigns in the secular order of interstate politics. It was not a role desired by the papacy, but one to which it had been reduced by the forces of absolutism and nationalism that began to emerge in the sixteenth century. The last years of Pius IX saw the international influence of the Holy See momentarily decline. There was a sentiment that agreed with the demeaning remark that the future function of the papacy would be to serve as "chaplains to the House of Savoy." This undoubtedly delighted some proponents of Realpolitik who wished to eliminate the moral voice of the Church and the peacemaking activity of the Holy See at the international level.

The problem was heightened (though also clarified) by the fact that Pope Pius IX had rejected a solution offered by the Italian Law of Guaranties, which on May 13, 1871, decreed that the pope was to enjoy all of his former prerogatives, recognition as a sovereign, and his traditional leadership in the Church. Representatives of foreign powers at the Vatican were conceded diplomatic rights and immunities, and the pope was to receive from the Italian treasury the equivalent of his previous income from the Papal States. Furthermore, the pope was left in full enjoyment of the Vatican and other properties in Italy with rights of extraterritoriality. But this legislation had no guaranteed standing or acceptance in international law. In addition, it could be annulled by any Italian government in the future, thereby subjecting the spiritual, sovereign independence of the Holy See to the pleasure of a secular state. The refusal of Pius IX, who was styled as the "prisoner of the Vatican," had the prudential advantage of underlining the independence of the Holy See from Italy. This was buttressed by his protest against the usurpation of papal territory and by a diplomatic rupture with the Quirinal.[1] The dispute, which came to be known as the "Roman Question," would not be settled until the conclusion of the Lateran Treaty in 1929 and raised some questions about the effectiveness of the Holy See as a force for world peace for several decades.

The problem was both political and legal, and its solution would rest in a multiplicity of sources—spiritual, ideological, and social. But the legal aspects must not be overlooked because there was a challenge to the very existence of the Holy See as an international juridical entity. International public law had come to be dominated during the late nineteenth century by the positivist school, which held that only states were sovereign and that territory was an essential attribute of the state. Some positivists concluded that the Holy See, having lost its territory, had also lost an essential component of sovereignty, and thus its international juridical personality was terminated. Although this position was held by some, the fact is that the Holy See continued to maintain diplomatic relations. Moreover, the pope as head of the Church vis-à-vis temporal sovereigns had antedated the diplomatic relations between temporal sovereigns themselves.

After the dissolution of the *respublica christiana*, the Holy See continued to be a subject of international law with full juridical personality, despite some growing opposition to the juridical integration of the Church in the international community after the Peace of Westphalia. Once the clear separation of the Church from civil

---

[1] See the Encyclical *Respicientes,* November 1, 1870.

power was confirmed by the French Revolution, liberalism held to the thesis of the external juridical insignificance of the Church. Attacks upon the Church at the domestic level by liberals, separatists, and Freemasons, however, did not cease.

Against this background, states after 1870 continued their diplomatic relations with the Holy See as well as with the new Kingdom of Italy, giving rise to what was called the "double diplomatic corps" in Rome.[2] This diplomatic corps and its relations with the Holy See forcefully contradicted the positivist theory. It is most doubtful that these diplomats would have engaged in diplomatic exchange or relations if the Holy See were not still considered to be a sovereign entity. The matter merits further comment.

At one end of the debate were the positivists who held that continued diplomatic representation at the Vatican could not accord with any legal principle to which they adhered. At the other end were certain Catholic writers who saw in the combination of the territory left to the pope, plus his spiritual authority, a sufficient basis for a claim of sovereignty. This was the curial thesis which asserted that the Italian invasion had not been complete and that some jurisdictional area (the Vatican and Lateran palaces) remained sovereign territory under papal control. This opinion was contested by some positivists, but the criticism was finally abandoned in 1929 with the signing of the Lateran Treaty. The abandonment of the positivist position that only temporal states had international personality would subsequently enable recognition of the international personality of international organizations as well.[3]

More interesting theories lay between these two views, for they illustrated a refinement of the concepts of sovereignty and international personality. One advanced the view that the Papal States had survived de jure but not de facto so that the pope was a dispossessed sovereign whose personality, having been conceded in the past, could still be recognized. The Holy See was like a state without territory or

---

[2] Robert J. Graham, SJ, *The Rise of the Double Diplomatic Corps in Rome: A Study in International Practice* (The Hague: Martinus Nijhoff, 1952).

[3] See chapter 1, "The Holy See as International Person and Sovereign," 1–16.

subjects. Another view held that the Catholic Church as such was a person of international law *sui generis*, a recognition accorded out of historical necessity. One position denied ordinary sovereignty to the Holy See, but recognized a "special" or "particular" sovereignty which allowed some international juridical personality. There was also the view that the pope was an artificial person of international law, created with the consent of the international community of states. Some theorists attempted to expand the category of subjects of international law to include every community possessing autonomous organization, independence, and equality with other entities according to the norm of *pacta sunt servanda*. But the majority of later authors abandoned such ambitious criteria and constructed personality on the factual basis of concordats and the right of legation.[4]

In the English-speaking world, noted more for its pragmatism than its theory, the tendency was to recognize the facts as such without surrendering the positivist position, acknowledging a limited exception. For example, J. B. Moore wrote in 1906:

> The Pope, though deprived of the territorial dominion which he formerly enjoyed, holds as sovereign pontiff and head of the Roman Catholic Church, an exceptional position. Though, in default of territory, he is not a temporal sovereign, he is in many respects treated as such. He has the right of active and passive legation, and his envoys of the first class, his apostolic Nuncios, are specially privileged. . . . The conventions which he concludes with States are not called treaties, but *concordats*.[5]

Oppenheim noted that the position of the Holy See prior to 1929 was widely discussed and many writers, including himself, were of the view that "although the Holy See was not an international person, it had by custom and tacit consent of most States acquired a

---

[4] Ibid.

[5] John Bassett Moore, *A Digest of International Law* (Washington, D.C.: Government Printing Office, 1906), vol. I, 39.

quasi-international position,"[6] and though not a state it was still a subject of international rights and duties.[7] These opinions reflected the conviction that only temporal and territorial sovereignty was recognized by international law, and that the Holy See enjoyed an exceptional position only insofar as custom and consent had assimilated it to its former status of temporal sovereign. Yet the underlying reason for this custom and consent is hinted at: the non-temporal sovereignty of the pope as head of the Catholic Church, a worldwide communion of peoples of all races and ethnicities.

The concept of spiritual sovereignty was developed by certain Catholic writers who did not opt for the curialist or other positions making concessions to the positivist insistence on territory and temporal sovereignty. This doctrine lay behind the previously mentioned position that the Church itself possessed international juridical personality, as did every community possessing an autonomous organization, independence, and equality. Some writers developed the idea that the Holy See as the juridical personification of the Church was analogous to the state as the juridical personification of the nation. The use of analogy was central to the theory. It has been argued that the Church has international juridical personality for the same reasons that states do. Both the Church and states are distinct, organized, and independent communities with which it is impossible to deal on any but an equal basis. While the Church is not a personality identical with that of the state, it is analogous to it. The Church's sovereignty, as Chapter 2 develops, existed before the principles of international law were laid down and could not have been created by other juridical persons who are subsequent subjects of international law.

After the Lateran Treaty in 1929, theorists such as Anzilotti, Le Fur, and Jarrige would sharpen the concept of spiritual sovereignty as flowing from an international personality which, equivalent to

---

[6] L. Oppenheim, *International Law: A Treatise*, 8th ed., ed. H. Lauterpacht (London: Longmans, 1984), vol. 1, §105, at 252.

[7] Marjorie M. Whiteman, *Digest of International Law* (Washington, D.C.: Government Printing Office, 1963), vol. I, 588–90.

that of the state, explained the case of the Holy See.[8] Furthermore, their respective examinations distinguish a category of law different from traditional international law but related to the same juridical order. In their view, when speaking of the spiritual sovereignty of the pope, one ought not to speak of international relations or inter-state relations, but of "intergroup" or "intersovereign" relations.

When Leo XIII became pope in 1878 he inherited Pius IX's position in the Vatican, but he quietly attempted to solve the Roman Question by negotiations with Italy. After several attempts at conciliation with the Quirinal had failed, he abandoned this approach and sought to pose the problem on the international plane.[9] While the Roman Question was not the only consideration in his foreign policy, it certainly was an important motive for his conciliatory strategy toward Germany (the *Kulturkampf* was completely over by 1887), toward France (the *ralliement* improved the climate, but this depended more on whether anticlericals were in power), and toward Russia (with which he reestablished diplomatic relations). Leo's policies, ecclesiastical as well as political, were characterized by a spirit of patient conciliation. In general, they were, with the exception of Italy, quite successful.

The pontificate of Leo XIII marked a great change in the attitude and style of the Holy See which enhanced its international capability perhaps more than an immediate solution of the Roman Question could have done. Although deprived of its territory, the Holy See was free of the shackles of temporal politics. The papacy now appeared more as the custodian of as supranational doctrine that was genuinely concerned about the destiny of world society. Leo abandoned the policy adopted since the French Revolution by which Rome, as far as temporal affairs were concerned, acted in a defensive manner.[10]

---

[8] See generally Dionisio Anzilotti, *Corso di Diritto Internazionale* (Padua: CEDAM, 1955), vol. 1; Louis Le Fur, *Le Sainte-Siège et le Droit de Gens* (Paris: Sirey, 1930); and René Jarrige, *La Condition Internationale du Saint-Siège avant et aprés les Accords du Lateran* (Paris: Rousseau, 1930).

[9] William Kiefer, SM, *Leo XIII: A Light from Heaven* (Milwaukee: Bruce, 1961), 109, 131.

[10] Henri de Riedmatten, OP, "La Politique International et l'Eglise Catholique," *LVI Schweizer Rundschau* (April-May 1967): 218.

He narrowed the gulf between the Church and liberal thought by developing the social teaching of the Catholic tradition and applying it to contemporary problems through his extensive corpus of encyclicals and other writings.

His first encyclical, *Inscrutabili* (1878), defended the right of the Church and religion as against the state. In a subsequent encyclical, *Diuturnum Illud* (1881), he defined the duties and powers of states. Three further encyclicals dealt with the problem of reconciliation between Catholic political theory and the modern non-Christian state—*Immortali Dei* (1885), *Libertas Praestantissimum* (1888), and *Sapientiae Christianae* (1890). To this was added his most famous encyclical, *Rerum Novarum* (1891), condemning the evils of laissez-faire capitalism and vindicating the rights of the working man. Pope Leo fostered a Catholic intellectual renaissance through his support of the Neo-Thomistic revival and his establishment of a biblical commission. He promoted the study of Church history by opening the Vatican archives to scholars, and he encouraged Catholics to engage in the experimental sciences to show that there was no conflict between science and religion. All of this strengthened the Catholic Church as a durable and credible transnational social force in the modern world.

Leo XIII reinvigorated the openness of the Church toward the needs of all humanity. He inaugurated an expansion of papal diplomacy that reached out to all peoples, regardless of religion. As Eppstein puts it, a change emerged in the scope of the papal role: Hitherto the mission had been conceived primarily in terms of keeping peace within the *respublica christiana*, but now the peacemaking efforts of the Holy See went beyond Catholic or even Christian states. Leo XIII dealt with Germany, the United States, and Britain, and deplored before the College of Cardinals the wars between Britain and the Boers, the Russians and the Japanese. While Catholics were spread around the globe, even though only a minority of governments professed Catholicism as an official religion, the pope contended that all nations must obey the law of God.[11] To this

---

[11] John Eppstein, *The Catholic Tradition of the Law of Nations* (London: Burns, Oates and Washbourne, 1935), 192–93.

increasingly universal papal activity, the loss of the Papal States posed no obstacle. In fact, various writers have testified to the increased world influence of the papacy after the confiscation of the Papal States in 1870.[12] Perhaps Leo XIII was compensating for the loss of territorial sovereignty and the consequences posed by this, but he demonstrated that the sine qua non of his international role was not a plot of ground but something more spiritual and universal—a transcendent and objective moral order for all peoples.

While the teaching on international relations took a secondary place in the prolific thought of Leo XIII, he nonetheless made substantive and significant contributions to its development both in word and in deed. In an important address to the College of Cardinals, *Nostis Errorem* (February 11, 1889), he declared that while war may sometimes be necessary, it had never failed to produce immense disaster and would continue to do so with modern armaments, which instead of insuring stability only increased the danger in war. As he argued,

> the vast number of soldiers and the stupendous armaments may for a while prevent an enemy from attacking, but they can never secure a sure and lasting peace. Moreover, armaments which are a menace are fitter rather to hasten than retard a conflict; they fill the mind with disquietude for the future. . . .[13]

In an apostolic letter to the world, *Praeclara Gratulationis* (June 20, 1894), Leo condemned the current arms race and conscription of young men into military service. In his view, the international tension generated by widespread rearming could not last much longer and could not be the normal condition of human society. As he

---

[12] See, e.g., Carl Conrad Eckhardt, *The Papacy and World Affairs* (Chicago: University of Chicago Press, 1937), 345–49.

[13] Harry Koenig, *Principles for Peace: Selections from Papal Documents Leo XIII to Pius XII* (Washington, D.C.: National Catholic Welfare Conference, 1943), ¶104 [different translation].

stated, "Yet we cannot escape from this situation, and obtain true peace, except by the aid of Jesus Christ. For to repress ambition and covetousness and envy—the chief instigators of war—nothing is more fitted than the Christian virtues and, in particular, the virtue of justice."[14]

More important than Leo's condemnation of the "armed peace" was his contribution to the development of arbitration, mediation, and conciliation as peaceful means of settling international disputes. In the late nineteenth century there was expanding interest in such means as a substitute for war so that in this respect Leo was at the cutting edge of international thought. The prevailing mood is described in a passage written by Dag Hammarskjold concerning his father's lifelong dedication to the international dispensation of justice:

> In trying to interpret the internationalism of which Hjalmar Hammarskjold was the representative, I find the key in this: *Civitas Dei* was a dream from the past. The attempts of our own age to create an international organization with a common executive had not yet seen the light of day. Instead we glimpse here the idea of a world community where nation-states should live under the protection of an internationalism which derives its strength from the logical nature of justice itself, not from arbitrary decree, and consequently in which the only needful international organ is of a judicial nature.[15]

Thus while in the latter half of the nineteenth century no statesman seriously suggested any limitation to the sovereign right of states to wage war, arbitration was acceptable since it proceeded by mutual agreement of the parties, and the arbitrator derived jurisdiction solely by the disputing states' consent. In *Diuturnum Illud* (June 29, 1881), Leo declared that wars in modern times had arisen from the failure to use arbitration, and since peacemaking was

---

[14] Ibid., ¶193.

[15] Sven Stolpe, *Dag Hammarskjöld, A Spiritual Portrait,* trans. Naomi Walford (New York: Charles Scribner's Sons, 1967), 14–15.

inherent in the office of pope, he was available for this task.[16] Four years later, he found himself taken up on his offer, becoming the first pope of the modern era to carry out public activity in favor of world peace. One of his more notable efforts in this regard was the resolution of a heated contest between Spain and Germany.

The Caroline and Palau archipelagos of Micronesia had been discovered by Spanish navigators in the sixteenth century. After the discovery, Spain exercised only intermittent acts of effective domination. Once foreign business interests had set up installations on these islands in the nineteenth century and found no Spanish authority there, Britain and Germany notified Madrid in 1875 that they did not recognize Spanish sovereignty within this territory. Spain did not protest at the time, lending credence to the view that the islands were *res nullius*. However, once German traders began to claim protection of the flag, Spain ordered an expedition to take formal possession. When Berlin told Madrid that it intended to proclaim a protectorate and a German commandant planted the imperial flag in August 1885, Spain protested vigorously and tensions were elevated. In September a clerical minister of the Spanish cabinet declared that no arbitration was possible unless it was that of the pope. Bismarck heard of the idea and found that it had merit (for domestic as well as international reasons). Preliminary *démarches* indicated that the Holy See would accept the duty, and despite

---

[16] *Diuturnum Illud*, No. 22, where the pope stated, "But from the time when the civil society of men, raised from the ruins of the Roman Empire, gave hope of its future Christian greatness, the Roman Pontiffs, by the institution of the Holy Empire, consecrated the political power in a wonderful manner. Greatly, indeed, was the authority of rulers ennobled; and it is not to be doubted that what was then instituted would always have been a very great gain, both to ecclesiastical and civil society, if princes and peoples had ever looked to the same object as the Church. And, indeed, tranquillity and a sufficient prosperity lasted so long as there was a friendly agreement between these two powers. If the people were turbulent, the Church was at once the mediator for peace. Recalling all to their duty, she subdued the more lawless passions partly by kindness and partly by authority. So if in ruling, princes erred in their government, she went to them and, putting before them the rights needs, and lawful wants of their people, urged them to equity, mercy, and kindness. Whence it was often brought about that the dangers of civil wars and popular tumults were stayed."

much opposition from European chancelleries, especially the Italian, the papal arbitration went forward.[17]

Pope Leo indicated during this period that he would prefer to act as mediator rather than arbitrator and this was accepted.[18] Mediation would not require him to set forth detailed proposals for rights of commerce and navigation, an involvement thought inappropriate for the moral authority of the Holy See. Through a diplomatic note of October 22, 1885, the Holy See proposed the following principles as a basis for negotiations: (1) recognition of the historic rights and sovereignty of Spain; (2) the need for effective exercise of sovereignty, absence of which had given plausibility to the German position; and, (3) the concession to Germany of appreciable privileges for commerce and navigation.[19] These proposals were accepted by both sides, and the conflict was resolved. The *pourparlers* went on in Madrid, Berlin, and Rome, and a protocol was signed in Rome on 17 November by the respective envoys to the Holy See.[20]

The Carolines mediation by Leo XIII was the first successful act of arbitration or mediation by the Holy See since 1702.[21] It not only preserved peace in Europe but also indirectly contributed to the termination of the *Kulturkampf* in Germany and raised the hopes of those who favored the new movement—reflective of the principal roles of the future League of Nations and the United Nations—toward peaceful settlement of disputes. Calvo declared that the decision was of great importance to international law and demonstrated the role of mediation in preserving the peace.[22] But the most certain historical result was a renewed prestige for the papacy in the international community, shown by the large number

---

[17] Koenig, 13, ¶72.

[18] Yves de la Brière, SJ, *L'Organisation Internationale du Monde Contemporain et la Papauté Souveraine,* Series I (Paris: Editions Spes, 1924), 247.

[19] Koenig, supra note 13, ¶51.

[20] La Brière, supra note 18, at 248–50.

[21] Eppstein, supra note 11, at 472. However, as Eppstein's work indicates, there were other offers of papal arbitration or mediation which were not accepted after they were made.

[22] Georges Goyau, "L'Eglise Catholique et le Droit des Gens," *Recueil des Cours* 6 (1925): 227–28.

of greetings and gifts from the sovereigns of the world, Catholic and
non-Catholic, on the sacerdotal jubilee of Leo in 1887. This
demonstration of affection and support for the Holy See had not
been observed for some time. While the Caroline mediation was
not the only reason, it was an important factor.[23]

Other requests for papal peacemaking followed. In 1890, Leo
was proposed as mediator in the boundary disputes between Britain
and Portugal and between Portugal and the Congo State. In 1893
the papal nuncio in Lima arbitrated a boundary dispute between
Peru and Ecuador; Venezuela called upon the pope in 1894 to
mediate with Great Britain in the Guiana boundary dispute. In
1895 the pope acted as arbitrator in a boundary dispute between
Haiti and the Dominican Republic. The following year Leo
appealed publicly to Emperor Menelik I of Ethiopia on behalf of
Italian war prisoners taken in the battle of Adowa. In 1898 the German foreign minister von Bülow proposed papal mediation between
Spain and the United States over the Philippine Islands, an offer
that Spain accepted but the U.S. refused. At the turn of the century,
the bishop of San Juan de Cuyo, Argentina, and the bishop of
Ancud, Chile, were instrumental in bringing about the arbitration
of a boundary dispute between their countries, an event commemo-
rated by the famous statue of the "Christ of the Andes."[24]

These peacemaking activities of the Holy See had an additional
impact on public opinion. The more internationally minded seg-
ments of the Catholic community joined the ranks of those who
supported arbitration and other peaceful means of settling international disputes. Some Catholics saw this as a proper exercise of
papal authority. A Catholic congress in Madrid in 1889 advocated
the assignment of the office of international arbiter to the papacy, as
did an Italian Catholic congress in 1896.[25] Others saw the pope as
a leader of the current trend in 1897 when the seventh Universal

[23] See Bernard O'Reilly, *The Life of Leo XIII, From His Personal Memoirs* (Philadelphia: John C. Winston, 1903), Chapter XXXV, 575–602 (Leo's Sacerdotal
Jubilee, 1887–88).
[24] See Eppstein, supra note 11, at 473. See Eckhardt, supra note 12, at 237.
[25] Goyau, supra note 22, at 229.

Peace Congress requested Leo XIII "to continue to make himself the champion of the great crusade for the brotherhood of the human race."[26] On the other hand, the pope's new role in international affairs appeared to some non-Catholics in a different light. Beales writes that Leo's zeal in reviving papal arbitration "met nowhere a stronger criticism than that of the internationalist bodies founded after 1867."[27] Since these groups were in the liberal tradition, strongly non-Catholic and secular minded in their ideals, there may have been some degree of antireligious or anti-Catholic prejudice at work. But it is also likely that they feared the revival of ad hoc papal arbitration as a threat to the establishment of the permanent arbitral tribunal, which they advocated as a necessary instrument for the effective dispensation of international justice.

Such fears, though understandable in the light of medieval history, were in point of fact groundless. The Holy See was favorably disposed toward the creation by states of a permanent arbitral tribunal. Perhaps the first public indication of this position was the joint appeal issued by Cardinals Gibbons of Baltimore, Logue of Armagh, and Vaughan of Westminster, on Easter Sunday of 1896.[28] Their statement, occasioned by the dispute between the United States and Great Britain over Venezuela, could not have been made without the prior knowledge and consent of the Vatican. It was an open invitation to

> co-operate in the formation of a public opinion which shall demand the establishment of a permanent tribunal of arbitration, as a rational substitute, among the English-speaking races, for a resort to the bloody arbitrament of war.[29]

The cardinals indicated that the difficulties were not insuperable, that such a court had once existed in a united Christendom and was being appealed to again, but that it was now up to governments,

---

[26] A. C. F. Beales, *The History of Peace: A Short Account of the Organized Movements for International Peace* (New York: Dial Press, 1931), 229.

[27] Ibid., 187.

[28] Goyau, supra note 22, at 229.

[29] Eppstein, supra note 11, at 172.

moved by public opinion, to establish a permanent arbitral tribunal, with defined jurisdiction, as a second line of defense after diplomacy had failed. Secular reasons supported such a plan, and the Church recognized their legitimate force and blessed whatever tended to the progress of man. But the main ground of their appeal, the cardinals declared, was the known character and will of the Prince of Peace.[30]

Pope Leo XIII himself had already suggested, in private, a permanent court of arbitration and would soon be involved in the planning of the Hague Conference of 1899. At a papal audience of 1893, Prince Lobanov of Russia raised the problem of the arms race. The pope responded with the suggestion of an agreement among nations on the limitation of arms, plus a juridical institution to judge international disputes. This international juridical body could eliminate the causes of war and make military preparations less necessary. Some observers believed that this conversation inspired the proposal of Czar Nicholas II in August of 1898 for an international conference to deal with the problem of the arms race.[31] Even if this observation remains in dispute, the fact is that a few days after the Russian minister of foreign affairs, Count Mouraviev, handed the invitation of the czar to the diplomats accredited to St. Petersburg, the Russian minister to the Holy See in Rome gave Cardinal Rampolla, the Secretary of State, a copy of the invitation on behalf of his government and at the express will of the czar, who wrote an accompanying letter expressing high esteem for the pope's peacemaking role and requesting his support. Rome's response was quick, as Rampolla conveyed to Mouraviev the pope's great interest in the project.[32]

---

[30] Ibid., 173.

[31] See Koenig, ¶217, Letter *Nous Pouvons* to Queen Wilhelmina of Holland, May 29, 1899, and ¶221, Allocution *Auspicandae Celebretatis* to the College of Cardinals, December 14, 1899.

[32] See Koenig, supra note 13, ¶¶202–6, First Diplomatic Note of Cardinal Rampolla, Secretary of State, to Count Mouraviev, Secretary of Foreign Affairs for Russia, September 15, 1898, and Koenig, ¶¶207–9, Second Diplomatic Note of Cardinal Rampolla, Secretary of State, to Count Mouraviev, Secretary of Foreign Affairs for Russia, February 10, 1899. See Koenig, ¶221, Allocution *Auspicandae Celebretatis* to the College of Cardinals, December 14, 1899, in which the pope mentions the efforts of the czar to the College of Cardinals.

The support of the Holy See was more than routine or idealistic. Cardinal Rampolla's reply, the following February, to a second note from Mouraviev on the agenda of the proposed conference revealed both a desire to contribute meaningfully to the planning and a shrewd appreciation of the significance of this development for world peace. Rampolla noted that the international consortium of nations lacked a system of legal and moral means to determine and make good the right of each without relying on immediate recourse to the use of force. In this situation the institution of arbitration and mediation was the most opportune remedy and was supported completely by the Holy See, which would prefer compulsory arbitration of all disputes. However, this may have been too much to hope for. As the cardinal noted,

> . . . perhaps we cannot hope that arbitration, obligatory by
> its very nature, can become in all circumstances the object
> of unanimous acceptance and assent. An institution of
> mediation, invested with authority, clothed with all the nec-
> essary moral prestige, fortified with the indispensable guar-
> antees of competence and impartiality, in no way restraining
> the liberty of the litigating parties, would be less exposed to
> meet obstacles.[33]

But the Holy See was not to attend the Conference now planned for The Hague. In February 1899 the Italian foreign minister notified St. Petersburg and The Hague that if the Holy See were invited Italy would not attend. The Quirinal was haunted by the Roman Question and feared that the papal representative would raise it at The Hague.[34] In vain, Russia offered guarantees that only previously agreed topics would be discussed. Italian anticlericals agitated and presented the theory that the pope was no longer sovereign because

---

[33] Koenig, supra note 13, ¶208, Second Diplomatic Note of Cardinal Rampolla, Secretary of State, to Count Mouraviev, Secretary of Foreign Affairs for Russia, February 10, 1899.

[34] See footnote 24 and accompanying text in chapter 1, "The Holy See as International Person and Sovereign," 7.

in losing his territory he had lost international juridical personality.[35] Russia, France, and Britain favored a papal presence at the conference. However, Berlin, in the Triple Alliance with Italy and only feebly enthusiastic over the initiative of the czar, let it be known that if one of the large powers abstained from the conference, Germany would not attend. Such an outcome would render the meeting useless. Thus, when the invitations were sent out by the Netherlands in April, the Holy See did not receive one.[36]

Instead of protesting the diplomatic slight, Pope Leo exercised a dignified attitude. He commended the spirit of the conference in a discourse to the Cardinals in April, and in May *L'Osservatore Romano* published an article that was quite sympathetic to the meeting. In addition, the pope tried to allay the fears of Italy by ordering the papal nuncio to absent himself from The Hague for several weeks.[37] Pope Leo blessed the Hague Conference in a letter to Queen Wilhelmina, but it was not read to the delegates immediately. Rumor had appeared in certain Italian papers that if the contents of the letter were publicized, the Italian delegates would create an incident or even walk out. The Queen thus waited until the last day of the Conference, July 29, 1899, to have its president give a public reading to the pope's letter. No incident was then possible and none occurred.[38]

Since the Permanent Court of Arbitration was established by the conference, and since the conventions concluded there were open to adherence by sovereigns not represented (who would then become high contracting parties capable of naming arbitrators to serve on future tribunals), there was still a possibility that the Holy See could be reintegrated into the assizes of the international juridical order. But Italy moved to prevent even this, desiring to lessen the international

---

[35] La Brière, SJ, supra note 18, at 264.

[36] Ibid., 263–66.

[37] See Eckhardt, supra note 12, at 238; Eppstein, supra note 11, at 174–75; and, Koenig, supra note 13, ¶¶210–13, Discourse *Rivedere Qui Oggi* to the College of Cardinals, April 11, 1899, and ¶¶217–19, Letter *Nous ne Pouvons* to Queen Wilhelmina of Holland, May 29, 1899.

[38] La Brière, supra note 18, at 269.

influence of the papacy and thus keep the Roman Question a purely Italian affair. To spare itself the odious role of despoiling the Holy See of this advantage after taking its territory, Italy persuaded Britain to play it. Lord Pauncefote, the British delegate, declared his government's position that no power could adhere to the protocols and be admitted to the Court without prior consent of all powers already represented. After much objection, the British view prevailed.[39]

Nonetheless, the Holy See had some resourceful friends at the conference. The original provision was that only states not represented at the conference could with unanimous consent eventually adhere to the protocols. But the rapporteur of the committee preparing the final draft was an eminent professor of international law, Louis Renault, who proposed in his oral report that the word *power* be substituted for *state*. This, as most involved with the drafting realized, would admit the possibility of the eventual admission of the Holy See to the Permanent Court of Arbitration. The principal Italian representative, Count Nigra, merely winked his eye behind his monocle and said, *"Je vois bien pourquoi!,"* but, judging the unanimity requirement a sufficient protection for Italy, made no objection to the change.[40]

Pope Leo protested the exclusion of the Holy See from the First Hague Conference,[41] and the same exclusion from both participation and adherence was repeated at the Second Hague Conference in 1907.[42] Despite the renewal of its increased status in world affairs, the Holy See would not be invited to a major international conference until 1951 when it was invited to a conference of plenipotentiaries who were to consider the plight of refugees and stateless persons.[43] It was ironic that just at the moment when its reintegration into the international community as a purely moral,

---

[39] Ibid., 271–72.

[40] Ibid., 270–75.

[41] See Eppstein, supra note 11, at 174, n. 1; and, Koenig, supra notes 13, ¶¶221–22, Allocution *Auspicandae Celebretatis* to the College of Cardinals, December 14, 1899.

[42] Eckhardt, supra note 12, at 238–39.

[43] *1951 U.N. Yearbook,* U.N. Sales No. 1952.1.30, 520, 527.

rather than both moral and temporal, power was solidifying, the Holy See was banned from a conference on peaceful settlement of disputes which it had inspired, promoted, and initially been invited to attend. But it is more ironic that by yielding to the pettiness of Italy, which refused to settle the Roman Question by international means, the powers meeting at The Hague excluded from the conference, its Conventions, and the Court the most venerable spokesman for and recently successful practitioner of peaceful means for international dispute resolution. This irony was accentuated by the fact that the pope had recently demonstrated himself on several occasions to be the leader of a transnational force capable of adding greatly to the moral support that these frail instrumentalities so desperately needed to achieve their intended goals.

It is not hyperbolic to suggest, as Eppstein does, that the exclusion of the Holy See from The Hague did "incalculable damage to the confidence of Catholic populations in the resolutions taken by their governments regarding arbitration."[44] A growing loyalty to the pope had set in after the events of 1870 and subsequent religious persecutions. In that context, the absence of the Holy See from The Hague only symbolized more dramatically the gulf between Church and state, between morality and politics. Papal presence would have meant papal approbation of the peaceful resolution of international disputes. The essential articles of the conventions of 1899 and 1907 would most likely have been promulgated and commented upon as obligatory rules of international morality in some pontifical document and then inculcated through the manifold teaching channels of the Church, creating an informed and influential public opinion, both Catholic and non-Catholic alike. La Brière noted that this was done regarding Christian teaching on capital and labor, the so-called "social question," with very efficacious results. However, while numerous Catholic movements grew up at the time that were concerned with social questions, there never were any comparable groups that dealt with the "international question."[45]

---

[44] Eppstein, supra note 11, at 174.
[45] La Brière, supra note 35, at 276–78.

The Hague Declarations and Conventions of 1899 and 1907 were certainly in harmony with the Church's natural law teaching and with contemporary needs. They constituted a major step toward the qualification of the kind of sovereignty that was responsible for the assertive behavior that inevitably led to war. Their weaknesses were notable, however. Parties to a dispute were not obliged to accept the Court's jurisdiction, and its decisions were not enforceable. Once arbitration had failed, the right of recourse to war was not abridged—in fact it was now enhanced. The attempt to humanize warfare by limiting its mode of conduct to certain well-defined and enforceable rules also seemed to make more acceptable the existence of armed conflict, as the first half of the twentieth century would suggest.[46] The compulsory arbitration or even the authoritative kind of mediation advocated by Rampolla in his second letter to Mouraviev had not been achieved. There was correlation, however, between the Catholic doctrine of the just war and international public law after the signature of the Hague conventions since a process of arbitration was now available. There emerged a moral obligation on all Christian states to agree to arbitration. Consequently, a resort to war in the absence of an agreement for arbitration was immoral.

More important was the sincerity of intention of the powers to implement what was agreed upon, a sincerity found lacking by many of the period. The dominant spirit of the age militated against peaceful conflict resolution. In a pessimistic letter written toward the end of his pontificate, *Pervenuti* (March 19, 1902), the aging Pope Leo lamented that "the repudiation of those Christian principles which had contributed so efficaciously to unite the nations in the bonds of brotherhood and to bring all humanity

---

[46] See, e.g., the 1899 Hague Declaration 2 Concerning Asphyxiating Gases, the 1899 Hague Declaration 3 Concerning Expanding Bullets, the 1907 Hague Convention V Respecting the Rights and Duties of Neutral Powers and Persons in Case of WAr on Land, and the 1907 Hague Convention XIII Concerning the Rights and Duties of Neutral Powers in Naval War. Along with other sources, these texts have been conveniently included in *Documents of the Law of War*, 3rd ed., ed. Robert Guelph (London: Oxford University Press, 2000).

into one great family," and the "system of jealous egoism, in consequence of which the nations now watch each other, if not with hate, at least with the suspicion of rivals."[47] He condemned the "fatal principles which have consecrated material power as the supreme law of the world" as responsible for the "limitless increase of military establishments and that armed peace which in many respects is equivalent to a disastrous war."[48] For this pope, a "lamentable confusion in the realm of ideas" had produced a general spirit of rebellion, and frequent popular agitations that are the prelude of much more terrible disorders in the future.[49] Hindsight shows that this was not merely pro forma pulpit rhetoric but a true reading of the signs of the times.

The policy of Leo XIII was to move the Holy See into the mainstream of international affairs. At his death in 1903, the favorite to succeed him was Cardinal Rampolla, who, as Secretary of State, was closely linked to this policy and would have likely continued it. But the choice of Rampolla was vetoed in the conclave by Austria, exercising a traditional right enjoyed also by Spain and France. Consequently, the new pope, Pius X (1903–1914), abolished the right of veto and changed the direction of the papacy. Known for his simplicity and holiness (and later canonized), Pope Pius has been called a "non-political" pope who was concerned with internal Church matters, especially the crisis of modernism.[50] But the picture of him drawn by many writers is a fictitious caricature. Falconi, for example, stated that Pius practiced an "ascetic absenteeism" from international affairs.[51] However, the evidentiary record shows this claim to be exaggerated.

By way of illustration, Pius X eased the restrictions on Catholic participation in Italian politics imposed by Pius IX and Leo XIII,

---

[47] Koenig, supra note 13, ¶234, Letter *Pervenuti* in which Leo XIII reviews His pontificate, March 19, 1902.
[48] Ibid., ¶235.
[49] Ibid.
[50] Herder correspondence, IV, 297.
[51] Carlo Falconi, *The Popes in the Twentieth Century: From Pius X to John XXIII* (Boston: Little, Brown & Co., 1968), 91.

and achieved a certain degree of rapprochement with the Quirinal. Although he experienced difficulty with Spain, Portugal, and especially France, where the Law of Separation of 1905 confiscated Church property and exiled members of religious orders, the role of the Holy See as peacemaker was less emphasized but not discontinued. In 1905, Colombia and Peru entered into a standing agreement to submit all their disputes except questions of independence and honor to the pope for arbitration in cases where direct negotiation had failed. In 1906 the Apostolic Delegate in Bogota played a role in the Putumayo boundary dispute between Colombia and Ecuador.[52] In 1909, Pius X was named sole arbitrator in the long-standing controversy between Brazil and her two neighbors, Peru and Bolivia, over the gold mines of Acre. The pope's suggestions resulted in treaties disposing of the principal questions.[53] In 1914 the pope supported efforts to bring about arbitration between the United States and Mexico.[54]

While Pius X did not develop the Church's teaching on international relations, neither was he silent. In 1905 he condemned the strident nationalism and the policy of "might makes right" being pursued by European powers.[55] The following year, in a message to the Fifteenth World Peace Conference in Milan, he blessed its efforts and again advocated the peaceful arbitration of disputes. On the founding of the Carnegie Endowment for International Peace in 1911, Pius wrote a special letter in which he praised the effort, which he called very important, to prevent war and to "remove even the anxieties of so-called armed peace" He added,

> This is especially true at the present day, when vast armies, instrumentalities most destructive to human life, and the advanced state of military science portend wars which must be a source of fear even to the most powerful rulers.[56]

---

[52] Eppstein, supra note 11, at 474.

[53] Ibid.

[54] Ibid.

[55] Eckhardt, supra note 12, at 259.

[56] Koenig, supra note 132, ¶266, Letter *Libenter abs* to Archbishop Falconio, Apostolic Delegate to the United States, June 11, 1911.

A comment in the *American Journal of International Law* praised this message and said that the pope had assumed the moral leadership of the world.[57]

As World War I appeared imminent, Pius issued appeals for peace in May and August of 1914.[58] During this time he uttered his well-known objection to the Austrian cause by responding to Franz Josef, "I do not bless war: I bless peace."[59] But it is a fact that after Sarajevo the Vatican Secretary of State, Cardinal Merry del Val, approved Austria-Hungary's ultimatum to Serbia and expressed the hope that she would stand firm and escape the dangers that threatened her from Slav nationalist movements. As the Austro-Hungarian charge d'affaire noted, his country was the "Catholic state par excellence" and so the "apostolic viewpoint and the martial spirit" coincided.[60] That Vatican support for Austria would lead to world war, however, was neither foreseen nor desired.[61] Pius X earnestly wanted peace in Europe but was powerless to preserve it. He died shortly after the outbreak of the most destructive war the world had ever known up to that time.

The First World War was the result of many causes that had been accumulating force in the period from 1870 to 1914. Certainly one of the most important of these was exaggerated nationalism. The Holy See was never happy with the growth of strong nationalism in Europe and favored at most a subordinated nationalism.[62] The attitude springs from Catholic teaching. As Renouvin put it,

> Roman Catholic doctrine is opposed, almost by definition,
> to aggressive nationalism. The internationalism of the

---

[57] See Editorial Comment, "The Pontifical Letter of June 11, 1911," *American Journal of International Law* 5(1911): 707–8.

[58] Koenig, supra note 13, ¶¶271–72, Allocution, *Ex Quo Postremum*, May 25, 1914, and ¶¶273–74, Exhortation, *Dum Europa Fere Omnis*, August 2, 1914.

[59] Quoted in Eckhardt, supra note 12, at 260.

[60] Pierre Renouvin and Jean-Baptiste Duroselle, *Introduction to the History of international Relations* (New York: Praeger, 1967), 211.

[61] See Koenig, supra note 13, at 273–74, Exhortation *Dum Europa Fere Omnis* to the Catholics of the Whole World, August 2, 1914, requesting Catholics throughout the world to pray for peace and the avoidance of war.

[62] See generally Eppstein, supra ¶¶note 11, at 347–63; and, Christine Alix, *Le Saint Siège et les nationalisme en Europe, 1870–1960* (Paris: Sirey, 1962), 146–49.

Catholic Church necessarily obliges the Holy See to view with suspicion any tendencies that would dispose Catholic nations to divide among themselves or damage Catholic solidarity.[63]

Church teaching on the rights and limits of nationality had hitherto been sparse except for the work of Taparelli, but it began to develop more rapidly under Leo XIII. The question received a good deal of attention from popes from that period on and the entire Catholic tradition until the Second World War, during which nationalism came to be seen as a threat not only to religious freedom and Catholic solidarity, but also to world peace and the solidarity of humankind.

Pope Leo XIII dealt specifically with the problem of nationalism primarily in terms of the Church–state conflict so prevalent in his reign. In *Sapientiae Christianae* (January 10, 1890) he wrote that the law of nature does indeed bid that Christians love their *patria* and defend it even with their lives. Nonetheless, they should be even more attached to the Church, for the good of the soul and everlasting life is higher than the good of the body and mortal life. Since natural love of country and supernatural love of the Church both come from God, they cannot conflict. But the order governing these duties is on occasion overturned by evil, so that the state seems to demand one thing and religious faith another—as would be demonstrated in the totalitarian states of the twentieth century. If the laws of the state are openly inconsistent with the rights of God, injure the Church, contradict religious duties, or do violence to the authority of Christ in the person of the pope, "then truly, to resist becomes a positive duty, to obey, a crime: a crime, moreover, combined with a misdemeanor against the State itself, inasmuch as every offense leveled against religion is a sin against the State. . . . "[64]

While commending that Catholics obey their lawful civil authorities, Pope Leo indicated that it might be proper for them to disregard orders to participate in an unjust war; furthermore, it is apparent from his other writings that he perceived clearly the causal

---

[63] Renouvin and Duroselle, supra note 60, at 193.

[64] Koenig, supra note 13, ¶115.

relation between excessive nationalism and war.[65] One can reason-
ably conclude, therefore, that although in his public statements he
confined himself largely to the religious issues, he also realized the
other problem of dual allegiance posed by nationalism, that of simultaneous loyalty to the state and to the whole human family. The two
aspects are connected intrinsically, and it was only a question of time
before they were related explicitly by *Sapientiae Christianae*.

In *The Catholic Tradition and the Law of Nations*, John Eppstein
included an essay on patriotism that gathered together what the tradition had to say on the role of nationality, and since his basic conclusions were widely held by Catholics between 1870 and 1914,
including the popes, it is worth summarizing here.[66] It helps to
explain, for example, the attitude of the Holy See toward the Habsburg Empire and the principle of national self-determination agitated before and during the peace conferences of 1919, and toward
that new international organization, the League of Nations.

Eppstein indicates that Church teaching has always valued the
family, clan, and people as unifying relationships, but has never let
them become absolutes or impediments to universal love and solidarity amongst the members of the human family. The same is true of
cultural heritage.[67] Taking the nation as an association in which man
finds his birth and his culture, the Church has respected nationality—but it has never held that state and nation were synonymous
terms or should necessarily coincide, though recognizing such coinci-
dence as at times extremely useful.[68] The rights arising from nationality are real and universal, to be respected by both Church and state.
However, national culture is only one factor contributing to the natural and ordered development of each person, and may never violate
the natural law, which brings fulfillment to all people, secures their

---

[65] Koenig, supra note 13, ¶22, Letter *Perlectae a Nobis* to Cardinal Guibert,
Archbishop of Paris, October 22, 1880, and ¶¶23–26, Encyclical *Diuturnum*
on the Origin of Civil Power, June 29, 1881.
[66] Eppstein, supra note 11, Chapter XIII, "The Rights and Limits of Nationality."
[67] Ibid., 348–49.
[68] Ibid., 352.

human rights, and draws them together.[69] True human love must be universal, unifying not only the home and *patria*, but all humankind. While the state has a real and important moral personality, it must be a responsible unit in the higher unity of the world. The role of patriotism is to keep the state united and thus able to fulfill its responsibility. Because of this hierarchy of loyalties, there is no conflict between true patriotism and international cooperation.[70]

Such was the official philosophy, but in practice there appeared the usual gap between the Church's teaching and the implementation of its positions in the world. Between 1870 and 1914, Catholics were certainly affected by nationalism, though probably less so than other groups. Conservatives tended to see Church and *patria* as natural allies against liberalism; liberals used the state against the Church. In some countries there was support for a national Church as part of its cultural heritage. In others nationalism itself tended to become a substitute religion, with an appropriate secular liturgy for the worship of the crown, the state, or the nation. In most cases, the Holy See came to be regarded more and more as a foreign agent outside the control of the state [the reverse of ultramontanism] both because it was religious and because it was supranational. The phenomenon of nationalism has been studied sufficiently to require no further investigation here. The question is to what extent it penetrated Catholic consciousness and consequently influenced, and was influenced by, the foreign policy of the Holy See.

Major Catholic political parties during this period avoided the pitfalls of excessive nationalism, but the clergy and faithful did not always exercise these principles. The French and German bishops generally gave active endorsements to all patriotic manifestations. In France between 1890 and 1914 most of the higher clergy were influenced by nationalist thinking, and during the Dreyfus affair Catholics were most nationalistic of all. In Austria-Hungary the clergy placed their moral influence at the service of the Habsburg dynasty. Nationalism was strong in the Christian Socialist party but

---

[69] Ibid., 355–56.
[70] Ibid., 361–62.

Catholic intellectuals had nothing to do with this trend. In Italy prior to 1867, clerical and lay Catholic circles were often fervently patriotic, but after 1870 they kept out of politics. Between 1904 and 1914 Catholics began to play a role once again, but were not active in the nationalist movement.[71]

Allied with nationalism was militarism, and opposed to both was pacifism. It is essential to note here the meaning of the term "pacifism" as used in the nineteenth century and through the period of the League of Nations. It does not necessarily mean absolute adherence to the principle of non-resistance in the Quaker sense, but is sufficiently broad to include a firm belief in the obligation to resort first to all possible means of peaceful settlement of disputes. Thus it is often used, especially where Catholics are concerned, to mean advocacy of a strict just war theory, arbitration, disarmament, and some kind of international organization to prevent war.

Since the beginning of the nineteenth century, as Renouvin has suggested, Catholic thinkers had been much more reserved than Protestants toward pacifism.[72] In some circles, the radical view of Joseph de Maistre was even influential—the idea that war was "divine in itself, since it was a law of the world" and the results of armed conflict "altogether eluded the speculations of human reason."[73] The vague internationalism of de Lammenais left some traces among Catholic socialists in 1848, some of whom were militant pacifists, but the influence did not affect the mass of the faithful.[74] In Germany, the Center Party initially opposed the militarist legislation advocated by Bismarck, but it was not a pacifist organization and abandoned its opposition to arms bills in 1897. It backed German foreign policy but avoided the Pan-German movement, whose excesses it condemned.[75]

Only in France and Belgium was there anything approaching a Catholic pacifist organization. In 1911 Alfred Vanderpol founded

---

[71] Renouvin and Duroselle, supra note 60, at 194.
[72] Ibid., 209.
[73] Ibid.
[74] Ibid.
[75] Ibid., 209–10.

the International League of Catholic Pacifists. He was a student of the history of the just war theory and the Church's efforts for peace and was a firm advocate of both. He tried in vain to obtain some sign of approval from Rome and when, with the support of the Bishop of Liege, he tried to organize an international ecclesiastical congress to open the way toward a Franco-German rapprochement. However, disappointment surfaced when only four French bishops agreed to send representatives.[76] There also existed a League of French Catholics for Peace numbering some seven hundred members. More important was the International Catholic Union for the Study of International Law According to Christian Principles, founded at Louvain in 1912. It was essentially a band of Catholic legal scholars discovering their own heritage rather than operating as a pacifist organization.[77] It survived the First World War, after which it was joined by larger and more important Catholic organizations that were pacifist in tendency. The shock of that war would be needed to produce anything resembling a significant Catholic peace movement.

Expansionist nationalism made this the great age of imperialism, yet one could look in vain for any contemporary Church teaching that really addressed the problem. The Church was in fact still operating on the principles laid down long before by thinkers such as Vitoria, and protested only the enslavement or mistreatment of colonial peoples, not their loss of political independence. The missionary opportunities offered by imperialistic adventures were most welcome, and many Catholic missionaries still identified Christianity with their own culture (despite all theology to the contrary) and considered loss of freedom a small price to pay for the advantages of civilization and the faith. They were aware that the Church condemned conquest as such, but did not seem to realize that the "civilizing mission" of imperialism was often a pretext for it. Full advantage, in case of doubt, was taken of the justifications

---

[76] Ibid., 210.
[77] Maurice Vaussard, "La Coopération International des Catholiques," *Le Problème de la Vie International* (Paris: Gabalda, 1927), 599.

listed by Vitoria for colonization, that is, discovery, just war, and request for intervention, so that the age of imperialism can hardly be said to have posed any new moral problem for Catholics.

In general, the colonial powers favored the missions, with a bias toward missionaries of their own nationality and religion. The missions did extraordinary work in education and social assistance, but always within the framework of Western culture. In many areas, this work subsequently produced charges of cultural aggression, while at the same time Western ideas of democracy and national independence learned at mission schools encouraged a nascent anticolonialism and a revival of traditions. The need for adaptation in missionary work was not clearly perceived, and there was a real danger that the Church would be considered an alien institution and Christianity an alien religion. Although there were some signs of a reemerging policy of adaptation under Leo XIII, such as the reestablishment of an Indian hierarchy among the Syro-Malabar Catholics of what is now Kerala, it was not until after World War I, and the new policy of Benedict XV, that the Church began to cut its ties with the colonial powers and put down deep roots into the soil of mission lands.[78] Thus the Church can be said to have acquiesced in and benefited from the age of imperialism but to have changed its policy in time to escape many of its negative consequences.

Despite the inroads of nationalism, the Church during this period was in a sense rediscovering its own universality. A new flowering of international Catholic conferences and organizations changed the climate of European Catholicism. It was the great age of international Catholic congresses. In 1888 the first of a series of Catholic international scientific congresses took place at the Institut Catholique in Paris. It was attended by more than three hundred scientists, a hundred cardinals and bishops, and some sixteen hundred prominent guests. Similar congresses were held in 1891, 1984, and 1897 with great success.[79] It was also an age of Eucharistic

---

[78] Jerome G. D'Souza, SJ, *The Church and Civilization* (New York: Doubleday, 1967), 144.
[79] Vaussard, supra note 77, at 595–97.

Congresses, the movement becoming international in 1881. A papal legate was first sent to the Jerusalem congress of 1893, and this became habitual after 1906. The apogee of the movement was probably the Chicago Congress of 1913, which attracted immense crowds.[80] This period also saw the growth of international pilgrimages to Lourdes and other shrines. Fostered and encouraged by the Holy See, these meetings raised the international consciousness of Catholics, mitigated the effects of nationalism, and contributed to world peace.

The first international Catholic non-governmental organizations were also founded during this era. In 1910 the International Union of Catholic Women's Leagues was established. The Holy See approved the organization and agreed to name its president.[81] One society affiliated to this union was an older organization founded in 1897, the International Catholic Association for the Protection of Young Women.[82] Other organizations that date from this period are the International Catholic League Against Alcoholism (1897), the World Union of Catholic Teachers (1910), and the Catholic Federation for Physical and Sports Education (1911). The founding of international Catholic organizations was also fostered by the Holy See, as it served to build a network of peaceful relationships among Catholics of different nations and involve them in the common problems of world society.

But of all the international Catholic movements and organizations that were founded or flourished between 1870 and 1914, the most important and effective, without any doubt, was the Catholic social movement. Concerned with social justice, the rights of labor, and improved working conditions for laborers, this movement, consisting of numerous organizations, was inspired by and allied with similar movements outside the Church. All of them shared a perception of the need to protect workers in an age of industrialization against the injustices arising from laissez-faire capitalism, through

---

[80] Ibid., 599–600.
[81] Ibid., 606.
[82] Ibid., 607–8.

intervention by the state at the national and international levels. It is especially important to consider here the participation of Catholic elements in this movement. This involvement was a prelude to cooperation between the Church and the future International Labour Organisation (ILO). The ILO was founded in 1919 in response to the agitation of the social question by a wide spectrum of forces during the previous half century.[83]

The ILO was designed to bring governments, employers, and trade unions together for united action in the cause of social justice, and emphasized the setting of international labor standards, to be drawn up into conventions or recommendations for acceptance by states. The need for such international cooperation had long been evident. As early as 1788, Jacques Necker declared that the Sunday rest could not be maintained unless it were observed in every country. The British social reformer Robert Owen presented two memorials to the Congress of Aix-la-Chapelle in 1818, asking the members of the Quintuple Alliance to protect their workers against exploitation. The French Protestant industrialist Daniel Legrand addressed a circular to European governments in 1837, requesting them to outlaw, among other abuses, night and Sunday work and the employment of children under the age of twelve. A year later, the professional revolutionary Louis Blanqui remarked that since the powers had made treaties to kill men, it was time they did the same in order to save and improve their lives. Nothing came of these efforts, but the idea gradually caught on as the social movement gained momentum.[84]

In that movement, Catholic forces came to play a prominent role. Wilhelm von Ketteler, Bishop of Mainz, deserves credit as the real founder of the Catholic social movement. In his *Discourse on the Labor Movement and Its Tendencies* (1869) he condemned treating labor as a commodity and advocated higher wages, days of rest, limitation of working hours, and prohibition of child labor; in

---

[83] John Lucal, SJ, "The Church and the ILO," *America* (May 31, 1969): 644–46.

[84] Adeodat Boissard, "La Coopération International dans le Domaine Social: Le Bureau International du Travail et les Associations Internationales de Politique Sociale," *Le Problème de la Vie International* (Paris: Gabalda, 1927), 455.

another document of the same year he proposed workmen's compensation and state inspection of factories.[85] Catholic involvement in the social question took place in a number of countries. In Austria the line goes back to Karl von Vogelsang, in France to Charles La Tour du Pin and Count Albert de Mun, and the Society of Catholic Workingmen's Groups founded in 1871. There were similar developments in Italy, Belgium, and Switzerland, where in 1884 Msgr. Gaspar Mermillod founded the International Union in Fribourg, which met annually to discuss current problems in labor-management relations. Cardinals James Gibbons of Baltimore and Henry Manning of Westminster lent powerful support to the cause of labor unions in the U.S. and Great Britain. Pope Leo maintained contact with these circles either directly or through Msgr. Jacobini, whom he had charged with that task. In addition, he frequently received the movement's leaders and pilgrimages of workers in audience at the Vatican.[86]

In 1884 Count Albert de Mun made a motion in the French Parliament that the government propose international legislation for the protection of workers and their families. Three years later the Swiss Catholic leader Gaspard Descurtins urged the Federal Council to call for an international labor conference, an initiative that led to the Berlin Conference of 1890 on labor questions. Despite the opposition of Bismarck, the conference had been strongly supported by Kaiser Wilhelm II, who wrote to Pope Leo that he had appointed Bishop Kopp, the Prince-Bishop of Breslau, as his own delegate. The pope replied that the conference responded to one of his dearest wishes, that he was very pleased at the appointment of Bishop Kopp, and that the combined action of governments and conformity of legislation would do much to attain the desired aim. Since religion was so important in instilling the principles of justice, the Church should

---

[85] Albert Le Roy, SJ, *The Dignity of Labor, the Part Played by Catholics in the Work of the International Labor Organization* (Westminster, MD: Newman Press, 1957), 19–20.

[86] Jean-Yves Calvez, SJ, and Jacques Perrin, SJ, *The Church and Social Justice: The Social Teachings of the Church from Leo XIII to Pius XII* (Chicago: Regnery, 1961), 78–80.

exert an influence in the solution of the social problem and would continue to do so.[87]

The great charter of the Catholic social movement, Pope Leo's encyclical letter *Rerum Novarum*, appeared in 1891 and laid down the basic principles that would shape the Church's teaching and Catholic action on socioeconomic questions in the modern world. It provoked a storm of protest from the liberal advocates of laissez-faire capitalism, including many Catholics, since it advocated state intervention in the economy when necessary for social justice. The encyclical did not specifically propose international labor standards, but two years later the pope gave unqualified approval to a proposal from the Swiss Catholic leader Descurtins for a congress of workers, delegates to be chosen without distinction of nationality, to promote an international agreement for the protection of labor. Leo wrote Descurtins that since commodities competed on the international market, domestic legislation alone would not provide adequate protection; differences in regulation would favor one country over another.[88] Benjamin Masse states that "[a]gainst this background it is easy to understand the sympathy and support which the Holy See has consistently given to the International Labor Organization."[89]

In 1900 the International Association for Labor Legislation was founded, with permanent headquarters in Basel. A private organization, it brought together experts to make studies and proposals for universal labor norms, and diplomats to agree on them. National sections were remarkably ecumenical: priests, rabbis, and ministers participated along with freethinkers, socialists, Catholic social leaders, industrialists, and trade unionists. The French section included both Albert de Mun and the socialist Albert Thomas, the first Director-General of the ILO. The Constitutive Assembly of the organization solicited the patronage of the Holy See as well as the collaboration of governments. The Holy See accepted the invitation and sent an official representative to all congresses of the IALL as

---

[87] Ibid.

[88] Le Roy, supra note 85, at 3–4.

[89] Benjamin L. Masse, SJ, *Justice for All: An Introduction to the Social Teaching of the Catholic Church* (Milwaukee: Bruce, 1964), 552.

well as an annual financial contribution. The association managed to draw up and obtain ratification of two conventions prohibiting the use of white phosphorous in matches and night work by women. Its work was interrupted by the outbreak of World War I.[90] This direct forerunner of the ILO was also a breakthrough in the Church's social outreach, the role of Catholic laymen involving the Holy See in an international organization, and ecumenical cooperation transcending all credal or ideological lines.

Thus even in an age of nationalism the partial reemergence of the Holy See in its traditional peacemaking role helped bring about an awakening of international consciousness and a new support for various forms of international cooperation among Catholics. The best evidence for this is a Catholic elite of internationally minded activists following the lead of the Vatican, and this linkage has been established. As for the impact of the new policy of the Holy See under Leo XIII on the mass of Catholics, it seems reasonable to assume that his teaching had some influence on attitudes. Yet, the verdict of Renouvin, based on his study, is that during the period from 1871 to 1914, "in nearly all European Catholic churches, nationalist sentiment triumphed over religious solidarity."[91]

But when Renouvin added that the "Vatican made no serious attempt to correct this tendency," that the involvement of Leo XIII in the Carolines mediation and the Hague Conference preparations were merely attempts to restore Vatican prestige, and that his condemnations of the "armed peace" were only "vague allusions" bereft of any intention to take the initiative, his judgment should not be allowed to stand unchallenged.[92] All evidence presented in this chapter demonstrates that Pope Leo took very seriously, as ends valid in themselves, both his own peacemaking role and his advocacy of a systemic change in the international dispensation of justice. Although it is impossible to prove that Leo did all he could to stem the tide of nationalism and militarism, it is a matter of record that he attempted

---

[90] Le Roy, supra note 85, at 4–5.
[91] Renouvin and Duroselle, supra note 60, at 210.
[92] Ibid., 210–11.

to do a great deal and, when measured against other world leaders of the time, probably the most. It is fair to deduce from his policy that he would have done far more had he been free from the severe limitations imposed by anticlerical attacks on the Church and Italian efforts to minimize his role in international affairs.

More balanced is this other conclusion reached by Renouvin in the same volume:

> It would be arbitrary, therefore, to attribute to the papacy a consistently hostile attitude toward certain kinds of nationalism during this period. After 1914, the attitude of the Holy See was entirely different.[93]

Though still unfair to Leo XIII, the changed attitude accurately reflects the efforts of Pius X and the contributions of Benedict XV (1914–1922). After 1914 the attitude of the Holy See toward excessive nationalism became unmistakable. Pope Benedict would meet head-on the fervor of militaristic nationalism in an unstinting effort to end the carnage of World War I and promote a truly effective international organization.

---

[93] Ibid., 194.

The Holy See and the Founding of the League of Nations: 1914–1920

P IUS X DIED on August 20, 1914, the day the German Army
entered Brussels. The conclave elected as his successor the Archbishop of Bologna and a former papal diplomat, Cardinal Giacomo
della Chiesa, who took the name of Benedict XV. Benedict's brief
pontificate (1914–1922) was stamped with the traumatic experience
of a war he unceasingly tried to end. There is no question that the
Great War became a turning point in the approach of the Holy See,
which now began to teach unswervingly the futility of war and the
absolute necessity of world organization. There is also little doubt
about Pope Benedict's attitude toward the First World War. It was not
a crusade against tyranny, but, as he stated, "this scourge of His
wrath,"[1] "this horrible slaughter, which for a whole year has dishon-
ored Europe,"[2] and "the darkest tragedy of human hatred and human
madness."[3] Language this strong from a longtime diplomat had not
been heard from the Vatican for centuries, and it was anything but

---

[1] Harry Koenig, *Principles for Peace: Selections from Papal Documents, Leo XIII to
Pius XII* (Milwaukee: Bruce, 1943), ¶275, Exhortation *Ubi Primum* to the
Catholics of the Whole World, September 8, 1914. [Slightly different transla-
tion.]

[2] Ibid., ¶387, Exhortation *Allorchè Fummo* to the Belligerent Peoples and Their
Leaders, July 28, 1915. [Translation differs a bit.]

[3] Quoted in Carlo Falconi, *The Popes in the Twentieth Century: From Pius X to
John XXIII* (Boston: Little Brown, 1967), 117.

popular. Yet despite the mortification and oblivion that he would suffer, Benedict would initiate a transformation in Catholic attitudes toward war and peace that endures to the present day.

Benedict repeatedly appealed to the secular powers to reconcile their differences peacefully. He made these appeals in September, November, and December of 1914, and again in January and July of 1915. But the belligerents were in no mood to negotiate. They expressed no sincere interest in the Christmas truce proposed by the pope for 1914. Consequently, Pope Benedict used the full forces of Vatican diplomacy and other structures of the Church to alleviate the horrors of war by helping to arrange, in a frenzy of diplomatic activity, the exchange of disabled prisoners and civilians of occupied territories, the hospitalization of the sick in neutral countries, the exchange of letters between war prisoners and their families, a day of Sunday rest for prisoners, truces to bury the dead, the identification and marking of graves, the provisioning of inhabitants of devastated regions, and the repatriation of prisoners after the war. In numerous public statements, he expressed compassion for the victims of war, especially in Belgium and Poland, voiced concern over treatment of prisoners and civilians, congratulated the Red Cross for its humanitarian efforts, contributed to war relief funds, asked for prayers for peace, demanded respect for international law, continued his own efforts against the bombing of open undefended cities, and exhorted Catholics to practice Christian charity and social action as a means toward peace.[4]

---

[4] Koenig, supra note 1, ¶333, Letter of Cardinal Gasparri, Secretary of State, to Gustave Ador, President of the Red Cross, February 19, 1915; ¶¶334–35, Letter of Cardinal Gasparri, Secretary of State, to Henry Sienkiewicz, President of the General Committee of Relief for War Victims in Poland, March 12, 1915; ¶336, Decree *Annuendo all Pia Domanda* issued by Cardinal Gasparri, Secretary of State, March 15, 1915; ¶338, Allocution *C'est avec Couleurs Bien Sombres* to M. Van den Heuvel, Minster of Belgium to the Holy See, March 17, 1915; ¶339, Letter of Cardinal Gasparri, Secretary of State, to Cardinal Mercier. Archbishop of Malines, April 6, 1916; ¶350, Letter of Cardinal Gasparri, Secretary of State, to Bishop Sapieha of Cracow, April 9, 1915; ¶341, Decree *Mossa dal Pio Desiderio* of Cardinal Gasparri, Secretary of State, April 9, 1915; ¶¶342–46, Letter of Cardinal Gasparri, Secretary of State, to Cardinal Amette, Archbishop of Paris, April 23, 1915; ¶¶383–84, Letter of Cardinal Gasparri, Secretary of State, to Bishop Scozzoli of Rimini, July 12, 1915; ¶¶397–400,

Ironically, the First World War was particularly scandalous for the Church since the main belligerents represented a large proportion of Catholic Europe. One commentator wrote:

> In each combatant state the national hierarchy supported the war and Catholics fought against Catholics, with apparently clear consciences under "just war" rules, morally supported by their respective hierarchies, applying the same doctrine on the morality of war, emanating from the same spiritual organization.[5]

In fact, Catholic bishops, theologians, and lay groups of the warring nations publicly accused each other of condoning military atrocities, libel and slander, and of ignoring their respective "just" claims in the conflict. The French and German hierarchies were especially involved, but the picture was one of a Church fragmented by nationalistic passion that belied any sense of Christian charity or universality. The same commentator oddly concluded: "The position of Benedict XV in this bizarre situation was one of complete impotence."[6] The conclusion is exaggerated—certainly the pope's voice was a moderating influence on many issues. Benedict's policy toward the war was one of moral outrage; however, this often proved to be ineffective against temporal leaders intent on obliterating their adversaries without giving much thought to anything else.

It is critical to understand the position of Benedict toward the First World War. Throughout the conflict, he almost never appealed to the distinction between just and unjust war; he did not repudiate

---

Letter of Cardinal Gasparri, Secretary of State, to Bishop Koppes of Luxembourg, August 17, 1915; ¶¶410–11, Letter of Cardinal Gasparri, Secretary of State, to the Duchess of Vendôme, October 31, 1915; ¶¶427–29, Letter of Cardinal Gasparri, Secretary of State, to the Minister of Russia, December 25, 1915; ¶435, Cardinal Gasparri, Secretary of State, Replies to the Petition of the American Jewish Committee of New York, February 9, 1916; and ¶436, Letter of Cardinal Gasparri, Secretary of State, to Archbishop Morganti of Ravenna, February 17, 1916. See Koenig, 200–317, for many other illustrations of Benedict XV's efforts related to peace and avoidance or minimization of the consequences of war.

[5] Herder correspondence, IV, (October 1967), 297.

[6] Ibid., 298.

the classic teaching of just wars, but by implication declared it a childish morality in an adult age, inadequate because it helped to nourish rather than extinguish war.[7] There was a clear reason for his policy of refusing to give clear directives to the clergy and faithful or to adopt a position himself in relation to the belligerent powers: each side was asking him to condemn the other as the aggressor. As a Curia cardinal remarked in a letter to Charles Loiseau:

> This century seems to demand of the Papacy of today precisely what it reproved in the Papacy in the past. It would like the present pontiff to hurl himself in the midst of the warring peoples thunderbolt in hand, sparing no one. Such advice may be generous, but we today are more modern and know what would happen to us if we followed it. The result would be that we should no longer be at peace with any nation once they became reconciled. Because, quite frankly, to follow this idea to the end we should have to condemn one after the other, and with great publicity, all nations, all social classes, and every category of sinner.[8]

But it is important to take stock of alternatives that the pope may have pursued. An encyclical condemning the war would have presented serious problems, possibly resistance by bishops and faithful on opposing sides. Minds were made up and passions would have prevented any serious theological examination, reflection, or discussion. A doctrinal stand requiring the inner assent of believers would have produced chaotic effects. Benedict therefore took an evangelical line on the war with the tragic result that he was unjustly accused of favoritism or cowardly neutrality, especially by Catholics on the Allied side. Even Leon Bloy, a spiritual and gifted man, frankly wrote in his journal for the years 1914–15 that the pope was a person of stupefying mediocrity since he accused no one and declared himself neutral; this was a monstrous declaration—the pope deceived infallibly.[9] This

[7] Falconi, supra note 3, at 118.
[8] Quoted in ibid.
[9] Ibid., 123.

bitterness persisted throughout the war and was not confined to conservatives. On November 17, 1918, the liberal Catholic Friedrich Baron von Hugel wrote to the excommunicated leader of modernism, Alfred Loisy, that it would be in the interests of the world and the Church to require the abdication of both Wilhelm II and Benedict XV.[10] Benedict's status as a neutral pope would later deny him the recognition he deserved. But many contemporaries questioned his proposals for peace and international organization.

Opponents of Benedict's policy usually forgot that where a point of ethics and international law was beyond dispute, such as the violation of Belgian neutrality by the Germans, he did not hesitate to speak out. It is significant that of all the neutral sovereigns and heads of state, the pope was the only one to protest this violation. The Holy See had not been a party to the Treaty of 1839 and thus need not have made a pronouncement. However, the president of the United States remained silent, and the Swiss Federal Assembly could not overcome the opposition of the German-speaking cantons. In an allocution of 22 January 1915 to the College of Cardinals, Benedict condemned "all injustice on whatsoever side it has been committed."[11] Though the language was not explicit, he received the thanks of the Belgian government and a protest from von Mühlberg, the Prussian minister to the Holy See.[12] A subsequent note from the Secretary of State, Cardinal Gasparri, to the Belgian minister to the Holy See was very explicit recalling that the German chancellor, Herr von Bethmann-Hollweg, had publicly confessed in the Reichstag that Germany had violated Belgian neutrality.

Pope Benedict attempted to influence Italy to remain neutral, and counseled Emperor Franz Josef to cede the Trentino to Italy to deprive the Italian interventionist movement of one of its most

---

[10] Ibid.

[11] Quoted in Koenig, supra note 1, ¶322, Allocution *Convocare Vos* to the College of Cardinals, January 22, 1915.

[12] Humphrey Johnson, *Vatican Diplomacy in the World War* (London: Basil Blackwell, 1933), 16. See Koenig, supra note 1, ¶¶363–77, Letter of Cardinal Gasparri, Secretary of State, to J. van den Heuvel, Belgian Minister to the Vatican, July 6, 1915.

persuasive arguments for entering the war, that of irredentism.[13] Of course Italy's intervention would not only widen the war, it would also put the Holy See in a very delicate position, since the Law of Guarantees of 1871 did not contemplate a state of war. When Italy did enter, however, the diplomatic representatives of the Central Powers voluntarily withdrew to Lugano, where they were allowed by Italy to correspond freely with the Vatican, but this was not regarded as a satisfactory solution by the Holy See. Although Benedict made public his sorrow over its entry into the war, his relations with Italy were remarkably smooth, despite several disturbing incidents involving the opening of Vatican mail and the expropriation of the residence of the Austrian ambassador to the Holy See, the Palazzo Venezia.[14]

At this point, Pope Benedict did not consider himself an apt mediator. He rather hoped that President Wilson could be persuaded to assume that role. Accordingly, he sent Cardinal Gibbons of Baltimore to Washington in September, 1915, but without positive results: The United States felt it could do nothing without a request for mediation by one of the belligerents.[15] During the same month, Benedict suggested the approach of guardedly disclosing a concrete peace proposal. A distinguished French prelate, visiting Rome to protest the pope's alleged pro-German attitude, pressed for an authoritative statement of the pope's views on peace. Cardinal Gasparri told him that according to the mind of the pope a just peace required five conditions: (1) France must preserve its territorial integrity; (2) Belgium must be independent; (3) Austria-Hungary should remain a great power, but this was not incompatible with territorial concessions to Italy; (4) Poland must be reestablished as a sovereign state; and, (5) the settlement of the Balkan question should exclude Russia from Constantinople and the Straits of Bosporus.[16] This proposal, which coincided remarkably with traditional British policy, produced no immediate reaction, but its

---

[13] Koenig, supra note 1, ¶367; Johnson, supra note 12, at 35–36.

[14] Johnson, supra note 12, at 18–19.

[15] Ibid., 22.

[16] Ibid., 21–22.

main features would appear again in the public peace proposal made by Benedict on August 1, 1917.

At this point, it seemed that any peace proposal based merely on the balance of power—that is, upon particular questions of national interest—was doomed to fail. However, there is evidence that a full year before the pope's peace proposal of 1917, the Holy See was already thinking in terms of transforming the global order through the establishment of an international organization or society of nations, that could provide the context and mechanisms necessary for peaceful settlement of the particular questions dividing the belligerents. In April 1916 there appeared in Rome a small pamphlet by a relatively unknown lawyer, Enrico Bafile, titled *"La formula della pace"* ("The Formula for Peace"), which proposed that a multinational organization be established to end the war. It received surprising publicity from the Catholic press. For example, the *Corriere d'Italia* reviewed the pamphlet even before it was put on sale. No internal evidence showed that the Roman Curia had any part in the work, for it contained no religious or moral statements and mentioned neither God nor the pope. Its theoretical base was pure law and positive science. Yet the influence of Pope Benedict was not hard to find: Bafile was related to Msgr. Tedeschini, who was very close to the pope, and there is little doubt that the work emanated from this environment and reflected the ideas of Benedict XV.[17]

Bafile began his pamphlet with the premise that since each party in the war claims to be fighting for justice, although in reality fighting for its own interests, the total victory of either side would be a calamity for the world. A settlement had to be arranged while both parties were equal in strength, and public opinion must be aroused to support this result. No just and lasting peace could be possible without compromise, but only if this were based upon law and right. But there can be no effective law without an authority capable of declaring and imposing it, hence the necessity for creating an international organ superior to the nations. To end this war

---

[17] Luigi Salvatorelli, *La Politica della Santa Sede dopo la Guerra* (Milano: Instituto per gli Studi di Politica Internazionale, 1937), 33, n. 8.

and prevent future wars, the authority needed to resolve conflict had to be handed over to an international organization capable of declaring the requirements of the applicable law and sufficiently empowered to maintain that law amongst its members and to defend it against non-members.

Membership in this body would be optional and open to neutrals who would put their armies at its service. Belligerents could do the same without defaulting on obligations to their allies, because these obligations have no end other than peace through justice. If this could be achieved by juridical means, then no nation could be justified in continuing the war, and it should join the new organization immediately. If any power rebelled against this plan, it would likely reveal its ulterior motives and appear responsible for the war and a traitor to humanity, thereby subjecting itself to possible military action by the forces of the organization. In any case, the multinational entity would be able to resolve under international law all existing and future conflicts. In essence, this would be the formula for peace.

The proposal did not receive a great deal of attention outside certain Catholic circles, especially in Italy, nor was there any official response. Nevertheless, perceptive observers in Europe were well aware that it represented the thought of Benedict XV. For example, the anonymous author of a famous article in *La Revue de Paris* of October and November, 1918, who attacked the Pope as anti-French, angrily rejected the papal thesis that the war was a vulgar power conflict rather than a crusade against tyranny, and declared that the Bafile book reproduced Benedict's ideas. The multinational organization proposed in *La formula* was not described in detail—it was called both a federation and a confederation—but it was certainly a novel idea. As an organization formed during the conflict, it was intended to include the belligerents, both sides, who would then participate in the resolutions of their conflicts. The author evidently believed that the horror of war manifested the immediate necessity of such an international organization. The belligerents initially disagreed, but they would come to see the necessity after their chosen method, the military solution, had run its course. Most important, the plan foreshadowed in a remarkable way the later proposals of Benedict XV, the concept of "peace without victory" advocated by Wilson in his speech to the U.S. Senate on January 22, 1917, and certain features of the new international organization—the League of Nations—that would in fact come into being.

Benedict, however, did not publicly propose such a radical solution in his own name, for the international community was not yet prepared for this kind of direct papal intervention. In 1916 the views of the Holy See would not have been received favorably by either side. The Central Powers seemed surer of victory than ever, and the Allies were spurred on to new efforts by their reversals and by their hope for American intervention. The signs of the acceptability of his proposal were more favorable in the spring of 1917. The new nuncio to Bavaria, Archbishop Eugenio Pacelli, made soundings in Munich and Berlin in May and June. In July the Reichstag passed a resolution in favor of a moderate peace introduced by a deputy of the Center Party. The nuncio in Berne urged the Vatican to take some initiative before the opening of the proposed international Socialist congress in Stockholm, which would support a peace without indemnities or annexations. Benedict decided it was time to act.[18]

On August 1, 1917, the pope submitted his proposal in the form of a letter to the belligerent peoples and their leaders.[19] Titled *Dès le Début*, the letter began with a statement of basic papal policy. This included impartiality toward all belligerents as their common father; assistance to all without distinction of person, nationality, or religion in accordance with the law of love; and a constant effort to bring both peoples and their leaders to a discussion of means to secure a just peace. The pope then reviewed his previous peace initiatives, pointing out that sufficient publicity was not given to all of them, and he dwelt upon the horrors of the war. He again called for peace and had no private political aim in doing so. His action was based on the supreme duty of his ministry and office. He now

---

[18] Johnson, supra note 12, at 24–25; Falconi, supra note 3, at 122.

[19] Koenig, supra note 1, ¶¶519–34, Exhortation *Dès le Début* to the Belligerent Peoples and to Their Leaders, August 1, 1917.

desired to put forward some concrete and practical propositions and invited the governments to agree on the following points:

1. The necessity to substitute the moral force of right for the material force of arms, followed by the simultaneous and reciprocal diminution of armaments and, as a substitute for armies, the institution of arbitration, with sanctions against the state which should refuse either to submit international questions to arbitration or to accept its decision;[20]

2. The abolition of all obstacles to the free intercourse of peoples: freedom of and common rights over the sea;[21]

3. An entire and reciprocal condoning of war damages, with certain adjustments to be made if necessary;[22]

4. A total evacuation of Belgium and France by third-party military forces; on the part of the other belligerents, a restoration of the German colonies;[23] and,

5. The settlement of territorial questions between Italy and Austria, between Germany and France, and in Armenia, the Balkan states, and Poland in a conciliatory spirit by the belligerents.[24]

These were the essential foundations on which the future reorganization of the peoples must be built, according to the pope. His points would make impossible the return of similar conflicts and would prepare the solution of the economic question so important to the material well-being of all the belligerent states. The pope said that he was animated by the hope of seeing acceptance of these principles that would witness the "speedy end of the terrible struggle which more and more seems to be a useless slaughter."[25]

---

[20] Ibid., ¶525.
[21] Ibid., ¶526.
[22] Ibid., ¶527.
[23] Ibid., ¶528.
[24] Ibid., ¶¶529–30.
[25] Ibid., ¶532.

The response which the pope's peace proposal evoked from the belligerent governments was extremely disappointing. The British reaction at first was to doubt whether a response would serve any useful purpose until the Central Powers admitted their guilt in regard to Belgium and promised its independence; indicated the amount of reparations that would be paid; declared their war aims; and, suggested measures to guarantee the future peace of the world. The French foreign minister, Ribot, was adamantly opposed to negotiations at this point and wished to make no reply to the pope's proposal. But France later agreed to associate itself with a British *note verbale* to the effect that the war had to continue until victory. Britain later associated itself with President Wilson's more detailed reply, transmitted to the pope on 28 August.[26]

Wilson responded that the pope's proposal would be a return to the *status quo ante*, which was unthinkable, would strengthen Germany, and perpetuate a regime whose word was completely untrustworthy. The president had originally indicated he might ignore the papal message entirely, but he was advised by Colonel House to respond to it, for refusal would discourage German liberals and hasten the collapse of the Kerensky regime in Russia. As the president's advisor stated, "I believe you have an opportunity to take the peace negotiations out of the hands of the Pope and hold them in your own."[27] Wilson then wrote a reply, but purposely ignored those aspects of the pope's plan pertaining to international organization. He was also vague about specifics in order to spare Allied feelings, for he could not say that their territorial claims did not interest the U.S. As a result of the pope's proposal, Wilson began to realize that American peace aims had to be expressed, and he wrote to House that the U.S. should ascertain what the Allies would insist on and then formulate their own positions.[28]

---

[26] Johnson, supra note 12, at 30–32.

[27] Letter of August 17, 1917, from Col. House to the President, *Intimate Papers of Col. House* (Boston,: Houghton Mifflin, 1928), vol. 3, 156–57.

[28] Johnson, supra note 12, at 32–33; *Intimate Papers of Col. House,* supra note 27, vol. 3, at 154.

Italy avoided a formal reply to the pope's proposal but on October 25, 1917, the minister for foreign affairs made an antipapal speech in the Parliament which was taken as the negative reply of the Italian government. Belgium thanked the pope for his solicitude on December 24 but its delay gave this response little effect. Of the other Allied and Associated Powers only Brazil sent a reply. The German response, forwarded to the pope on September 19, was a great disappointment after the hopeful signs of the summer. The note not only failed to mention Belgium but said nothing of any territorial settlement, though lip service was paid to arbitration. Austria sent a reply the following day in the form of a personal letter from the emperor to the pope. This letter supported disarmament, freedom of the seas, and arbitration. The terms of peace should allow the empire to develop in security, and Austria was not directly concerned with the status of Belgium.[29]

In spite of these rebuffs, the pope and Cardinal Gasparri did not let the matter drop. They continued their efforts through contacts and correspondence, to explain and elaborate the plan, and to press for an exchange of proposals.[30] One of these subsequent communications is of particular importance to an understanding of Benedict's first and key point and the essential strength of the international organization he envisaged. A letter of Cardinal Gasparri to Lloyd George, written on September 28, 1917, detailed the means for obtaining the "reciprocal and simultaneous disarmament universally desired." The pope considered that the only practical way of effecting this was through

> a pact among civilized nations, including non-belligerents, requiring the simultaneous and reciprocal suppression of compulsory military service; the institution of a tribunal of arbitration to decide international controversies; and the imposition of a general boycott as a sanction against any

---

[29] Johnson, supra note 12, at 33–36.
[30] Ibid., 35.

nations that might attempt to re-establish obligatory military service, or might refuse to submit an international question to arbitration or to accept the decision thereon.[31]

The same three steps were set forth in a letter of Gasparri to Archbishop Chesnelong of Sens of October 7, 1917, clarifying *Dès le Début*. The Cardinal employed the term "Court of Arbitration" in his correspondence.[32] Both letters argued that voluntary military service would provide the forces necessary for the maintenance of public order. By the same token, this type of defense scheme would not supply the enormous armies required for modern war. Thus the pope's proposal would produce,

> without any disturbance of public order, almost automatically a complete disarmament, with all the benefits directly consequent thereon: a lasting international peace (as far as that is possible in this world), and the restoration of sound finances in the various nations in as short a time as possible.[33]

From this it is clear that Benedict expected the nations to apply economic sanctions against the state which would refuse to submit international questions to arbitration or to accept an arbitral decision. Small volunteer armies would avoid war as the means of acquiring justice. War itself would be replaced by non-violent economic isolation, and then only as a last resort when arbitration had failed.

By November 1917, however, it was clear that the pope's peace proposals were not being given serious consideration and that his attempt at mediation was failing. The Allies were unwilling to settle for a moderate peace, and Germany refused to give any guarantees on Belgium. It is clear that the Entente leaders considered the papal proposal pro-German, and it did coincide with certain secret German

---

[31] Koenig, supra note 1, ¶541, Letter of Cardinal Gasparri, Secretary of State, to Lloyd George, Prime Minister of England, September 28, 1917.

[32] Ibid., ¶549, Letter of Cardinal Gasparri, Secretary of State, to Archbishop Chesnelong of Sens, October 7, 117.

[33] Ibid., ¶542, Letter of Cardinal Gasparri, Secretary of State, to Lloyd George, Prime Minister of England, September 28, 1917.

and Austrian moves that the Allies considered a trap.[34] But basically the powers were not ready to stop the war because the tide of battle had not yet turned definitively in anyone's favor. Concern for immediate military advantage and future territorial arrangements gave the war a revitalized momentum, which repressed the thought that aims could be settled by compromise in a "peace without victory." This momentum made inopportune the proposal that states should no longer seek security in arms but in a new and untried international system.

From the outset of the First World War, the Holy See had entertained hopes of obtaining a seat at the peace conference that would construct a new international order. When Italy entered the war in the spring of 1915, the Vatican feared a repetition of previous Italian maneuvers, because of the Roman Question, to exclude the Holy See from international conferences. Indeed by the end of that year, this fear was justified. The secret Treaty of London, signed between Italy and the Allies on April 26, 1915, was Italy's price for entering the war and promised territorial and other concessions. One of these addressed the status of the Holy See and was contained in Article 15, which stated

> France, Great Britain and Russia pledge themselves to support Italy in not allowing the representatives of the Holy See to undertake any diplomatic steps having for their object the conclusion of peace or the settlement of questions connected with the present war.[35]

According to the Italian premier at the time, his government exacted this promise to prevent the Holy See from being in a position to demand the internationalization of the Italian Law of Guarantees.[36]

---

[34] Johnson, supra note 12, at 30; Maurice Pernot, *Le Saint-Siège, L'Eglise Catholique et la Politique Mondiale* (Paris: Armand Colin, 1924), 35–36.
[35] Article 15, Treaty of London, in *The Major International Treaties 1914–1973: A History and Guide with Texts,* ed. J. A. S. Grenville (London: Methuen & Co., 1974), 26.
[36] Johnson, supra note 12, at 38–39.

Although the Treaty was secret, the pope seems to have learned of it by the end of 1915,[37] and the entire document, as well as other secret engagements made by the czar with the Allies, was revealed by the Soviet government after the October Revolution of 1917.[38] Once the existence of Article 15 became public knowledge, the pope encouraged protests against it, but the Allies remained firm. In England, Lord Stanhope told the House of Lords that the pope was like any other neutral sovereign: His representative could not be admitted to the peace table without the consent of all belligerents.[39] Lord Robert Cecil carefully stated in the House of Commons that the scope of the provision was simply that England would support an Italian refusal to give that consent; it did not constitute a promise to oppose any action of the Holy See to bring about peace.[40] Thus Article 15 does not seem to have been framed in order to prevent the pope from acting as mediator and was, consequently, not the primary cause of the Allied rejection of Pope Benedict's peace proposal of August 1, 1917. On the other hand, it must have had some influence, for if the pope's proposal had been accepted, papal mediation would most likely have followed, after which it would have been difficult to refuse the Holy See a place at the peace conference.[41]

The popular reaction to the pope's peace plan was even less friendly than the official responses. English public opinion was hostile. Even the *Tablet*, a British Catholic journal, rejected the proposal on the grounds that Pope Benedict imperfectly understood the military situation (which was presumably the determining factor).[42] In Germany there was some sympathy for the plan among leading Catholics, but their voices were muted. Only the Socialist organs praised the Pope's intentions. The journal *Vorwaerts* said on August 17 that the papal plan was closer to the ideas of the Socialist

---

[37] Walter H. Peters, *The Life of Benedict XV* (Milwaukee: Bruce, 1959), 169.
[38] Johnson, supra note 12, at 37.
[39] Ibid., 37–38.
[40] Ibid.
[41] Ibid., 38.
[42] Ibid., 30.

International than was the position of the French foreign minister.[43] In Italy, the Catholic and Socialist press was generally favorable, while nationalist and liberal organs were opposed. Pope Benedict was called "Maladetto XV" by extreme nationalists[44] and, after the battle of Caporetto a few days later, was blamed for contributing to that defeat, since certain Catholic organizations had joined the Socialists in spreading peace propaganda among the Italian soldiers.

It was in France that the pope's plan encountered the strongest opposition among Catholics. Ultramontanes and freethinkers joined in condemning what Clemenceau called a "peace against France" and a "peace against violated justice."[45] While Clemenceau castigated Benedict as *"le pape boche,"* the equally anti-Catholic German General Erich Ludendorff called him *"der französiche Papst."*[46] Several French bishops tried to interpret the papal plan in a manner that was least hostile to the Allies, occasioning numerous letters and replies from the Holy See. But the general reaction among Catholics, including many of the hierarchy, was still very negative.[47] This reaction was epitomized by a ceremony in the Church of the Madeleine in Paris on December 10, 1917, during which celebrated Dominican preacher and scholar Père Sertillanges, in the presence of the Cardinal-Archbishop of Paris and many governmental and civic leaders, forcefully rejected Benedict's plan for peace and called for France to fulfill its divine mission by continuing the war to the bitter end and imposing "the peace of the soldier." As Père Sertillanges exhorted:

> Most Holy Father, we cannot at this time hold to your words
> of peace. . . . Our enemies are still powerful, untouched by
> invasion; your solemn reproaches have not made them

---

[43] Ibid., 35–36.

[44] Falconi, supra note 3, at 115.

[45] Johnson, supra note 12, at 30.

[46] Peters, supra note 37, at 172; D. A. Binchy, *Church and State in Fascist Italy* (London: Oxford University Press, 1941), 638; John F. Pollard, *The Unknown Pope: Benedict XV (1914–1922) and the Pursuit of Peace* (London: Geoffrey Chapman, 1999), 94.

[47] Pernot, supra note 34, at 36.

renounce the anti-Christian principles that have guided them. . . . We feel constrained to bring our enemy, if we can, to experience anguish, the only lesson he seems capable of learning. We shall conquer him. . . . Our peace will thus not be a conciliatory peace. It will not be the peace of the diplomats, nor the peace of Stockholm . . . it will not even be— and we regret it with all our heart—the peace of a paternity thrusting himself between the two camps: it will be the peace of a bitter war fought to the end, the peace of just power smashing violence, the peace of the soldier![48]

What angered public opinion most was that the pope's proposal identified neither conquerors nor conquered, neither unjust aggressors nor victims. Pernot called it *"la paix blanche,"* saying that the pope was attributing an equality of right to all the belligerents and should have realized the negative response to such a move.[49] The public did not want to hear that the war through which they had suffered was not a noble crusade for justice but, in the words of the pope himself, "a useless slaughter." This famous phrase, which became infamous as it shook the world's conscience, had been kept in the document by the pope against the advice of his closest advisors. Falconi suggested that the pope's single-mindedness shows the moral greatness of Benedict. He could have achieved a diplomatic victory, perhaps, without so total a condemnation of war. But his overriding goal was to stop the war as soon as possible and secure the definite suspension of all wars. By subordinating diplomatic to moral and evangelical considerations, he forfeited considerable, if momentary, prestige.[50]

Pope Benedict's peace proposal of 1917 was certainly not rejected as utopian. Five months later Woodrow Wilson's Fourteen Points, sharing some of the pope's idealism as to the new world order,

---

[48] Maurice Vaussard, "L'Eglise Catholique, la Guerre et la Paix," *Guerre et Paix* (Lyon: Chronique Social de France, 1953), 134. [Lucal translation.] See Falconi, supra note 3, at 120.

[49] Pernot, supra note 37, at 35.

[50] Falconi, supra note 3, at 120.

received a tremendous ovation from the same circles that had ignored or criticized *Dès le Début*. Wilson's first four points corresponded to Benedict's first and second: open covenants, freedom of the seas, removal of economic barriers, and the reduction of armaments to levels necessary for domestic safety. The president's last point called for a general association of nations, a concept implicit in Benedict's first. The territorial changes proposed by Wilson were, of course, quite different. Wilson's points were based on the principle of nationality and much more favorable to the Allies. But apart from territorial questions, the Fourteen Points were widely acclaimed as giving Wilson the moral leadership of the world, something Benedict never received, and the question necessarily arises as to why this was so.

It is noteworthy that Woodrow Wilson, like Benedict XV, had made *démarches* toward mediation in 1916, and his efforts were met with equally poor results.[51] The following year, he had also, like the pope, spoken out as a neutral against a victor's peace imposed on the vanquished. In his address to the United States Senate on January 22, 1917, he advocated "peace without victory," a phrase which, like Benedict's "useless slaughter," he had kept in his text despite the objection of a close adviser, Secretary of State Lansing.[52] Benedict hailed this address as "the most courageous document which has appeared since the beginning of the war," and said it "revives the principles of Christian civilization."[53] Many others agreed, and the speech was widely acclaimed and won Wilson the support of those holding different perspectives on the war. But when the neutral pope tried the same approach a few months later, his renewed efforts were met with little enthusiasm or approval.

In August 1917, there remained some minimal chance for a negotiated settlement. The pope's peace plan was viewed primarily in terms of its territorial aspects and only secondarily as a moral appeal for a new world order. His first point received little atten-

---

[51] Ray Stannard Baker, *Woodrow Wilson: Life and Letters* (New York, Charles Scribner's Sons, 1946), vol. V, 412.

[52] Ibid., 407–14, 425.

[53] "Pope Lauds Wilson Speech: Calls It 'Most Courageous Document' Issued in the War," *New York Times* (January 26, 1917): 2.

tion: The question was what each nation would finally get after all the bloodshed. By January 1918, a negotiated peace was virtually impossible, and so Wilson's Fourteen Points were viewed as an idealistic statement of war aims and a blueprint for the world after an Allied victory. The Fourteen Points acted as a seductive peace appeal to the people and leaders of the Central Powers, while they stimulated great moral fervor on the Allied side. Wilson was in a position to offer a plan that would provide a framework for peace discussions, although few realized the implications of his proposals or how much they contradicted the secret treaties already reached among the Allied Powers. It was a case where the idealistic offer of a belligerent was more effective than the practical proposal of a neutral. Pope Benedict called the war a "useless slaughter," but President Wilson insisted that the Allies were fighting a war to end war. This was much more appealing to the spirit of the time. In comparing and contrasting Pope Benedict's peace proposal with the Fourteen Points of President Wilson, a well-known French Catholic, according to one of Benedict's biographers, is said to have exclaimed, "The President has sent out an Encyclical and the Pope a Protocol."[54]

Catholic commentators have been fond of pointing out the similarities between Benedict's proposal and Wilson's Fourteen Points in the area of international organization, even to the point of saying that *Dès le Début* was "an exact anticipation" of the President's program.[55] Their motive seemed designed to give the pope credit for being the first sovereign to propose reduction of armaments, compulsory arbitration, and sanctions—thus linking him to the League of Nations. La Brière declared that until August 1, 1917, no chief of state had formulated precisely the second and third of these principles, later stated explicitly in the Fourteen Points. Despite the failure of contemporaries to admit this, he argued that history would ultimately do justice to Benedict XV for making the first categorical affirmation of these necessary reforms in international public law

[54] William Barry, "Benedict XV: Pontiff of Peace," *The Dublin Review* 170 (January 1922): 171.

[55] See Falconi, supra note 3, at 121; Peters, supra note 37, at 163; and Pollard, supra note 46, at 128.

that would later find their way into the treaties of 1919 and 1920.[56] Benedict does deserve this credit, which he rarely gets from anyone except these commentators, but it would be a mistake to conclude that the Fourteen Points were simply a repetition or duplication of his ideas. There are significant differences that should not be overlooked. The same is true, in other ways, of *Dès le Début* vis-à-vis the League Covenant and the entire series of peace treaties that finally ended the Great War.

The Fourteen Points differed from the pope's plan in several ways. Of the first four points offered by Wilson, only two—freedom of the seas and reduction of armaments—are explicitly mentioned in Benedict's proposals. The pope probably favored open covenants, and the Holy See later registered several concordats with the League. More importantly, Wilson was silent on the pope's key point, that is, compulsory arbitration with economic sanctions. Benedict emphasized the need for a process in three steps: (1) substitution of right (the French *droit*, which includes the Anglo-Saxon notion of law) for material force, followed by (2) simultaneous and reciprocal arms reduction, and finally, (3) compulsory arbitration with economic sanctions. Wilson certainly endorsed the first step, which appears in the Preamble to the League Covenant, and stated the second so impressively in his fourth point that his language is found in Article 8/1 of the Covenant. But the concept of compulsory arbitration with sanctions is not contained in the Fourteen Points. Moreover, only a weak version of arbitration full of ambiguity appears in the Covenant (Articles 12–16).

Perhaps the most famous of Wilson's Fourteen Points, placed last for emphasis, was his proposal for a "general association of nations." The idea had been in his mind since August, 1914. It had formed a central pillar of his peace program since May, 1916, and it received brief mention in his address of January 22, 1917—but this fueled the ambitions of the president's critics.[57] This concept is only

56 Yves de La Brière, SJ, *L'Organisation International du Monde Contemporain et la Papauté Soveraine, Series I* (Paris: Editions Spes, 1924), 45–48.
57 Baker, supra note 51, vol. V, at 416.

implied in the pope's proposal, and then just to the extent that the community of nations would have had to operate collectively in the enforcement of sanctions. Significantly, however, Benedict later developed his thinking on the subject—perhaps influenced by the views of Wilson and others, and the founding of the League of Nations. In the encyclical *Pacem Dei Munus* of May 1920, he would express the desire that

> all States, putting aside mutual suspicion, should unite in one league, or rather a sort of family of peoples, calculated both to maintain their own independence and safeguard the order of human society.[58]

As will be argued, this was a likely endorsement of the League of Nations in principle or concept rather than in its actual implementation, but it marked an advance in the pope's thought.

Moving to the more concrete terms of the peace settlement, which would be vital to the success of any future organization of states, the reciprocal condonation of war damages (with adjustments for exceptional cases) found in Benedict's third point, but in none of Wilson's fourteen, now appears a far wiser course than the imposition of the huge indemnities that caused so much economic disaster and bitter hatred in the interwar period and helped bring on another world conflict. As for the territorial proposals in the pope's fourth and fifth points, it has been well argued that history proved them to have been more realistic than the president's Fourteen Points and certainly better than the actual peace settlement. Benedict's plan would probably have left France without all of Alsace-Lorraine, but it would have saved many French lives and left the country no more insecure than it actually was. For Belgium, a speedier liberation would have offset advantages from reparations. Italy would not have acquired discontented Germans and Slovenes. Poland might have been smaller but more secure between a friendly Germany and Russia.

---

[58] Koenig, supra note 1, ¶678, *Encyclical Pacem Dei Munus Pulcherrimum* on Peace and Christian Reconciliation, May 23, 1920.

Benedict did not desire the dismemberment of the Austro-Hungarian Empire and many historians eventually agreed with him. Peace in 1917 would have left the empire shaken and badly in need of reform, but many new problems in Central Europe could have been avoided. A "Vatican peace" would not have involved the wholesale dismemberment of Turkey's Asiatic empire, but it would have freed Armenia, which the Treaty of Lausanne did not. Turkey certainly would have been compelled to grant the Arabs greater autonomy. Benedict's solution would also have prevented the bloodbath which terminated the attempt to create a "greater Greece" on the eastern shores of the Aegean. Lastly, the extinction of Germany's colonial empire did not preserve peace. A settlement leaving the Reich with territorial losses in Alsace-Lorraine and Poland and no gains to show in compensation for these losses would have compromised the prestige of the Prussian military class. This would not be forgotten by many Germans in the coming decades.

Although it was not a detailed plan for a new international organization, Pope Benedict's proposal would have provided a firmer foundation for such a structure than that enjoyed by the League of Nations. Because his peace would have originated not from victory but from a cessation of hostilities, it would have been in itself a kind of manifesto that war was no longer an acceptable solution to international problems. It would have probably been a more stable peace insofar as it was less vindictive. It would also have been less traumatic because it corrected certain defects in the *status quo ante* rather than making a drastic shift in the balance of power. From the pope's peace initiative, a new international structure would likely have arisen, built according to a step-by-step process until it was capable of dealing with nationalist aspirations and territorial adjustments in an atmosphere free from the passions of war. This body would have been universal, not a society for victors and invited neutrals. It would also have been more pacifist than the League, in that the sanctions it applied to offenders would have been economic rather than military; consequently, it would have required smaller armed forces than the League system. Lastly, this new structure could, and in all probability would, have been transformed into a genuine society of nations along the lines of the League, but stronger in dealing with threats to peace and security.

As Francis Walters has stated in *A History of the League of Nations*, the pope's peace proposal of 1917 "made no effective impression at the time."[59] But, Walters also noted, it made a contribution as one of many examples of "The League idea in the First World War," along with the schemes formulated by the British League of Nations Society, the American League to Enforce Peace, the Fabian Society, Wilson in his Fourteen Points, and by government committees such as the French Committee headed by Leon Bourgeois and the Phillimore Committee in Great Britain.[60] It should be noted that in 1918 and 1919 Benedict's plan received far more attention from proponents of the League idea on the continent, especially in Germany, than it did in the Anglo-Saxon countries. Catholics as a whole were more disposed than others to grant it favorable consideration.[61] Benedict XV did not stop the war or influence the peace to any great extent, but he did inspire some people at the time, and his wisdom has influenced many more since.

As the war ground to a close in 1918, the Holy See still hoped that in some way it would be invited to the peace conference that would remake the world. Reliable reports indicated that in July 1918 Cardinal Gasparri obtained the assistance of the Belgian government to inquire about a modification of Article 15 of the Treaty of London, which would exclude the Holy See from postwar peace deliberations. Catholic bishops of the world also asked that the Holy See be invited to the peace talks. The mission of Msgr. Bonaventura Cerretti to Paris, before he was named nuncio there, was also connected with this effort. However, the promise made to Italy, plus the personal dispositions of leaders beginning with

[59] Francis Walters, *A History of the League of Nations* (London: Oxford University Press, 1952), vol. I, 18–19.
[60] Ibid., 15–24.
[61] "Favor League Plan to Safeguard Peace: Cardinal Gibbons Sends Letter to Taft," *New York Times* (7 February 1919): 2.

Clemenceau and Wilson, rendered all of these efforts to reserve a place for the Holy See in peace deliberations futile.

When it became clear that the Holy See would be excluded, Benedict promised, in an allocution of December 24, 1918, his prayers and his "firm resolve to secure to the just deliberations of the world congress the support of Our influence among the faithful. . . ."[62] Nonetheless, some saw in this an indication that he still wanted to take part. On March 19, 1919, *L'Osservatore Romano* denied this interpretation. Still, the pope would have wished to participate but only if there were a prospect of a truly conciliatory peace. This was something in which the victors of the war displayed little interest. However, even before the conference opened in January, 1919, Benedict was already on record as supporting the proposal for a League of Nations. In a letter to Cardinal Gasparri on November 3, 1918, he said that he longed for the day when "universal concord will unite the nations in a League fruitful of good."[63] More important, his special New Year's message to America praised Wilson and expressed the hope that the Peace Conference might result in a new world order with a League of Nations, the abolition of conscription, and the establishment of tribunals to adjust international disputes. The message stated:

> On the eve of the new year, in which humanity is at last to enjoy the blessings of peace, we are glad to send cordial greetings to the American people as the champions of those same principles which have been proclaimed by both President Wilson and the Holy See, ensuring for the world justice, peace and Christian love. In this solemn moment, when a new era in the history of the world is about to begin, we pray that the Almighty may shed His light upon the delegates

---

[62] Koenig, supra note 1, ¶610, Allocution *É la Quinta volta* to the College of Cardinals, December 24, 1918.

[63] Koenig, supra note 1, ¶597, Letter *Dopo gli Ultimi* to Cardinal Gasparri, Secretary of State, November 8, 1918; see Richard Arès, SJ, *L'Eglise Catholique et l'Organisation de la Société International Contemporaine (1939–1949)* (Montreal, 1949), 19.

who are meeting in Paris to settle the fate of mankind, and especially upon President Wilson as the head of the noble nation which has written such glorious pages in the annals of human progress. May the conference be of such a nature as to remove any resentment, abolish forever wars among brothers, establish harmony and concord and promote useful labor. Out of the peace conference may there be born that League of Nations which, by abolishing conscription, will reduce armaments; which, by establishing international tribunals, will eliminate or settle disputes; which, placing peace upon a foundation of solid rock, will guarantee to everyone independence and equality of rights.[64]

Benedict's praise of Wilson indicated where his hope for international organization lay. In a letter dated November 27, 1918, Cardinal Gibbons of Baltimore urged Wilson not to visit Rome without seeing the pope, who thought very highly of the American president.[65] On January 4, 1919, Pope Benedict greeted President Wilson with extended hand. Their conversation lasted for about twenty minutes, and Wilson then talked with Cardinal Gasparri. Vatican spokesmen said that the visit, which had been anticipated with immense interest, brought great satisfaction to the Holy See.[66] During their time together, the pope expressed his appreciation of Wilson's efforts in bringing ideas the pope advocated closer to implementation. Still another hearsay account relayed that Wilson relieved the pope's doubts about the League and converted him to the main lines of his plan.[67] In any event, in the popular mind the names Benedict XV and Woodrow Wilson became associated with the proposed league of Nations. Alfred

---

[64] "Pope Hopes for Foundation of League of Nations; Invokes Divine Help for Wilson in Peace Mission," *New York Times* (January 2, 1919): 1.

[65] Quoted in Peters, supra note 37, at 165–66.

[66] "Wilson Confers with Pope, Leaves for Genoa; Accepts Popular Acclaim as Approval of His Ideas; Calls for Millions to Check Starvation in Europe," *New York Times* (January 5, 1919): 1.

[67] *New York World* (17 March 1919): 2; *Congressional Record,* 66th Cong. vol. LVII, part I, 139, remarks of Sen. Sherman.

Verdross, the outstanding Austrian international legal authority, stated that only when the American president and the pope became its spokesmen did the proposal for an organization of states penetrate the chancelleries of the world.[68]

The Paris Peace Conference opened on January 18, 1919. A week later the Conference enacted the resolution creating the League of Nations. In April the draft of the Covenant was presented, and on June 28 the Treaty of Versailles, of which the League Covenant was an integral part, was finally signed. During the conference, the Holy See publicly supported the concept of a League of Nations. Cardinal Gibbons, certainly acting with Vatican approval, gave Wilson badly needed support at home by writing a letter to William Howard Taft in favor of the League which was read at the Atlantic Congress for a League of Nations on February 6, 1919.[69] In March, *L'Osservatore Romano* printed an article which was understood to embody the views of the Holy See. It said that the League "might have been constituted in a simpler manner," and outlined its proper function in terms of compulsory arbitration with economic sanctions, following *Dès le Début*. But it added, significantly, that a society should be formed of civilized nations willing to accept such arbitration, including those defeated in the war.[70]

There were also indications that the Holy See was hoping that the proposed League could be dissociated in some way from the peace settlement. Cardinal Gibbons said in an interview on April 3, 1919, that consideration of the League should come only after the signing of the peace treaty, which was needed quickly because of unrest in Europe.[71] The Holy See was becoming increasingly disenchanted with the progress of the peace talks as was indicated by an article in *Civilta Cattolica* titled "The Hypocrisy of Politics and the Failure of

---

[68] Alfred Verdross, *Völkerrecht* (Wien: Springer, 1959), 39.

[69] "Favor League Peace Plan," *New York Times* (February 7, 1919): 2.

[70] See "Vatican Holds League Might Be Simpler: Semi-Official Organ Recalls that Pope Suggested Such a Project in 1917," *New York Times* (March 13, 1919): 2.

[71] "Wants Peace Signed First—League Can Wait Says Cardinal Gibbons, Alarmed Over Bolshevism," *New York Times* (April 4, 1919): 2.

the Peace Conference." This article condemned a priori all that might result from a conference that was solely political and atheistic.[72]

During the conference, the Holy See was accused of trying to participate officially, since it had sent churchmen to Paris who were to follow and influence the solution of questions touching on the interests of the Church. In June, Cardinal Gasparri released this statement to the press:

> It has been repeatedly stated that the Holy See was making efforts to obtain a seat at the Conference, but the truth is that nothing was further from our thought. Monsignor Cerretti, who is now in Paris, was merely entrusted by the Holy Father with the task of trying to save flourishing German missions in Africa and Australia.[73]

Paragraphs 122 and 438 of the proposed treaty, dealing with the expulsion of German nationals and the administration of mission property, constituted threats to Catholic missionary activity. Cerretti secured a favorable modification of these provisions, and Pope Benedict later thanked Wilson for his assistance in this matter.[74]

There was another issue followed by another papal representative. Msgr. Francis C. Kelley, the head of the Catholic Extension Society (an American Catholic organization supporting the missions), was sent to bring up the case of the exiled Mexican bishops. In this connection, he promoted the inclusion in the draft Covenant of an article on liberty of conscience originally proposed by the British. The text was redrafted at the request of President Wilson and became known as the religious liberty clause. When it came up for discussion at the tenth meeting of the Commission on the Covenant, Colonel House, who was presiding, notified the members of the Commission that Wilson favored inclusion of the article. However, the representatives of Britain, France, Serbia, and Greece

---

[72] "L'Ipocrisia Nella Politica—E Il Fallimento del Congresso per la Pace," *Civilta Cattolica* III (1919): 3.

[73] Quoted in Peters, supra note 37, at 169.

[74] Koenig, supra note 1, ¶635, Allocution *Nobis Quidem* to the College of Cardinals, July 3, 1919.

signaled their opposition. The Commission recommended the omission of the article, and Wilson subsequently withdrew his support. Kelley later wrote that this failure to ensure that the Covenant protected freedom of conscience cost the League considerable Catholic support. As he said,

> Catholics would have been for the League if that right had been properly recognized. As it was they were against it. The whole Catholic press could have been rallied to support the League but it had nothing to rally around. President Wilson was right, and it is to be regretted that, weakening at the last moment, he thus lost the cause. I say "thus lost the cause" because it was plain that the Commission would not have opposed him on the point.[75]

The usual explanation for the defeat of the religious liberty clause was that the Japanese delegation had suggested adding to it a statement on the equality of nations that Britain and the U.S. found unacceptable. Japan had previously attempted to have this principle included in the preamble, but had been successfully opposed by these same two powers, who feared that it would provide legal grounds for a Japanese challenge in the league to the racially discriminatory immigration laws of the U.S., Australia, and New Zealand. When Baron Makino of Japan argued that while it was right to proclaim that no one should suffer on account of one's religion, this should also apply to race or nationality, the British and Americans found the baron's position both unanswerable and unacceptable. In addition, France opposed any statement on religious freedom on the grounds that it was not a proper subject for inclusion in the Covenant. With this kind of formidable opposition, the clause was defeated.[76]

Msgr. Kelley, who lobbied extensively for the religious liberty clause, stated that his chief opponent in the Commission, Eleuthe-

---

[75] Francis Clement Kelley, *The Bishop Jots It Down* (New York: Harper, 1948), 256.

[76] Walters, supra note 59, vol. I, at 63–64.

rios Venizelos of Greece, claimed to have killed the provision because of the addition on racial equality. But he also testified that he himself had ascertained from the Japanese that adoption of their proposal was in no way a condition for their support of the religious liberty clause. Kelley suspected that Clemenceau feared that it would be an implied censure on his own anticlerical past.[77] The conclusion seems evident that Britain, the U.S., and France, with the support of Greece and others, saw how it would be convenient to eliminate two objectionable provisions with one effort. The spokesman of the Holy See thus found himself allied with an Asian power in the cause of human rights, against countries of the so-called Christian West. Kelley later wrote that the omission of the religious liberty clause was really the failure of liberalism. As he argued,

> It was liberalism's chance but the liberals muffed it. The persecuted Jews of Germany are paying the bill today. Both Protestants and Catholics elsewhere will be paying it tomorrow. It has given its death sentence to the League because, by failing to stand against religious persecution, it cut the ground from under the inalienable things. In the scales of modern statesmanship, as against wealth and power, they were seen to be as light as a feather.[78]

The Paris Peace Conference was also the occasion for serious discussion of the Roman Question between representatives of the Quirinal and the Vatican. When Msgr. Kelley was in Paris, Cardinal Mercier invited him to investigate the possibilities of raising the Roman Question. On May 17, Kelley had a conversation with Orlando, the Italian premier, in which they examined in detail various proposals, including a territorial solution with an outlet to the sea as well as a guarantee through the League of Nations. Reporting to Rome on May 22, Kelley placed the matter before Cardinal Gasparri and Msgr. Bonaventura Cerretti, the Secretary of the Congregation for Extraordinary Ecclesiastical Affairs. After conferring with

---

[77] Kelley, supra note 75, at 257–60.
[78] Ibid., 358.

the pope, Cerretti went to Paris to see Orlando, taking along a proposal drawn up at the Vatican.[79]

In his conversation with the Italian premier in Paris on June 1,
1919, Cerretti proposed that Italy support membership for the Holy
See in the League. This would provide a suitable means for securing
an international guarantee for a territorial settlement, since the
League guaranteed the territorial integrity of its members. Orlando
agreed and asked if the dignity and prestige of the Holy See would
be maintained in the League, since it would be on the Council and
take part in the most important functions. Cerretti replied that the
pope would belong to the League as a head of state. Orlando said it
was essential that the pope participate as a head of state and not of a
religion. Otherwise, the caliph and the grand rabbi would demand
membership in the League, which would be out of the question. The
settlement then tentatively agreed upon corresponded roughly to
that of the Lateran Treaty of 1929, minus the financial compensation
and basic legal changes by Italy. But since Orlando hinted at possible
difficulties with the king and people, it was understood that the subject might have to be postponed and taken up at a later date.

It seems clear that Orlando had felt himself under pressure to conclude an agreement, since the Allies, in April and May of 1919, were
denying Italy's aspirations and using the Roman Question against it.
Upon his return to Rome, however, Orlando was defeated in Parliament and resigned. His successor, not feeling the same pressure, discontinued the negotiations begun with Cerretti. It is possible that if
Orlando had not been defeated, the League may have been asked to
admit the Holy See to membership as a state.[80] On the other hand,
there are those who hold that it is not clear at all that Benedict really
desired membership in the League, that his overriding goal was an
international guarantee for any agreement with Italy, and that the significance of the Cerretti mission should consequently not be over-
drawn.[81] While crucial evidence may not be available on this point,

---

[79] Oliver Earl Benson, *Vatican Diplomatic Practice as Affected by the Lateran
Agreements* (Liège: Georges Thone, 1936), 18–19.

[80] Benson, supra note 79, at 18–19; Kelley, supra note 75, at 261–76.

[81] Peters, supra note 37, at 169–70.

several observations can still be made. It was the Holy See and not Italy that originally suggested League membership as part of the agreement. An agreement would have been possible without the Holy See's membership in the League. Moreover, Benedict XV consistently showed a high respect for the League and a desire to participate actively in international affairs. Subsequent denials of a desire for membership and disillusionment with the League cannot be projected backward to 1919 and can be sufficiently explained by other reasons.[82]

There were strong indications that even before the Treaty of Versailles was signed on June 28, 1919, the Holy See was already discontented with the peace settlement. It did not hide its disappointment in the ensuing months. In August, *Civilta Cattolica,* whose editor was in close touch with the pope, criticized the treaty as the opposite of true reconciliation.[83] He argued that it was a perpetuation rather than a conclusion of the conflict, inspired by the spirit of revenge.[84] Benedict pointedly declared over and over again that no peace was possible without the spirit of Christian charity, and it was clear that he considered the spirit of the peace settlement too vindictive to assure the future peace of Europe.[85] On December 16, 1919, in an allocution to the College of Cardinals, he deplored the hatred still evident between nations and the excessive nationalism of some ecclesiastical hierarchies. He concluded with the wish that the League might succeed in reconciling victors and vanquished.[86] The unstable peace that weakened his faith in the League's future only increased his hope that peace could still succeed.

But despite the pope's advocacy of the League concept, the attitude of most Catholics toward the League was either one of opposition or apathy. Church leadership attempted to win them over but it was a formidable task. One principal reason for Catholic opposition,

---

[82] Anne O'Hare McCormick, *Vatican Journal: 1921–1954* (New York: Farrar, Strauss and Cudahy, 1957), 20–21.

[83] "La Guerra Sociale Dopa la Pace di Versailles," LXX *Civilta Cattolica III* (August 30, 1919): 271.

[84] Peters, supra note 37, at 174.

[85] Koenig, supra note 1, ¶¶643–45, Letter *Amor Ille* to Cardinal Amette, Archbishop of Paris, October 7, 1919.

[86] Falconi, supra note 3, at 126; *The League* II (February 1920): 189.

especially on the continent, was the ideological stance of the League's most vocal supporters, especially the Freemasons and the Socialists. The Masonic organizations of the Allied and neutral countries, meeting in Paris in June 1917, had proposed a League that was to be a kind of international super-state, with a universal parliament and universal democracy inspired by secular humanism and having a moral, spiritual, and pedagogic mission to all peoples. Such utopianism, viewed as derived from the bourgeois tradition of humanitarian pacifism based on Rousseau, may have created among Catholics suspicion and incredulity toward a League of Nations. Certain German Catholic writers indiscreetly called the League "a Masonic excrescence." In France and Belgium, the fear of Masonic influence was very strong. Catholics everywhere also disliked and distrusted the internationalism and pacifism of their other enemies, the Socialists, who during the war had begun propagating the idea of a League based on Marxist ideology.

If some Catholics opposed the League because of its friends, others were certainly influenced against it by its enemies. An important factor in Catholic opposition to the League was the widespread nationalism that feared any loss of national sovereignty. In France the influence of Charles Maurras and his *Action Française* cannot be ignored. The simple word "pacifism"—a term evoking the idea of international organization—produced shock among French Catholics under the sway of Maurras and his positivist outlook. In Italy, the attitude toward the League was less nationalistic and more apathetic. The Roman Question provided an outlet for nationalism, and it was only later that interest in international questions developed, stimulated by contact with the ideas of French and German Catholics. In the U.S., the efforts of Cardinal Gibbons were directed against Catholic nationalism as well as dislike of Wilson, and a deep apathy or pessimism concerning the League. Irish Catholics seemed much more interested in the Irish question, while German and other Catholics with roots in Central Europe were more concerned about their relatives abroad. The American Church, largely immigrant and poor, was heavily isolationist and illustrated the general view that the League attracted the intellectuals more than the working classes.

Anti-Catholic nationalists, on the other hand, feared that the Church, as a world force, wanted to make the League an instrument of the Vatican. Enemies of the League in the U.S. played upon such fears. For example, on June 20, 1919, U.S. Senator Lawrence Sherman of Illinois warned his colleagues that of the forty potential members of the League, some twenty-four would be "spiritually dominated by the Vatican," which was reason enough for the U.S. not to join.[87] As he said, "The peril lies in the claim of papal power, never abjured, never disavowed. . . . Shall the United States commit itself to the mercy of a power from which our ancestors delivered us?"[88] Sherman continued by asserting that, "The Vatican is a most earnest advocate of the Covenant of the League of Nations."[89] He also recalled Wilson's audience with Benedict XV, and entered into the Congressional Record the pope's August appeal, the secret treaties, and an article from the *Masonic Chronicle* accusing the Vatican of meddling in politics and throwing its influence in favor of Germany.[90] Thus fear of the League as being dominated by one's ideological and unpatriotic enemies was not confined to Catholics.

Catholics who saw the League as a creature of secular humanism, were disturbed because the Covenant did not mention the name of God. The document seemed to indicate "an attempt to construct the framework of a society of States without the one essential, spiritual foundation."[91] In addition, it was evident that there would be no place in the organization for the pope, and this was considered a poor return for his long tradition of peacemaking. Nothing sapped the confidence of Catholics in the League as much as these omissions.[92] It was viewed by Catholic publicists, more than it was at the

[87] *Congressional Record,* supra note 67, at 1437.
[88] Ibid.
[89] Ibid.
[90] Ibid.
[91] John Eppstein, *The Catholic Tradition of the Law of Nations* (London: Burns, Oates and Washbourne, 1935), 319.
[92] Ibid., 319–20.

Vatican, that the League reflected the same policy of deliberate hostility to the Church shown in Article 15 of the Treaty of London. Article 1 of the Covenant restricted membership to fully self-governing states, dominions, or colonies, but did not allow for the possible admission of "powers," as had the Hague Conference of 1899.

Finally, the League did not seem to draw much inspiration from the Catholic tradition on international relations. The British Phillimore Committee, which on July 3, 1918, reported its investigation of "various schemes for a League of Nations, as well as other devices which have been proposed or attempted for the avoidance of war," completely ignored the ideas of Taparelli and Benedict XV.[93] This showed in the Covenant, which Catholic internationalists, even those who supported the League, felt was not strong enough. La Brière, for example, worked hard for the new organization but still could write that it should be based on the principle of compulsory arbitration with sanctions, and should collaborate with the papacy to give international law and the decisions of international tribunals real efficacy.[94] It was not hard for Catholics to see that the ideological origins of the League were in the liberal internationalist tradition. This tradition included the views of Grotius, absolute national sovereignty, the secularization of politics, empiricism and rationalism, Deism and the Enlightenment, the positivist school of international law, and the secular views of humanism and progress. While this tradition was not necessarily perceived as evil, it did present a worldview and a concept of the nature of man-in-community quite different from that of the Catholic tradition.

Even Catholic friends of the League would have misgivings and recognize forces and influences behind the League that were unfriendly to the Church. If Masons and Socialists did not seem to predominate, there were always the Protestants. After all, the principal proponents of the League in the Christian world were Protestants, and its headquarters would be in Geneva, the city of John Calvin and

---

[93] Ibid., 313.
[94] La Brière, supra note 56, *La Collaboration de Rome avec Geneve*, Chapter XII, 281–309.

the "Protestant Rome." Msgr. Giovannetti has summed up this Catholic uneasiness by stating that:

> Finally, there was the "League spirit" (the Calvinist–Protestant–Masonic "Geneva spirit") which set the Holy See and Catholics generally on their guard from the beginning, whereas the League needed to win the confidence and sympathy of all concerned.[95]

To the great mass of Catholics, including many sincere proponents of international organization, the League of Nations seemed something alien, generated by enemies of the Church, and a possible threat to Catholicism. Of course, this image impressed itself in varying degrees. The pope was undoubtedly affected by these negative sentiments to a certain extent, but he did not oppose the League. The same is true of the many Churchmen who spoke out in favor of its adoption, despite the "League spirit" and the defects of the Covenant, since the new organization should be given a chance. The public silence of Benedict on the League question during 1919 and early 1920, together with the endorsements of Church leaders, indicated that the Holy See still approved the establishment of the proposed League of Nations. This support did not prevent, however, serious reservations about its future success.

The League Covenant, after all, aimed at the same goal of world peace through law as *Dès le Début*. Although its mechanisms for peaceful settlement of disputes and for sanctions were weaker and it did not make disarmament the first step toward peace, its provisions were in general accord with Christian principles and the Catholic tradition. While the League was not constituted as a universal world organization, there was a thrust toward universality in the Covenant in that neutral states were from the first invited to join. It was understood that despite its origins in a peace conference

---

[95] Alberto Giovannetti, "Catholics and the International Community," CXLIV *American Ecclesiastical Review* (February 1961): 77. Msgr. Giovannetti was the first Permanent Observer of the Holy See to the United Nations in New York and served from 1964 to 1973.

of victors, the League could eventually include the Central Powers as well as all other states willing to assume the obligations of membership. Despite the "League spirit" that alarmed Catholics, the organization included or would soon include several states with large Catholic populations. Among these were Belgium, Bolivia, and Spain who were named as members of the League Council, in addition to France and Italy. The Secretary-General of the League, Sir Eric Drummond, was known to be an outstanding Catholic. There were also Catholics of note in the Secretariat then being organized. This supplied some evidence that there was no ideological problem for Catholics, despite earlier fears. Lastly, there would undoubtedly be Catholic delegates who could counter the influence of influential anti-Catholic liberals in the decisionmaking process of the League.

Another factor in the early history of the League also tended to alleviate Catholic fears: the establishment of the International Labour Organisation. The ILO was almost a natural outgrowth of the Catholic social movement. The first International Labour Conference, held in the fall of 1919, was a distinct success in spite of dire predictions to the contrary. Six important conventions were concluded (later ratified widely) and agreement was reached on other important questions. The ILO also appointed its governing body and agreed to the admission of Germany and Austria in the first real act of reconciliation after the war.[96] All of these factors taken together made it clear to the Holy See that there was really only one possible decision if peace was to be obtained, and that was to promote the adoption of the Covenant as it stood and to support the existing League in the practical order, even if it was not the ideal world organization from a Catholic perspective.

Despite his reservations about the League, and in the face of strong Catholic opinion, Benedict worked quietly to support the League. He was especially concerned about what the U.S. would do, and on July 24, 1919, Cardinal Gibbons authorized a statement

---

[96] Walters, supra note 59, at 79–80.

advocating American participation in the League.[97] Gibbons reportedly issued this statement at the request of the White House, which was concerned that American Catholics were much opposed to Wilson because of his Mexican policy, especially his refusal to do anything to alleviate religious persecution. But the support of Gibbons was not enough to change the minds of many American Catholics who "by that time had fashioned their own idea of Wilson and Wilsonianism."[98] The pope was greatly disappointed when the U.S. Senate voted against entering the League. Anne McCormick wrote of an audience she had with Pope Benedict some time later in which evidence of his disappointment surfaced. As she indicated,

> The Pope went on to question us about America. He was curious as to the real causes of what seemed to him the reversal of public sentiment in regard to the League of Nations, which (perhaps he felt himself to be not without a part in its formulation) he called "a great conception." I was told by a Vatican official that no one in Europe had more faith in President Wilson than the Pope, or more deeply regretted his defeat by the Senate.[99]

Support for the League also came from Catholic prelates abroad. The Belgian Cardinal Mercier stated in September 1919 that he was not one of those hostile to the League and prayed that it might be blessed and given that spiritual breath of life which it needed to

---

[97] "Gibbons Predicts Agreement on the League of Nations," *New York Times* (July 25, 1919): 1. The *New York Times* stated that Cardinal Gibbons of Baltimore had authorized issuance of the following statement: "It is my firm conviction that after thorough and honest discussion in both Houses of Congress both parties will finally arrive at a common agreement based upon a just and sincere League of Nations that will give us a reasonable guarantee against the horrors of war in the future, as well as grounded assurance of lasting peace without in any way impairing American sovereignty or surrendering any American right, and without involving us in entangling alliances. I am sure that an early adoption of the League of Nations will infuse intense joy throughout the United States without distinction of part and will be hailed with satisfaction by the allied powers of Europe."

[98] See McCormick, *supra* note 82, at 20–21.

[99] Ibid., 20–21.

succeed.[100] The journal *League of Nations Union* reported in January 1920 that Catholics everywhere were rallying to the support of the League, citing the recent pastoral letter of Archbishop Whiteside of Liverpool that exhorted Catholics to support the movement to give life to the League of Nations.[101] The archbishop made a strong statement. He referred to Pope Benedict's peace proposal of 1917. The archbishop said that Catholics should have no doubt about supporting the League:

> International justice ultimately and in its last analysis is based on the natural law, of which God is the Author. This League of Nations is a genuine attempt to form on questions of public policy an international conscience. Since the days when the Catholic Church ruled the consciences of all Christians, it is the first step in that direction which the world has seen. Catholics, as directed by the Supreme Pontiff, cannot hold aloof from this movement. If for no other reason it is for them at least to see that the international conscience of the future is guided by that revealed truth of which the Catholic Church is the custodian and the interpreter.[102]

Other Catholic leaders also endorsed the League of Nations. Cardinal Dubois, Archbishop of Rouen, declared that he welcomed with joy the establishment of the League. This caused a French Catholic newspaper, *La Croix,* to comment that the Cardinal's attitude was particularly interesting and that the Catholic press, which had either withheld its opinion or expressed hostility to the League, was favorably impressed by his remarks.[103] Cardinal Amette, Archbishop of Paris, supported the idea of the League of Nations. In Austria a well-known leader of the Catholic peace movement, Doctor Metzer of Graz, published four essays on the League and Catholic international organizations in *Die Neue Zeit.* He said that the Christian principles in the League would receive due recogni-

---

[100] *The League* II (November 1919): 63. See Eppstein, supra note 91, at 312.
[101] Eppstein, supra note 91, at 310–11; see *The League* II (January 1920): 142.
[102] Quoted in Eppstein, supra note 91, at 311.
[103] *The League* II (December 1919): 101.

tion.[104] These and many similar endorsements of the League would most likely not have been made without the prior knowledge of the favorable attitude of the Holy See. There is strong evidence that even papal diplomacy was employed to promote popular support for the League. The papal nuncio to Switzerland used his influence to persuade the Conservative Party in that country to favor the League of Nations. On November 19, 1919, the Swiss Parliament voted to enter the League, a decision ratified by a nationwide plebiscite the following May.[105]

The League Covenant was an integral part of the Treaty of Versailles, and so the League would come into official existence only when sufficient ratifications brought that treaty into force. It was not a perfect peace settlement in the eyes of Benedict XV, nor did it provide the proper context for a successful League, but there was no alternative available. The new organization would have to conquer the vindictive harshness of the peace and the rampant nationalism of the period in order to survive. However, given the whole Catholic tradition, this first real step toward international organization since the collapse of medieval Christendom had to, in all good conscience, be supported by the Holy See. The alternative would be for the Church to turn its back on the plight of humankind and fail its essential responsibility. In any event, there was little doubt that the Treaty of Versailles would come into force despite the refusal of the United States Senate to ratify it. The expected soon happened, and on January 10, 1920, the League of Nations was born.

---

[104] *The League* II (February 1920): 190.
[105] Walters, supra note 59, at 92.

The Holy See and the First Years
of the League: 1920–1922

W HAT WAS the comprehensive attitude of the Holy See
toward the League of Nations that officially came into
existence on January 10, 1920? To this question contradictory
answers have been given, ranging from the view that the pope
warmly approved the League and desired membership, to the
counterposition that he ignored or even opposed the League as a
possible rival to his own position. Vatican policy in 1919 and early
1920, as has been shown, fostered attempts by Church leaders to
persuade governments and the Catholic faithful to support adoption of the Covenant. However, this did not imply total approval
of the League. The pope maintained a discreet public silence during this period, not broken until his encyclical *Pacem Dei Munus*
of May 23, 1920, wherein he addressed the necessity of justice
and charity for peace to succeed. The answers to the question
posed at the beginning of this chapter have thus turned largely,
though not exclusively, on the interpretation of this encyclical. For
this reason, as well as its own intrinsic merit as an outstanding
Christian statement on international peace, this document merits
close attention.

In *Pacem Dei Munus*, Pope Benedict rejoiced that peace had
begun to shine at last. But anxiety remained, "for if in most places
peace is in some sort established and treaties are signed, the germs

of former enmities remain. . . . "[1] Treaties are insufficient without forgiveness, and love of enemies as a component of the biblical law of love applies also to peoples. "The Gospel has not one law of charity for individuals and another for States and nations, which are indeed but collections of individuals."[2] The pope noted that in addition to charity, the nations are being drawn together by a new sense of interdependence and modern communications. As a sign of reconciliation amongst parties who were in strong disagreement with one another, Benedict relaxed the papal prohibition against official visits to the Quirinal by the heads of Catholic states, without in any way renouncing the rights claimed by the Holy See against Italy. The key paragraph of the encyclical states,

> Things being thus restored, the order required by justice and charity re-established and the nations reconciled, it is much to be desired, Venerable Brethren, that all States, putting aside mutual suspicion, should unite in one league, or rather a sort of family of peoples, calculated both to maintain their own independence and safeguard the order of human society. What specially amongst other reasons, calls for such an association of nations, is the need generally recognized of making every effort to abolish or reduce the enormous burden of military expenditures which States can no longer bear, in order to prevent these disastrous wars or at least to remove the danger of them as far as possible. So would each nation be assured not only of its independence but also of the integrity of its territory within its just frontiers.[3]

Benedict promised that the Church would not refuse its aid to "[s]tates united under the Christian law in any of their undertakings inspired by justice and charity, inasmuch as she herself is the most perfect type of universal society," possessing in her organization and

---

[1] Harry Koenig, *Principles for Peace: Selections from Papal Documents—Leo XIII to Pius XII* (Milwaukee: Bruce, 1943); *Encyclical Pacem Dei Munus Pulcherrimum* on Peace and Christian Reconciliation, May 23, 1920, ¶662.

[2] Ibid., ¶675.

[3] Ibid., ¶678.

institutions a wonderful instrument for achieving brotherhood, temporal well-being, and eternal salvation. He recalled the Church's role in pacifying and uniting Europe and quoted Augustine's famous description of the role of the celestial city in maintaining peace on earth.[4] Toward the end of the encyclical, Benedict declared,

> We fervently exhort all the nations, under the inspiration of Christian benevolence, to establish a true peace among themselves and join together in an alliance which shall be just and, therefore, lasting.[5]

It should be understood that this remarkable encyclical did contain some ambiguity. The League of Nations is not mentioned by name, although papal style at that time avoided specific names whenever possible. But reference to the League seems clear, given the historical context in which the encyclical was written and promulgated. Certainly the aims of the League are given the warmest possible endorsement. But was the League of Nations the "family of peoples" desired by Benedict? The pope advocated a society embracing all states, but the League did not. As the Covenant's first article stated, admission to the League was not automatic.[6] He also stressed the need to put aside all mutual suspicion; however, some members of the League continued their suspicions about particular states, especially former belligerents. The concept of the family was a favorite idea of the pope, but there was little familial spirit among the states of Europe in 1920. For example, many of the pope's public statements reflected the fact that the end of the war did not bring an end to enmities. Benedict also placed great emphasis on the reduction of armaments as a principal purpose of his league,

---

[4] Ibid., ¶679.

[5] Ibid., ¶680.

[6] As Article 1(2) of the Covenant states, "Any fully self-governing State, Dominion or Colony *not named in the Annex* may become a member of the League if its admission is agreed to by two-thirds of the Assembly, provided that it shall give effective guarantees of its sincere intention to observe its international obligations, and shall accept such regulations as may be prescribed by the League in regard to its military, naval and air forces and armaments." [Italic added.]

something contained but not emphasized strongly in the Covenant.[7] He pledged collaboration with "States united under the Christian law," but then urged nations (including non-Christian ones) to act "under the inspiration of Christian benevolence," and unite in a single alliance. Evidently this Christian law and benevolence were expected of all peoples, which was a revolutionary theological concept in 1920 and not easily understood by Catholics who had been recently engaged as belligerents in a devastating war.[8] The pope did not say whether this alliance was the existing League of Nations, a different organization, or possibly an improved League, universal in membership and animated by a new spirit of fraternal concern even for former enemies.

The encyclical *Pacem Dei Munus* was not particularly well received, and its abstract quality may be one reason the reception was unenthusiastic. The pope appeared to be endorsing the aims of the League without endorsing explicitly an organization that he realized was far from perfect. Commentators and historians have put quite different interpretations on *Pacem*. McKnight states that Benedict ignored the League outright and cited Carlo Sforza's view that the pope refused to endorse the League because that might have been interpreted "as a renunciation of the supreme and distant aims of the Church," and because he distrusted an institution in which "no Pope could have a part, for a Pope can hardly admit of sitting as an equal among equals."[9] But in fact Benedict did not ignore the League. The historical context of *Pacem* made his allusion to it unmistakable, and he later communicated with officials of the organization itself. As for Sforza's imputation of motive, the Pope did not fear that his actual endorsement of a universal "league, or rather a sort of family of peoples" would be misinterpreted as a renunciation of Church goals. In addition, the Cerretti-Orlando talks demonstrate that Benedict was willing at one time to sit as an equal amongst equals.

---

[7] Koenig, supra note 1, ¶678.

[8] Ibid., ¶679.

[9] John McKnight, *The Papacy: A New Appraisal* (New York: Rinehart, 1952), 405, n. 70.

While some might argue that Benedict ignored or criticized the League in *Pacem* because it did not correspond to his ideas,[10] especially universality, his thoughts were otherwise. Benedict must have been thinking of the absence of the United States from the League and, even more, of Germany and the other defeated nations. But Benedict did not ignore the League in *Pacem* if that document's emphasis on universality was an indirect appeal to the U.S. to join the League and to the League to admit Germany and the other defeated nations. This was the interpretation of a good number of its readers.[11] Another commentator indicated that the pope was interested in the League and the primary proponent of the idea even if the Holy See were not to be a member. If the organization were to be concerned with issues transcending the purely temporal, the Church's cooperation would be likely.[12] But nowhere in *Pacem* did the Pope claim a role of leadership for the papacy in a secular international organization, the kind of organization he himself advocated and to which the Church would give its aid. Nor did he say that unless the League was founded on Christian principles (a suggestion that he nowhere entertained), the cooperation of the Church would not be forthcoming. He only requested that the organization operate according to Christian principles.

A prominent Vatican diplomat, Archbishop Cardinale, writing in more recent times, states that "Benedict XV refused to recognize the League of Nations because in his enlightened opinion, as subsequent events were to prove right, it lacked the necessary foundations for insuring a lasting peace."[13] This diplomat certainly had more ready access to the Vatican sources than did other scholars, yet even

---

[10] Carlo Falconi, *The Popes in the Twentieth Century: From Pius X to John XXIII* (Boston: Little, Brown, 1967), 126; Walter H. Peters, *The Life Of Benedict XV* (Milwaukee: Bruce, 1959), 177.

[11] Herder correspondence, IV (October 1967), 298.

[12] See Sisley Huddleston, "The Vatican's New Place in World Politics," *Current History* XIII, No. 2 (November 1920): 75, where the author comments on others' views but points to primary sources, including Benedict XV's *Pacem*, to reveal accurately the Holy See's views on the League and related issues.

[13] H. E. Cardinale, *The Holy See and the International Order* (Buckinghamshire: Colin Smythe, 1976), 231.

his statement could be misinterpreted. Benedict certainly did not recognize the League of Nations in the diplomatic sense, for there were no means available to do so. But the pope's subsequent direct communication with the League in 1921 suggested some recognition. Still, *Pacem* reflected Benedict's conviction that the League was not built on a sufficiently strong foundation. This view is reinforced by an examination of the history of the first five sessions of the League Council, from January to May 1920. The Council had been prevented by the Supreme Council of the Allied Powers from considering the key questions arising from the peace treaties. Its performance on discussions about the Saar, the status of Danzig, the Swiss neutrality guarantee, treaties concerning protection of minorities, conflict in Russia and Poland, and plans for Russian relief did not contribute to a world peace that was badly needed.[14]

Other commentators saw *Pacem* as a genuine endorsement of the League. One wrote that the pope

> gave his express support to the League of Nations but called for the strengthening of the covenant and for the admission of all states to its membership so that it could be really effective.[15]

It is hard to accept the adjective "express," but this commentator demonstrated great familiarity with papal documents and seemed to have mastered the art of discerning the meaning of carefully drafted discretion. As for his remarks on the Covenant and universality, these indications are present in *Pacem*. The Canadian Jesuit Richard Arès stated that in *Pacem* Benedict declared himself in favor of the aims of the League. Since the preamble of the Covenant showed that the pope's conditions for collaboration were quite close to being realized, it was no surprise when he later entered into direct communication with the League.[16] Arès was optimistic about the preamble of

---

[14] See generally Francis Walters, *A History of the League of Nations* (London: Oxford University Press, 1952), vol. I, 86–102.

[15] Herder correspondence, IV (October 1967), 298.

[16] Richard Arès, SJ, *L'Eglise Catholique et l'Organisation de la Société International Contemporaine* (Montreal, 1949), 19.

the Covenant already satisfying Benedict's concept of Christian principles; the pope could have entered into direct communication with
the League whether or not he believed that the organization was
meeting the conditions laid down in the encyclical.[17]

Cardinal Gibbons, an experienced Church leader in the United
States, interpreted *Pacem* as an endorsement of the League. On October 21, 1920, the cardinal announced his strong support for the
League and based this chiefly on the encyclical's text. He added his
name to a list of 15,500 American clergymen who had taken a firm
stand for the League, and praised the Covenant in specific ways as
corresponding to the wishes of the pope.[18] Gibbons emphasized the
provisions of the Covenant for preventing war that were in accord
with papal teaching, rather than dealing with Catholic objections to
the Covenant or the League itself. But his statement was designed to
influence American opinion in favor of the League so that the organization could become universal—or at least include the United States,
whose membership was viewed as critical to the organization's success.

Despite the ambiguity in *Pacem Dei Munus*, rumors spread in
the summer of 1920 that the Vatican had already applied for admission to the League. One observer attributed this to the fact that the
League had held its last meeting in Rome, adding that there was
much semi-official talk about the Holy See's possible membership.
He reported that the Vatican had denied any papal representation in
this sense, but insisted that the matter would have to be seriously
considered, since there remained a possibility of the Holy See's continuing interest in membership. Lastly, he identified questions in
which the Holy See's position in international relations had been
raised; however, he rhetorically pointed out that the Holy See and
the League, if they could speak with the same moral voice, would
represent a united "verdict" that would be difficult to defy. Of the
Holy See, he said, "Its authority is a moral authority, its power is a
spiritual power, its weapons are persuasion and not force."[19]

---

[17] Ibid., 20.

[18] "Cardinal Gibbons Firm for League: Delay Imposed Alone Will Reduce Wars
to a Minimum He Says," *New York Times* (October 22, 1920): 6.

[19] Huddleston, supra note 12, at 207.

The idea that the Vatican should belong to any postwar League had been propagated in Germany during the war. In 1919 Joseph Müller renewed a theory he had already raised in a 1916 publication, that the pope should be included in the postwar international settlement as peacemaker, arbitrator, mediator, and guarantor of peace. He argued that the Holy See should cooperate in all the international organizations to be set up, especially in the League and the Court, and that the pope's position should be that of the highest moral authority with at least the honorary presidency.[20] German Catholic writers were particularly favorable to an international role for the Holy See and found in the League a means of bolstering the prestige of the papacy. There also appeared a number of articles in German publications in 1918 and 1919 proposing a positive role for the Holy See.[21] The question of some kind of representation for the Vatican at the League was also dealt with at the Third Inter-Allied Conference of Associated Societies for a League of Nations, which met at Brussels in December 1919. A committee of this Conference decided that although the Holy See was not a state, it was a power, and there was no important reason for its exclusion from the League. A motion was allowed to be introduced, for consideration at the next meeting, which declared that it was earnestly desired and hoped that the Holy See should become a member of the League of Nations.[22]

In December 1919 a French statesman, Denys Cochin, said in an interview that the League was a continuation of the mission of the Church, to whom suffering peoples appealed for intervention against state oppression. Since the temporal power of the pope was no longer necessary, it should be replaced by a supranational independence

---

[20] Oliver Earl Benson, *Vatican Diplomatic Practice as Affected by the Lateran Agreements* (Liège: Georges Thone, 1936), 184.

[21] Benson, supra note 20, at 184; La Brière, Chapter XIII, 281–319.

[22] *The League,* II (January 1920): 142. See *New York Times* (December 6, 1919): 3, where a brief report from Brussels stated, "The Committee of the Conference of the Associations for the League of Nations decided today [December 5] that the Holy See could not be regarded as a nation, but expressed the view that it was a power, and that there was no important reason for the exclusion of the Vatican from representation in the League of Nations."

guaranteed by the Christian members of the League. While the pope should not necessarily be a member of the League, there should be an advisory voice for him in the League's activities.[23] Maurice Pernot stated that Benedict was obsessed with assuring the Holy See an eminent role in world politics and, excluded from the peace conference, wanted the Holy See to enter the League.[24] During the negotiations between Cerretti and Orlando in 1919, the Holy See expressed its interest for membership in the League as a means of solving the Roman Question. But Eloy Montero suggested that the papacy changed its mind very soon after the failure of these conversations. It was thought preposterous that the pope should be cited before the Hague tribunal or an arbitral commission, and it would be difficult for the Holy See to have to decide, for example, in a controversy between France and Germany—two countries with large Catholic populations.[25]

The Vatican subsequently denied that it had any desire to enter the League, in an article in *L'Osservatore Romano* on April 15, 1921. Luigi Salvatorelli argued that this was not a question of dissatisfaction, but meant that the League as it had come to be constituted was not the kind of organization in which the pope could suitably participate, and cited *Pacem* as an indication of this.[26] On the other hand, the same author maintained that Pope Benedict, with discreet reserve, still held to a policy of the possible entry of the Holy See in a reformed League of Nations.[27] At this stage, it would be sensible to

---

[23] *The League,* II (February 1920): 189–90; Richard Arès, SJ, *L'Eglise Catholique et L'Organisation de la Société International Contemporaine* (Montreal, 1949), 20; Yves de La Brière, *L'Organisation International du Monde Contemporaine et la Papauté Souvraine* (Paris: Editions Spes, 1924), I, 55–58; Msgr. Bresson in Alban de Malezieux du Hamel, *Le Pape et la Société des Nations* (Albert Mechelinck, 1932), 47; John Eppstein, "League of Nations," *New Catholic Encyclopedia* (Washington, D.C., 1964), vol. 8, 588.

[24] Maurice Pernot, Le Sainte-Siège, *L'Eglise Catholique et la Politique Mondiale* (Paris: Armand Colin, 1924), 41.

[25] Eloy Montero, *La Santa Sede en el Orden Internacional* (Madrid: La Editorial Catolica, 1943), 34.

[26] Luigi Salvatorelli, *La Politica della Santa Sede dopo la Guerra* (Milano: Instituto per gli Studi di Politica Internazionale, 1937), 35.

[27] Ibid., 95

say that: (1) the prudence and reserve of the Holy See toward the new international organization certainly did not include plans for its immediate membership; but (2) the possibility of membership in an improved world organization was not excluded; and, (3) at the very least, some kind of advisory role or participation in the League without the onus of membership was always desired by Pope Benedict XV.

W. A. Purdy concludes that Benedict XV gave his blessing to the League in principle and could hardly have done otherwise, since its basic purpose was to prevent aggressive war.[28] In a similar vein, others concluded that Benedict wished to see formed a true family of nations and thus had reservations about the League. For example, C. Fenwick argued that the endorsement of the pope was not unqualified, since, foreseeing the problems posed by the peace settlement, he laid down conditions—conditions that were not fulfilled by the members of the League, despite the ideals proclaimed in the Covenant.[29] *Pacem Dei Munus* was not well received, especially in the United States, since it seemed to offer only abstract principles for peace. As a statement for the record of history, it has generated more confusion than clarity. Still, one can sensibly conclude that Benedict wished to give qualified support to the League so as to rally the mass of Catholics to promote, influence, and work to improve it.

Many Catholics never understood Benedict's teaching on international questions, although he had endeavored from the outset to give a new orientation to Catholic attitudes on war and peace. This line was followed, somewhat more hesitantly, by his successor, Pope Pius XI (1922–1939), who praised patriotism but condemned inordinate nationalism as a source of evil. While the Holy See may have supported or encouraged the development of Catholic pacifist groups, these movements were, in reality, the work of an elite of internationally minded Catholics. The situation paralleled that of the late nineteenth century, when Pope Leo XIII attempted to rouse

---

[28] W. A. Purdy, *The Church on the Move: The Characters and Policies of Pius XII and John XXIII* (London: Hollis and Carter, 1966), 127.

[29] Fenwick, *New Catholic Encyclopedia*, vol. XI, 38–41.

Catholics on social questions. The nationalism of the interwar period remained as impervious to papal pleas as the conservatism of the 1880s and 1890s, but in each case a few Catholics did respond actively and helped swing the Church a few degrees in the papal direction. In that sense their efforts were not entirely lost, but they failed to leaven the Church as a whole.

In the period just after the First World War, the Catholic international elite began to speak out and to organize. Conscious of the defects of the League, this elite still claimed its substantial conformity with the Christian ideal of peace and asked that the new organization be given the cooperation necessary to its smooth functioning and improvement. Catholic fears of the League began to moderate as a result. Yves de La Brière, SJ, describing the change in December of 1920, noted that with the war over, the treaties signed, the League Council having met eleven times and the Assembly once, the League had come out of a "dream palace" into the real world of politics, and promised to be a real forum for considering world problems—a praiseworthy development of international law.[30] The policy of the Catholic international elite, inspired and encouraged by the Holy See, can perhaps best be shown in the remarks of the Bishop of Lausanne and Geneva, Marius Besson, at religious services in the Catholic cathedral of Geneva on the eve of the first meeting of the Assembly of the League. The bishop asked the blessing of God on the deliberations about to begin and said:

> Because the principle of the League is a fact in conformity with the Gospel, because the League is adapted, at least indirectly, to the Catholicity of the Church, because it is perfectible—it would be preferable, rather than closing ourselves up in passive opposition, to try to improve what is there and to give the League the complete support of Catholics.[31]

---

[30] Yves de La Brière, SJ, *L'Organisation Internationale du Monde Contemporain et la Papauté Soveraine, Series I* (Paris: Editions Spes, 1924), 55.

[31] Ibid., 66; du Hamel, supra note 23, at 47.

The elite of internationally minded Catholics came principally from Western Europe, and was well-informed in the international field. It was a heterogeneous group united by a belief in the Church's responsibility to work for peace. With a good proportion of jurists, writers, professors, union leaders, and some political activists, the group contained both clerics—such as Cardinal Mercier, Primate of Belgium, and Don Luigi Sturzo in Italy—and active laymen like John Eppstein of England, the Swiss Gonzague de Reynold, Maurice Vaussard and Paul Claudel in France, and the Germans Joseph Müller and Friedrich Ritter von Lama. The elite supported the League from both left and right political perspectives. In France, Msgr. E. Beaupin was a member of the progressive Sillon movement, while the prolific Jesuit scholar and publicist Yves de La Brière was the counterpoint. These men of talent would seek to coordinate at the international level the activities of the various Catholic organizations to which most of them belonged, to speak with an effective Catholic voice in world affairs, to stir up Catholic support for the League, and to provide a kind of functional linkage between the Holy See and the new organization in Geneva.

The Catholic elite, believing that the Church had a message relevant to the international community, strongly favored relations between the Holy See and the League, and Vatican membership with some recognition of the pope's superior moral authority. This line was especially evident among German writers, as noted earlier. Political realists for the most part, these Catholics understood that the League was not the Masonic or Socialist conspiracy or superstate they had feared, and so they avoided the disenchantment felt by some former apologists of the League idea who now thought the organization little more than an improved Hague Conference. As La Brière put it in 1922, increased communications and interdependence required a permanent organization and more complex juridical ties among nations, and the League was another step in the direction taken for the past fifty years toward collective solutions and services provided by international offices and bureaus. The League had already had some successes, for example, in the Aaland

Islands and Upper Silesia issues. But it was unable to reform international morality by reconciling growing international divisions. The Catholic attitude toward the League, said this spokesman for the elite, should be to support it in principle, correct its weaknesses, support its just interventions, summon it to defend Catholic interests, and promote its collaboration with the Holy See.[32]

Members of the Catholic international elite quickly perceived the need for united action transcending national boundaries. As a result, a number of new international Catholic organizations were rapidly founded, and this trend continued throughout the decade. The organization that would have the closest contact with the League of Nations was the Catholic Union of International Studies (Union Catholique d'Etudes Internationales), an outgrowth of the Fribourg Union reestablished in 1917 by Baron de Montenach.[33] Gonzague de Reynold, like de Montenach a prominent Swiss Catholic, joined the Catholic Union. Foreseeing during the war that a League would be formed, de Montenach realized that if Catholics were to influence it they would have to study those questions affecting the interests of the Church, such as the disposition of the Holy Places under the British mandate in Palestine. Should the Holy See not participate in the settlement and the League, it was up to Catholics to occupy the position the Vatican might have had. This meant forming an effective organization that inspired respect and trust at the League of Nations. Thus, the Union had to engage in action as well as study, to search for Christian solutions to the problems of peace, to act as a Catholic presence and influence at the League, and to protect the organization from those who would make it "the temple of humanitarian religion."[34]

The Catholic Union of International Studies was approved in principle by Pope Benedict in February 1920. Its constitution was adopted in November of that year. The Union would have a permanent secretariat in Fribourg, be in regular communication with the

---

[32] La Brière, supra note 30, at 58–59.

[33] Ibid., 58.

[34] Gonzague de Reynold, *Mes Mémoires,* Tome III (Genève: Editions Générales, 1963), 499.

Holy See, and coordinate the work of member organizations in various countries. Some of these member groups already existed in France. They included the Societé Gratry pour le Maintien de la Paix entre les Nations (founded in 1906), La Ligue des Catholiques pour la Paix, and La Ligue Internationale des Pacifistes Catholiques (begun by Alfred Vanderpol in 1911). All went to make up the French section of the Union.[35] The English affiliate, the Catholic Council on International Relations, was started in 1923, while in the United States the Catholic Association for International Peace was begun in 1926.[36] The Catholic Union brought together a distinguished international elite and produced a number of important papers and studies. It formulated positions consonant with Catholic teaching and made these known to governments and public opinion with considerable success. It was in frequent communication with the League secretariat, either through informal contacts made by its leadership or through official statements, and was influential in the League Committee on Intellectual Cooperation, of which Gonzague de Reynold was a member.

Other new international Catholic organizations also appeared. In 1920, Cardinal Mercier presided over the first meeting of an organization he had founded, the Union Internationale d'Etudes Sociales, which came to be known as the Malines Union. It produced several studies, most important of which was *A Code of International Ethics*, published in 1937. In the same year, a group of Swiss, Italian, Spanish, and Dutch students founded an international union of Catholic students which took the name of Pax Romana, with an international secretariat at Fribourg. This organization collaborated later with the League Committee on Intellectual Cooperation.[37] There was also founded in 1920 the International Federation of Christian Trade Unions (IFCTU), which was strongly, though not

---

[35] Yves de La Brière, SJ, *L'Organisation Internationale du Monde Contemporain et la Papauté Souveraine, Series III* (Paris: Editions Spes, 1930), 9–31.

[36] Harry W. Flannery, "CAIP Fights for International Peace," XXIX *U.S. Catholic* (September 1963): 25–28.

[37] Maurice Vaussard, "La Coopération Internationale des Catholiques," *Le Problème de la Vie International* (Paris: Gabalda, 1927), 602–5.

exclusively, Catholic and participated in the International Labour Organisation (ILO). In 1921, the First Catholic Peace Congress was held in Paris, bringing together the White Cross Societies, which had been formed by Catholics in France and Germany to work for peace during the war. This event was for a time repeated annually under the auspices of Pope Pius XI.[38]

It was in France that international Catholic organizations were most active during the 1920s. Frenchmen were leaders in the Catholic Union of International Studies, and also published the *Bulletin Catholique International*, which included among its collaborators a good number of outstanding Catholic intellectuals. In addition, French Catholics were active in organizations not strictly confessional in nature, such as the Groupement Universitaire Français pour la Societé des Nations and Marc Sangnier's Comité International d'Action Democratique pour la Paix. Just after the war, Sangnier had been inspired by Benedict XV to work for peace, and he launched a series of international congresses for peace (Congres Democratiques Internationaux) which generated a good deal of interest. Outside France, Central Europe had the most Catholic peace organizations in this period. In Germany, there was the Friedensbund Deutscher Katholiken, founded by the Dominican pacifist Franziskus Stratmann, OP. Catholics were also active in the Quickborn Movement and the Liga fur Völkerbund. Austria, Hungary, and Czechoslovakia had similar organizations. All of these groups met together annually, either at Sangnier's congresses or those of the Internacio Katholika (IKA), another international federation which flourished for a time in the 1920s.

The interwar period was also notable for the great number of international organizations founded along functional lines. The Holy See fostered this structuring of the forces of world Catholicism, not only to promote peace but also to develop a certain Catholic enthusiasm against ideological opponents. While not pacifist, these organizations certainly worked for peace in functionalist terms. From the International Congresses of Catholic Youth, founded in

---

[38] A. C. F. Beales, *The History of Peace* (New York: Dial Press, 1931), 301–2.

1921 with a permanent secretariat in Rome, to the International Federation of Catholic Associations of Doctors, established in 1936 in Vienna, no less than fourteen such international Catholic non-governmental organizations (NGOs) were founded, nine in the first decade and five in the second. They represented youth, charitable agencies, education, social work, journalism, labor, radio, film, employers, nurses, and doctors. Like most Catholic NGOs, their energy came largely from Western Europe, especially France and the Low Countries. They lacked the basic resources of money and personnel, but they did have an effect on their membership and the Church, and cooperated with organs of the League insofar as this was possible. They would work more closely with the United Nations and its specialized agencies after a period of reorganization and augmentation in the years immediately following the Second World War.

The League of Nations was in official existence for only two years of the pontificate of Benedict XV and in full operation for little more than one. This left the pope comparatively little time to observe the new organization in action and to develop modes of contact with it. In keeping with his attitudes toward the peace settlement and the League's spirit and structures, and his own exclusion from it, Benedict adopted an overall policy of discreet reserve and watchful waiting vis-à-vis Geneva. Still, the Holy See was keenly interested in how the League would deal with the many problems confronting the postwar world. With some of them, it had a more direct concern and responsibility, for example, urgent humanitarian questions, the general issue of religious freedom, and particular problems involving the rights of Catholics and the Church. Issues with this kind of religious orientation could not be ignored or passed over in silence, and so communication between the Holy See and the League was soon established, even as the two institutions were developing their postures toward each other.

The Holy See was in private contact with the League during its early years. For example, in February of 1921 Pope Benedict appealed to Geneva for the protection of Christians in Asia Minor who were menaced by the Turks.[39] However, the only public communication sent directly to the League from Benedict XV concerned another people in danger, the Russians, threatened by famine in their war-ravaged country in the years immediately following the First World War.[40] At the 15th Plenary Meeting of the Second Assembly, on September 21, 1921, President van Karnebeek of the Netherlands, opened the meeting and read the following telegram:

> The reports arriving from Russia become even more grave, and the misery is so great that only the united effort of all, the collaboration of both people and government, can bring about a remedy. Hence, We address, by means of your Excellency, the Representatives of the nations reassembled there, and We appeal to their sense of humanity and fraternity in order that adequate measures may quickly be taken to save the unhappy Russians.[41]

The telegram was signed "Benedictus XVP." The president made no comment but proposed that "this important communication which we have had the honor receiving" be referred to Committee No. 6, which was considering a motion on Russian relief offered by Dr. Fridtjof Nansen of Norway. The Assembly agreed.[42]

Committee No. 6 reported to the 24th Plenary Meeting on 30 September, and the occasion provided an opportunity for two Catholic delegates to the Assembly to show initiative in exploiting the occasion and for the Assembly itself to respond to the pope's gesture of friendship and confidence in the League. The Committee's rapporteur, Mr. Motta of Switzerland, was a prominent Catholic friendly to the Holy See, as was its chairman, Count de Gimeno of Spain. Motta concluded his report by noting that the chairman of the Committee

---

[39] See "Pope Appeals to League: Asks Protection for Christians in Cilicia, Menaced by Turks," *New York Times* (February 3, 1921): 6.

[40] Koenig, supra note 1, ¶719, Letter *Le Notizie* to Cardinal Gasparri, Secretary of State, August 5, 1921.

[41] Ibid., ¶720, Telegram of Benedict XV to the League of Nations, September 1921.

[42] Records of Second Assembly, Plenary Meeting, 293.

asked the Assembly to decide to transmit the text of the resolutions which we adopt to His Holiness Pope Benedict
XV, through the President of the Assembly. The Committee enthusiastically concurred in this suggestion of its chairman. I think the Assembly will do the same. It is only right
that it should applaud the generous action of Pope Benedict XV, the great guardian of souls. We are also happy to
recall that, in appealing to us, His Holiness has acted in a
manner which transcends pure and simple courtesy, and
which has a great moral significance. By his action he has
given striking proof of the sympathy he feels for the League
of Nations and for the ideas of peace, collaboration and fra-
ternity for which it stands in the world. [Loud applause.][43]

Dr. Nansen, the High Commissioner of the Geneva Conference and a delegate of the joint committee, then made a dramatic
plea for funds, saying that voluntary organizations alone could not
do the job. He would continue his appeal to private charity from
which he had received many gifts, including 1,000,000 lire from
the pope—but he needed 5,000,000 pounds from the League, half
the cost of a battleship. If there was no help, within two months the
fate of twenty to thirty million people would be sealed.[44] The problem was that the machinery for Russian relief was too cumbersome.
The Supreme Council of the Principal Powers had just set up an
International Relief Committee, which in turn had called a conference for Brussels in October to deal with the Russian question.
Many delegates thought that the Assembly thus had no more than a
hortatory role. This was the view of Committee No. 6, and it prevailed. There was also opposition to proposed relief programs that
might help the Bolsheviks. The delegate from the Serb-Croat-
Slovene State attributed the famine to the Soviet government and
said his country would not contribute a penny.[45] It is interesting to
note that Benedict XV was not bothered by the possibility that the

[43] Ibid., 545.
[44] Ibid., 545–48.
[45] Ibid., 546.

Soviets might receive some indirect assistance. The Holy See did not take an intransigent line with the Bolshevik government at first, for which it was criticized by czarist elements.[46]

The final text of the resolution adopted at the 25th Plenary Meeting mentioned in its preamble the statement of Dr. Nansen and the appeal of the pope, but it did little more than appeal to private organizations and encourage relief efforts generally. The resolution asked the president of the Assembly to transmit to the pope a copy of the decisions as a sign of the League's appreciation of his message, and to express the Assembly's gratitude for so generous an action. Count de Gimeno of Spain thanked the Assembly for adopting his suggestion that the pope be notified.[47] Still, Benedict XV was disappointed by the League Assembly; he never got the "prompt and effective action" he asked for. Perhaps the pope and Dr. Nansen commiserated with each other at the latter's audience on November 2, 1921, when the latter officially thanked the pope for his contribution to Russian relief. At any rate both men went ahead and did what they could to solve the problem, regardless of the Assembly's decision.[48]

The results of this first public communication between the Holy See and the League can be viewed in different lights. As acts of mutual recognition, the papal telegram and the Assembly's applause gave witness to a spirit of friendship between Geneva and the Vatican that encouraged supporters of the League, especially the Catholic elite. Despite the substantive failure of the Holy See to become a member of the League, the form was successful and left the door open to similar contacts in the future. The event also enhanced the claim of the Holy See to active participation in the international community, and reinforced its juridical personality *opinio juris.* The image of the pope was improved by his support for a humanitarian cause transcending denominational and national lines and by his association with Nansen, a sympathetic public figure who needed

---

[46] See infra note 75, and accompanying text.
[47] Records of Second Assembly, Plenary Meeting, 573.
[48] League of Nations, *Official Journal,* Special Supplement, No. 6: 36–38.

support at the time.[49] Furthermore, the role of Catholic laymen in the League as mediators between the two institutions was clearly demonstrated. In a quiet way this amounted to a show of Catholic influence in the League as well as a concern for its effective operation. On the other hand, the failure of the Assembly to fulfill the pope's first public request for Russia was a setback for Benedict, and reinforced a public impression of League impotence (or indifference). Critics of the League, especially Catholics, were provided with new ammunition that could be directed at the League and its shortcomings. At the very least, the whole affair could have had a better outcome for the parties concerned.

Another question dealt with by the League in its early years in which Benedict XV and his successor, Pius XI, took a keen interest, was the economic crisis of Austria. The war and the brutal peace imposed at Versailles had left the nation truncated, impoverished, and suffering from famine and misery. Benedict, with Austria in mind, made two appeals for the relief of suffering in Central Europe during 1919.[50] While aid from the Allies kept the Austrian people from starvation in the years 1918–21, the country was still not self-supporting. As Benedict declared outspokenly in a letter to Cardinal Gasparri dated January 24, 1921, Austria did not have the means to exist as a state and conditions there were "absolutely intolerable."[51] The pope said that he could not remain silent and asked the secretary of state to call this serious matter to the attention of the diplomatic corps accredited to the Holy See. In the spring, the League Council, at the request of the allies, prepared a plan of financial and economic reconstruction for Austria, but the refusal of the U.S. to

---

[49] See "Nansen Tells Pope of Relief Plans," *New York Times* (November 2, 1921): 13; see Walters, supra note 14, at 150.

[50] Walters, supra note 14, at 205–6. See Koenig, supra note 1, ¶¶646–49, Letter of Cardinal Gasparri, Secretary of State, to Cardinal Bourne, Archbishop of Westminster, October 29, 1919; ¶¶650–53, Encyclical *Paterno Iam Diu* on Christian Charity for the Children of Central Europe, November 24, 1919; and ¶694, Letter *Plane intelligimus* to Cardinal Piffl, Archbishop of Vienna, and to the other Bishops of Austria, November 26, 1920.

[51] Koenig, supra note 1, ¶706, Letter *La Singolare* to Cardinal Gasparri, Secretary of State, January 24, 1921.

postpone its claims rendered the project futile. Consequently, in the next few months the Austrian krone became practically worthless. Financial assistance from Britain, France, Italy, and Czecho-Slovakia early in 1922 again prevented collapse, but by August a new crisis was imminent. The Allies, unwilling to continue this process, submitted the entire problem once again to the League.[52]

Despite widespread predictions of failure, the League Council officially accepted the Austrian assignment on August 31, 1922, and formed a special committee, which included Msgr. Ignaz Seipel, the Austrian chancellor, to supervise a comprehensive plan (already in formation) for economic and financial reconstruction. But the Council shrewdly postponed Austria's public appeal to the League until a few days later, when the Assembly opened its third session. Msgr. Seipel's address to the Council was thus heard by nearly fifty delegations, and his straightforward but moving speech had its intended effect.[53]

The next day, in the Assembly, Giuseppe Motta put the general sympathy for Austria into far more emotional words. Other speeches followed, and the Assembly was visibly moved to take action.[54] Within five weeks arrangements for a loan and League economic controls were completed and protocols signed. The scene immediately changed for the better. The loan was successfully floated the next summer, the Austrian budget was in balance by 1924, the government assumed full control in 1925, and by 1926 the League's commissioner had left Vienna.[55]

The rescue of Austria was thus visibly successful and it strengthened support of the League. The organization responded to popular sympathy, recognized the international economic common good and the power of unified action, and demonstrated that it could act

---

[52] Walters, supra note 14, at 208.

[53] As Prof. Walters stated, "It would be hard to imagine a more effective advocate in any international gathering than this quiet, ascetic, supremely intelligent priest, whose clerical-garb seemed to set him apart from the other delegates." See Walters, supra note 14, at 208.

[54] Ibid.

[55] Ibid., 209–10.

swiftly and decisively. In addition, the Council started a new trend by employing the financial, economic, and legal expertise of the Secretariat and technical organizations of the League in Austrian reconstruction. To make use of a permanent international institution was, in 1922, a brilliant innovation. Lastly, and perhaps most important to peace, the operation of the League demonstrated a spirit of reconciliation toward a defeated power and thus increased hope in the reality of brotherhood among peoples.

Catholics shared these perceptions along with everyone else, of course, but added a few impressions of their own. The League had, intentionally or not, responded to papal appeals for Austria, a Catholic country whose chancellor was a cleric opposed by the Socialists but aided by the League. The League initiative also fulfilled Pope Benedict's repeated exhortations to mutual forgiveness and Christian charity. Again the role played by prominent Catholics at Geneva came to light—men like Motta and Gabriel Hanotaux, the French representative on the Council's Austrian Committee. This was a source of satisfaction for many in the Catholic community.

Two major Catholic concerns in the Middle East became acute during the pontificate of Benedict XV and were eventually dealt with by the League in one way or other. The primary concern was the disposition of the Christian Holy Places under the proposed British mandate for Palestine. This issue aroused a good deal of Catholic feeling and consequently dragged on through the League for several years. The other concern worth mentioning here was the plight of Christians in Turkey from 1914 to 1923. While primarily Greek and Armenian minority groups, one-tenth of the Christian population was in union with Rome. They had been tolerated by the Ottomans (each rite constituting a "nation"), and through special international agreements called "capitulations" had been accorded protection by Russia (Orthodox Greeks and Armenians), France (European Catholics plus uniate Greeks and Armenians), and Italy (certain Catholics, by agreement with France and with the tacit consent of the Sublime Porte). But the advent of war in 1914, the enfeeblement of the empire, the rise of the Nationalists under

Mustapha Kemal and their rejection of the Treaty of Sèvres, resentment over the Armenian Republic, the Greek invasion, Allied occupation, war with Russia—all brought suffering, persecution, deportation or death to Christian minorities in Anatolia and aroused worldwide concern.[56]

Pope Benedict appealed to the League on February 3, 1921, to protect Christians in Cilicia, but little effective action was taken.[57] As the Turkish counteroffensive mounted in September of 1922, Nansen brought the problem of Greek and Armenian refugees before the Third Assembly, and repeated an earlier proposal that the League act to end the war in Asia Minor. The Assembly moved quickly to authorize Nansen to extend his Russian relief services to these refugees and recommended action by the Council. That body voted 100,000 Swiss francs for administrative costs out of the "Unforeseen Expenses" account, while pledges of financial aid were received from various states. On Nansen's other proposal, however, the major powers blocked any immediate League moves to settle the conflict and proposed a peace conference instead.[58] The autumn of 1922 saw a good deal of diplomatic activity, in which the Holy See participated vigorously, in order to stop the bloodshed. There followed the abolition of the Sultanate by Kemal's Nationalists, and the convening of the Conference of Lausanne on November 20. The situation of Christians in Turkey was still critical, however. On December 5, Cardinal Gasparri sent the Conference a strong diplomatic note appealing "in the name of humanity, that immediate and effective steps be taken on behalf of the safety of the cruelly persecuted population."[59]

The Treaty of Lausanne, which was finally signed during the following July, abrogated the capitulations and prohibited foreign intervention. It also promised civil equality and religious freedom to minorities and authorized the League Council to consider any alleged

---

[56] See La Brière, supra note 30, at 166–84, for an in-depth discussion.
[57] See supra note 39, and accompanying text.
[58] La Brière, supra note 30, at 122–23; *Monthly Summary* II, 222.
[59] Koenig, supra note 1, ¶756, Diplomatic Note of Cardinal Gasparri, Secretary of State, to the Conference of Lausanne, December 5, 1922.

violation of these rights. Kemal agreed to all of this. He persuaded the
Greek, Armenian, and Jewish communities to declare they wished no
special treatment, but he then ignored them.[60] La Brière cited the
problem of minorities in Turkey as another reason for regular and
official collaboration between the Holy See and the League. As the
League was charged by treaty to guarantee the security of the Catholic
faithful in Anatolia, the Holy See watched over the same faithful as
part of its divine mission.[61] Unfortunately, the League was never successful in any of its attempts to protect minorities, most of which
were in East and Central Europe. Despite the Minorities Treaties
devised in 1919, which carried a League guarantee, and the hearing of
petitions by the Council, the League could do little more than exert
moral pressure against an offender.[62] Walters notes that there were
two functions in which the League failed so notably that in 1945 they
were not assigned to the United Nations: one was the protection of
minorities, the other disarmament. It is significant that the Holy See
had a particular interest in both and was keenly disappointed in the
failure of the League to perform them.[63]

That Benedict XV considered disarmament the key to peace
can hardly be doubted, and so the Holy See was particularly disturbed by the failure of the League in this regard. Article 8 of the
Covenant called for the reduction of armaments to the lowest point
needed for domestic security and the enforcement of international
obligations, but the efforts of the First Assembly to start a move in
this direction were not successful. It asked the Council to name a
commission, which did not meet until July 1921, issuing an incomplete, preliminary, and mainly negative report.[64] That same month
the League lost the initiative when the U.S. announced the Washington Conference and its intentions to pursue peace through alternative means. In August, Pope Benedict made known his views on
the subject in an indirect way, through Cardinal Gasparri and the

---

[60] Walters, supra note 14, at 404.
[61] La Brière, supra note 30, at 184.
[62] Walters, supra note 14, I, at 402–11.
[63] Walters, supra note 14, II, at 813.
[64] Walters, supra note 14, I, at 143–44.

Roman correspondent of the U.S. National Catholic Welfare Conference, Msgr. Enrico Pucci.[65] Pucci revealed that the Holy See was in general accord with the proposals of President Harding, but still advanced the position, expressed by the pope in 1917, of the pressing need for disarmament, compulsory arbitration, and economic sanctions. Pucci also reported that a further Vatican proposal, completing that first peace plan, had been contained in a second, unpublished note to the belligerents from Gasparri in 1917 and would have been made public by him in an interview, had not Wilson's reply constituted "an answer permitting no discussion of the Pope's peace proposals." What the Holy See had stated then, and still advocated in 1921, was that the simplest, most feasible, and most effective means of disarmament was the abolition of conscription, the "tax of blood."[66]

According to Pucci, the Holy See had studied the question of disarmament very carefully and considered the steps to be taken if a nation rejected peaceful settlement and resorted to arms. Gasparri, he reported, concluded that if conscription were abolished this danger would be minimal, since volunteer military service would provide sufficient force to maintain order but not enough to make offensive, aggressive war possible. If disarmament and compulsory arbitration were accepted by all nations, any state in revolt could be dealt with by economic boycott or sanctions, which were no less effective in the long run than a resort to arms. This approach would be duplicated decades later by the U.N. in dealing with recalcitrant states. The Holy See hoped these papal considerations would influence the Washington Conference through moral persuasion since it neither took part in the conference nor drafted any document concerning it.[67] However, Pope Benedict sent a telegram to President Harding at the opening of the conference on November 10, 1921,

---

[65] See "Pope Is In Accord with Harding Plan: Thinks Disarmament Agreement Should Carry Pledge to Abolish Conscription—Views of 1917 Unchanged—Benedict XV Would Have Published Them Here, but for Wilson's Reply to Peace Note," *New York Times* (August 29, 1921): 2.

[66] Ibid.

[67] Ibid.

saying that he was praying for its success in achieving true disarmament.[68] Again he mentioned the conference favorably in an allocution to the College of Cardinals on November 21.[69] Moreover, the Holy See was probably responsible for an article in the *Corriere d'Italia* of November 15 which reported the pope as saying that the abolition of conscription was the simplest way to disarmament and would pave the way for obligatory arbitration to resolve international conflict. While President Harding's initiative was a satisfactory beginning, the long-range good of humanity required something along the lines of what the Holy See had indicated, as the best way to guarantee a just and lasting peace.[70]

The Washington Conference met from November 1921 to February 1922 and produced three treaties and a number of secondary agreements. Its most important achievement was the Five Power Treaty for the limitation of naval armaments. Although it had an ameliorating effect on international relations, this conference left the basic problem of disarmament unsolved.[71] Benedict XV died during its deliberations, on January 22, 1922, and his successor, Pius XI (1922–1939) sent an unofficial representative to the Genoa Conference the following spring, but that meeting was destined to fail.[72] For the next twelve years, from 1922 to 1933, the question of disarmament was continuously in the forefront of League aims and activities, but all efforts failed in the end.[73] Had Benedict lived until 1924, he would probably have supported the Geneva Protocol, which essentially linked disarmament to compulsory arbitration of disputes not resolved by the Permanent Court of International Justice or the Council. Although its provisions concerning the recalcitrant state differed somewhat from the ideas of Pope Benedict, the

---

[68] Koenig, supra note 1, ¶724, Telegram to President Harding of the United States at the Opening of the Arms Conference in Washington, November 10, 1921.

[69] Koenig, supra note 1, ¶¶725–27, Allocution *In Hac Quidem* to the College of Cardinals, November 21, 1921.

[70] "Pope Would Clinch Peace; Urges Abolition of Conscription as Way to Disarmament," *New York Times* (November 16, 1921): 5.

[71] Walters, supra note 14, at 163.

[72] Ibid., 164–67.

[73] Ibid., 217.

Geneva Protocol generally corresponded to his basic notion of three steps—disarmament, arbitration, and sanctions—leading to the substitution of reason for armed conflict in international dispute resolution. This was Benedict's great contribution to the theory and practice of international relations.

Despite his exclusion from the Peace Conference and the League, Benedict XV appreciably strengthened the international position of the Holy See during his brief pontificate. He restored diplomatic relations with France and initiated them with England, Holland, Finland, Poland, Czechoslovakia, and Latvia.[74] His policy had a strong eastern direction, shown by his interest in Turkey, Palestine, and especially Russia. He appealed to Lenin to respect religious freedom,[75] set in motion the diplomatic moves that resulted in contact with the Soviets at the Conference of Genoa in 1922,[76] worked for a rapprochement with the Eastern Orthodox Church and the improvement of conditions for Catholics in Russia, and established the Sacred Congregation for the Oriental Church and the Pontifical Oriental Institute.[77] Benedict also reached out to Protestants, approving the Malines Conversations on interfaith problems between Lord Halifax and Cardinal Mercier, although he declined to attend an ecumenical conference.[78] He also restored a measure of internal peace within the Church by ending the anti-Modernist campaign initiated by Pius X.[79] He also initiated gestures of reconciliation toward Italy. In asking an intermediary to forward a copy of *Dès le Début* to Victor Emmanuel III, the pope referred to the latter as the "King of Italy," the first official recognition of Italian unity by the Holy See.[80] In 1919 the Orlando-Cerretti conversations attempting to resolve the Roman Question were

---

[74] Koenig, supra note 1, at 127.

[75] Ibid., ¶625, Telegram of Cardinal Gasparri, Secretary of State to Lenin, Founder of the Union of Soviet Russia, march 12, 1919.

[76] Carlo Falconi, *The Popes in the Twentieth Century: From Pius to John XXIII* (Boston: Little, Brown, 1967), 141.

[77] Ibid., 139–41.

[78] Ibid., 142–43.

[79] Ibid., 130–34.

[80] Walter H. Peters, *The Life of Benedict XV* (Milwaukee: Bruce, 1959), 195–96.

begun. In *Pacem Dei Munus* he relaxed the ban on visits by heads of Catholic states to the Quirinal. Finally, in the last year of his life, he sent Cardinal Gasparri to meet secretly with Mussolini on the Roman Question and thus paved the way for the Lateran Treaty of 1929.[81]

Benedict XV modernized the international function of the Church by initiating a revolution in Catholic missionary practice. He was determined to "plant" the Church definitively in the mission territories, with an indigenous clergy and episcopate and greater adaptation to local cultures, languages, and art. Reviving the approach of Matteo Ricci and Robert De Nobili, he advocated greater study and appreciation of the older civilizations of Asia and the tribal cultures of Africa. His encyclical *Maximum Illud*, published on November 30, 1919, paved the way for the integration into the family of nations of the less developed or developing nations. Realizing that this policy depended upon the freedom of the Catholic missions from interference by the imperial powers, he secured from the Paris Peace Conference the Church's rights in relation to the missions,[82] and he attempted to withdraw the missions in China from French protection. Leo XIII had aspired to establish diplomatic relations with China but French opposition had caused him to desist. Benedict renewed the effort and was temporarily successful until France sent a threatening note to Peking, signed by the Allies, and the Chinese government capitulated. Benedict did not relent. He named the Bishop of Canton as Apostolic Visitor to China, leading to the appointment of the first Vatican envoy to Peking under Pius XI. This change in missionary policy was one of the greatest innovations ever attempted by a pope.[83]

Benedict initiated a new policy of greater openness to the values of non-Christian civilizations, but he remained always a European Catholic. While he believed in Christian values as a universal substratum for world peace, he appealed earnestly for this peace as

---

[81] Ibid., 194–96.
[82] Falconi, supra note 76, at 144–45.
[83] Ibid., 143–48.

something possible in a religiously diverse world.[84] He was certainly a European, but it was Europeans who were making war, many of them people of his own flock, and who thus needed his message most of all. Furthermore, his mission policy showed a perception of Christian values in non-Christian civilizations. His assistance to the suffering on both sides of the Great War and to all peoples in need afterward won him and the papacy both respect and affection. Turkey was especially grateful.[85] There is a statue of him in Istanbul bearing the inscription

> To the Great Pope of the World's Tragic Hour—Benedict XV—Benefactor of the People—Without Discrimination of Nationality or Religion—A Token of Gratitude from the Orient 1914–1919[86]

These words sum up his achievements in international relations as well as his charity, yet in the Christian world there is no similar monument to his name. He was perhaps born too soon, too pacifist, and too internationalist for his times, and too "modern" in his thinking on the relationship of the Church to the world. He sought to involve the Church in world politics, not as a power perfects its own interests, but as a transnational or supranational force building peace for all.

Pope Benedict XV left his mark on world history and his peace efforts would come to be appreciated in later years. He stimulated a Catholic elite to break new ground in international thought and action. He was a positive force supporting the League in his first years, and he enlarged the horizons of Catholics everywhere. Despite the opprobrium he earned by his attitude toward the First World War, his "pacifist idealism" became better understood in later years.

---

[84] Jacques Leclercq, *The Christian and World Integration* (New York: Hawthorn, 1963), 48–49.

[85] Maurice Vaussard, "L'Eglise Catholique, La Guerre et La Paix," *Guerre et Paix* (Lyon: Chronique Social de France, 1953), 136; Peters, supra note 81, at 186; Carol Conrad Eckhardt, *The Papacy and World Affairs* (Chicago: University of Chicago Press, 1937), 261.

[86] See Peters, supra note 81, at 186.

As was said of him: "It is one of the ironies of history that it has taken another World War to reveal Benedict's accomplishments in their true historical perspective."[87] Yet for most people, including many Catholics, he remains an unknown figure. This aspect of Benedict as the forgotten pope of peace is also captured by a statue, the only one of him outside Istanbul that the ordinary traveler would ever see. In St. Peter's in Rome, at one side of the chapel where Pius X is buried, the figure of Benedict kneels in prayer, wearing neither tiara nor miter, and looking very much like a simple priest. Although he was in life very much "the pope" when insisting on the right of the Church to freedom and of humanity to peace, this is probably the way he would want to be remembered.

As the *New York Times* editorial, tribute to him said,

On no other Pope, perhaps, has rested so thankless and difficult a task, such a burden of disaster, so violent a pressure of hostile opinions, interests and nations fighting for existence, as made the first four years of Benedict XV's pontificate a continual anxiety and sorrow to himself and brought on him many complaints and resentments, rather inevitable than justified. We ought to be able to regard him now not only with more charity, but with more justice than was his lot when each side was soliciting his favor and finding fault with him.[88]

---

87 Koenig, supra note 1, at 127.
88 Editorial, "Benedict XV," *New York Times* (January 23, 1922).

The Holy See, the League and the Mandate for Palestine

O F ALL THE ISSUES debated by the League in its early years, none caused more concern at the Vatican than the British Mandate for Palestine, which endangered centuries-old rights of the Church over the Holy Places. Since it is impossible to understand the position of the Holy See on this question without looking at the origin of these rights, a brief historical survey is in order.[1] It will also serve to underscore the importance to the Church of the Holy Land, and to unravel some of the complexities of a region situated at a crossroads of the world and sacred to the three great monotheistic and historical religions. For Jews, Palestine is the land of the patriarchs and prophets, of David and the kings, the cradle of a People and its Promised Land. For Moslems, it is the home of their ancestors Abraham and Ishmael, and Jerusalem is the third most sacred city in the world because Mohammed was taken up into heaven from there. For Christians, the Holy Land, especially Jerusalem, was definitively sanctified by the earthly life of Jesus and constitutes the central religious sanctuary of the world.

---

[1] See S. E. Mons, Jean Louis Tauran, Secretary for Relations with States, Symposium Commemorating the 50th Anniversary of the Pontifical Mission for Palestine, United Nations Headquarters, October 25, 1999; and S. E. Mons, Renato R. Martino, Statement before the 4th Committee of the United Nations, United Nations Headquarters, November 3, 1999.

Over the centuries, possession of the Holy Land, or a vigorous presence within it, became for each faith the sign of a living spiritual heritage, of contemporary religious fervor, and of the worldwide concern of its adherents. A struggle for control of Palestine resulted, which continues to the present day. For Christians it is ironic that the land where Christ proclaimed peace and love among men should be the scene of such dissension and conflict, especially quarreling among different Christian churches for control of a particular shrine. Yet the Holy Land as a great symbol has also presented a challenge to the three great religions acknowledging the Bible—the "People of the Book," as Islam puts it—to co-exist peacefully in a sacred place. Their efforts to do so have brought bloodshed, to be sure, but have also produced toleration, if not brotherhood, and a complex history of agreements, accommodations, and arrangements intertwined with the politics of the powers in control and those assuming the role of protector of a particular faith. In this part of the world, religion and world politics have gone hand in hand.

The heart of the Holy Land is Jerusalem, the city of peace. Captured from the Jebusites by King David, Jerusalem remained in Israelite hands some four hundred years. After domination by Babylonians, Persians, and Greeks, Jewish rule was restored for another century until the city fell to Rome in 63 B.C. Jerusalem and all of Palestine was part of the Roman Empire for almost seven hundred years. For nearly half of this period, the sites connected with the life Christ were in Christian hands. Constantine's mother, Helen, began building churches and shrines in these places, which soon attracted pilgrims from all over the world. For Christians, this was the golden age—unaffected by the transfer of power to Byzantium—when the Holy Land became almost indelibly impressed in the consciousness of Christians as the most sacred land in the world. A Persian invasion interrupted this period briefly in the early seventh century, but the real danger was to come. In 638 Jerusalem was taken by Arab forces and the adherents of a new religion, Islam, now dominated the region. With Europe passing into the Dark Ages of barbarian rule and Constantinople too weak to expel the invaders, the problem of the Holy Places, the access and control of the shrines, was posed for the first time.[2]

The Moslem rulers of Palestine followed a policy of toleration in religious affairs. However, there were exceptions. The Moslems erected shrines sacred to Islam, such as the famous Dome of the Rock on the site of the Jewish temple. The Patriarch of Jersualem, a prelate of the Eastern Church in union with Rome, came to be named by the caliphs, and soon sought assistance and support from the rulers of the Frankish kingdom in Europe. This need for Christian support, plus the presence of Frankish monks in the Holy Land and commerce between Palestine and Europe, led to an exchange of embassies between Baghdad and the Frankish court beginning in 765, a relationship that reached its apogee between Charlemagne and the famous Caliph Haroun-al-Rashid (of "Arabian Nights" fame). This relationship resulted in an informal Frankish protectorate over Christians and the Holy Places lasting to 840. After a period of persecution under the Fatimid rulers—during which the Church of the Holy Sepulchre was destroyed by Caliph Hakim—toleration was restored and the caliphs allowed the emperor to exercise a protectorate over Christians and the Holy Places. The Church of the Holy Sepulchre was rebuilt (1027–48) and pilgrimages resumed.[3]

Within a short time, Palestine was invaded by the Seljuk Turks, who took Jerusalem in 1071 and exercised intolerance toward Christians, resident or pilgrim. Armed pilgrimages now became necessary, and this need of military force to defend the right of access led to the proclamation of the First Crusade in 1096. During the entire period of the Crusades, almost a century and a half, there was both a Catholic king and a Latin patriarch in the Holy Land. The Holy Places remained in Christian hands for the most part and were enriched and restored. The Crusades ultimately failed in their quest to procure Christian dominion over Jerusalem. However, one purpose had been achieved: Even after the restoration of Arab rule in 1239, pilgrimages continued and Christians could live in relative

---

[2] B. Collin, *Le Problème Juridique des Lieux-Saints* (Paris: Sirey, 1956), 10.
[3] Ibid., 12.

peace. Western powers obtained various benefits for Christians in the Holy Land during this period by means of diplomacy. Relations between Naples and the Sultan of Egypt were the most important, since they resulted in the confirmation of the Franciscan order, already in the Holy Land for a century, as custodians of the Holy Places. This Custody, as it was called, was juridically established in the second quarter of the fourteenth century by treaty and resulted in the supervision of many Holy Places by the Franciscans, who enjoyed this right in the name of the Catholic Church. The permanent presence of Latin religious in the Holy Places was a new element, and occasioned interventions on behalf of the Franciscans by Naples, Venice, Aragon, Burgundy, and France.[4]

When the Ottoman Turks took Jerusalem (1516–17), a new phase in the issues surrounding the Holy Places began. The spirit of the Crusades had faded away, but it was succeeded by the involvement of the Holy Places in European public law and world politics, as well as severe interconfessional strife between Christian churches. In 1535, Francis I of France and Suleiman the Magnificent signed the first treaty regarding the Holy Land to be called a "capitulation." Although preceded for two centuries by a series of agreements with European states guaranteeing the protection of their subjects and providing for consuls, the capitulations gave Christians the protection of their own law (the law of the Ottoman Empire was Islamic law) and a kind of extraterritoriality for their property. Many such agreements would be signed in the future, such as the Capitulations of 1604 with France, in which the French king was named the protector of pilgrims and the Holy Places. During the seventeenth and eighteenth centuries, the Sublime Porte signed capitulations with almost all western states.[5]

Ottoman policy favored the Greek Orthodox and a concentration of power in the Patriarch of Constantinople, who received investiture at the hands of the sultan and was head of the Greek "nation" in the empire. The Greeks were able to increase their control over certain Holy Places at the expense of Latin Catholics. Thus,

---

[4] Ibid., 22–23.
[5] Ibid., 27–33.

the Capitulations of 1740, favorable to Catholics, were upset in 1757 when the Orthodox took over many shrines in Jerusalem and Bethlehem. Catholics objected vigorously, but the action was confirmed by the sultan. This division came to be known as the Status Quo and comprised an incredibly complicated set of regulations as to which Christian Church should control, use, and maintain each shrine or part thereof (some shrines are occupied jointly). As confirmed by a *firman* of 1852, the Status Quo applied to seven Christian sites (and two Moslem and Jewish Holy Places).[6] Contention between Christians eventually involved European powers: Russia became the patron of the Orthodox, France of the Latin Catholics. This rivalry was a factor leading to the Crimean War, which resulted in greater religious freedom for Christians.[7] Russia used the religious issue again in 1877 to mask its drive to the Straits of Bosphorus. This goal was not attained, but at the Congress of Berlin (1878) the Status Quo was confirmed without French protest.[8] However, France continued as protector of Latin-rite Catholics in Palestine, and this role was confirmed by the Holy See.[9]

In addition to Christian–Moslem tensions, interconfessional strife among Christians and big power rivalry in the Near East, another factor appeared to complicate the situation—Zionism. Catholics generally were not favorable to the movement. When its founder, Theodore Herzl, had an audience with Pope Pius X in 1904 and sought his support, the pope replied, "It is not pleasant to see the Turks in possession of our Holy Places . . . but to support the Jews, that we cannot do."[10] In May 1917, Msgr. Eugenio Pacelli—the future Pius XII—helped the Zionist leader Nahum Sokolow obtain an audience with Pope Benedict XV, whom Sokolow reported as extremely cordial and sympathetic.[11] But in fact the Holy See at the

---

[6] Ibid., 34–49.

[7] Ibid., 40–51.

[8] Ibid., 56–58.

[9] Ibid., 62–65.

[10] Pinchas Lapide, *Three Popes and the Jews* (New York: Hawthorn Books, 1967), 284.

[11] Ibid., 274–75.

time was not in favor of the establishment of a Jewish home in Palestine, and was alarmed at the Zionist pressure on both the Allies and
the Central Powers that had begun to build during the First World
War. Zionists in Germany and Austria-Hungary were negotiating
with their governments in an effort to obtain from Turkey certain
rights in Palestine for the Jews of the world. The Zionist group in
Great Britain, led by Baron Rothschild and Dr. Chaim Weizmann,
exerted pressure upon the government to grant a national home for
Jews in Palestine in the event of Allied victory during the Great War.

With the situation on the battlefront uncertain, the need
appeared great in London to obtain friends for the Allied cause and
to influence Russian Jews who had been active in overthrowing the
czarist regime and favored the continuation of the war with the
Central Powers. On November 2, 1917, Lord Balfour, Secretary of
the Foreign Office, addressed a letter to Baron Rothschild, stating
that the British government viewed with favor the establishment in
Palestine of a national home for the Jewish people. It was clearly
understood that nothing would be done to prejudice the civil and
religious rights of non-Jewish communities in Palestine. The Balfour Declaration caused a storm of indignation and protest among
Arabs, since Britain had promised them independence for the whole
of the Middle East including, as the Arabs thought, Palestine. The
reaction of the Holy See was also dubious. The Balfour Declaration
seemed perplexing in itself, and with the imminent liberation of the
Holy Land from Moslem domination, as Turkey appeared certain to
be defeated, it threatened both those rising expectations and traditional Christian rights in Palestine.[12]

Catholic hopes were not dashed, however. In January 1918 a
British monsignor, Arthur Stapleton Barnes, stated that Great Britain,
then occupying Palestine, would name Pope Benedict protector of
the Holy Places.[13] In June, London softened the effect of the Balfour
Declaration by assuring the Arabs that Jewish settlement in Pales-

---

[12] Sergio I. Minerbi, *The Vatican and Zionism—Conflict in the Holy Land:
1895–1925* (New York: Oxford University Press, 1990), 197–98.
[13] "Britain May Name Pope; Expected to Name Him Protector of Shrines of
Palestine," *New York Times* (January 21, 1918): 3.

tine would not interfere with or threaten the political and economic freedom of the Arab population. Subsequent assurances promised freedom and independence for the Arab population and a government based upon the consent of the governed. Catholics generally did not reflect on what this might mean for the Holy Places. What seemed of paramount importance was the defeat of Turkey by Christian powers. With the defeat of Turkey, Jerusalem was in the hands of France, England, and Italy—three nations that played a great part in the Crusades. Restoration of Christian control of the Holy Places would be accomplished with the Franciscans returning to shrines taken from them a century and a half before.

The term "Holy Places" as used in the international forum over the centuries has acquired both a general and a restricted sense. Obviously there are places in the Holy Land sacred to Judaism and Islam—the Wailing Wall, Rachel's Tomb, and the Dome of the Rock are prime examples—and so one can properly speak of Jewish and Moslem Holy Places. But unless the term is so specified or clear from the context, it usually refers to the far more numerous Christian sites. Of these there are hundreds, including 94 of major importance. The key shrines are Gethsemane and the Mount of Olives, the Via Dolorosa with its churches and chapels, the Basilica of the Holy Sepulchre, the Cenacle, the Church of the Dormition, and, in Bethlehem, the Basilica and Grotto of the Nativity. In the nineteenth century, discussion of the Holy Places was generally confined to the last four, but there are many more. Since the fourth century, Christians of the world have been building, adorning, and endowing churches, shrines, hospices, convents, monasteries, and schools in the Holy Land, many of which now have historic as well as religious value and represent a vested property interest. Again, the term "Holy Places" can be used as an umbrella term to cover all the traditional rights of religious communities living in the country, even those unconnected with access and control of shrines, for example, recognition of Church marriages and schools.

The Paris Peace Conference of 1919 was to decide the future of the Holy Land, and accordingly received a memorandum from the

Franciscan superior in Jerusalem, the Custodian of the Holy Land, outlining traditional Catholic rights and asking for the restoration of the Status Quo Ante of 1740. This was countered by a memorandum from the Greek Orthodox community, stressing prior occupation of the Holy Places by the Greeks before the Crusades, and the repeated confirmation of the Status Quo of 1757 by the European powers.[14] The Conference also heard indirectly from Benedict XV. In a speech of March 10, 1919, to the College of Cardinals, the pope said,

> But there is one matter on which We are most specially anxious, and that is the fate of the Holy Places, on account of the special dignity and importance for which they are so venerated by every Christian. Who can ever tell the full story of all the efforts of Our Predecessors to free them from the dominion of infidels, the heroic deeds and the blood shed by the Christians of the West through the centuries? And now that, amid the rejoicing of all good men, they have finally returned to the hands of the Christians, Our anxiety is most keen as to the decisions which the Peace Congress at Paris is soon to take concerning them. For surely it would be a terrible grief for Us and for all the Christian faithful if infidels were placed in a privileged and prominent position; much more if those most holy sanctuaries of the Christian religion were given into the charge of non-Christians.[15]

The Holy See was mobilizing its forces in opposition to what it considered a Zionist and Protestant policy on the part of Britain. In April, Cardinal Gasparri publicly stated a preference for the internationalization of Palestine, while Msgr. Cerretti lobbied among the delegates to the Peace Conference.[16] The decision of the Conference to classify Palestine as a mandate meant that the United King-

---

14 Collin, supra note 2, at 173–90.

15 Harry Koenig, *Principles for Peace: Selections from Papal Documents—Leo XIII to Pius XII* (Milwaukee: Bruce, 1943), ¶617, Allocution Antequam Ordinem to the college of Cardinals, March 10, 1919.

16 "Behind the Pope's Palestine Note," *New York Times* (July 2, 1922): sect. 2, 12.

dom would rule the country for some years to come. It was understood that Britain would be named as mandatory power by the Mandates Commission of the Supreme Council of the Allied Powers. London had worked this out with the Quai d'Orsay and, by careful design, had occupied the area over which it wanted to keep control for strategic purposes.[17] It also meant that the League would have a role in the future of Palestine, confirming the mandate agreement and receiving reports through its Permanent Mandates Commission. The Allied Mandates Commission predictably assigned the Mandate for Palestine to Great Britain, and this was confirmed by the Supreme Council of the Allied Powers at San Remo on April 25, 1920. But the particulars of the mandate still had to be drafted and approved by the League.

An indication of these concerns had already been provided by an article in the *Corriere d'Italia* in early July 1920. Occasioned by a joint effort of the pope and King Victor Emanuel to obtain custody of the Cenacle, the article charged the Jews with having opposed the work of the Franciscans for centuries and said that the king of Italy, as heir to the sovereigns of Naples, was now claiming the Cenacle on behalf of the Franciscans. In April, 1919, the sultan had agreed to restore the Cenacle to Italy, but England had refused to give its consent. The population of Palestine was only ten percent Jewish, but Jews occupied all the public offices, while the English governor of Jerusalem, Sir Herbert Samuel, was both a Jew and a fervent Zionist. Some Arabs were preparing to rise up against what they perceived to be Jewish domination.[18]

The draft Mandate for Palestine was first presented to the League Council for approval in February 1921. Although not debated at that time, the text became public and it received a critical reaction from the Holy See. Article 13 stated that the Mandatory Power was granted all responsibility in connection with the Holy

---

[17] Collin, supra note 2, at 71–74.

[18] "Pope and King Seek Care of Zion Shrine—Vatican and Italian Monarch Unite in Effort to Recover Holy Places for Christians—England in Opposition—Unwilling to Offend Hebrews and Mohammedans, Who Now Hold Desired Spots," *New York Times* (July 9, 1920): 17.

Places, religious buildings and sites, including that of preserving existing rights, assuring free access and freedom of worship. It could also make agreements with the administration of Palestine to implement these responsibilities. The immunity of purely Moslem shrines from interference by the Mandatory was guaranteed. This was a grant of enormous power and complete responsibility, as well as a solid indication that the Status Quo would not be changed.[19] Draft Article 14 was just as unacceptable to the Holy See. This draft stated that:

> The Mandatory undertakes to appoint as soon as possible a special Commission to study and regulate all questions and claims relating to the different religious communities. In the composition of this Commission the religious interest concerned will be taken into account. The Chairman of the Commission will be appointed by the Council of the League of Nations.[20]

Thus the Commission, entirely dependent on the British government, could not only determine and designate the Holy Places, but resolve all disputes concerning them. In effect, Britain was taking over the role of the Ottoman Empire regarding the Holy Places.[21]

The Holy See opposed the terms of the draft mandate not only in principle, but also because of the tenor of British policy in Palestine. In a consistorial allocution of June 13, 1921, Pope Benedict spoke plainly by saying,

> When the Christians by means of the Allied troops regained possession of the Holy Places, We joined with all Our heart in the general exultation of men of good will; but Our joy was tempered by the fear that as a result of so splendid and joyous an event the Israelites might find themselves in a position of preponderance and privilege in Palestine. To judge by the present situation, unhappily what We feared has come about. It is in fact known that the position of

---

[19] Collin, supra note 2, at 86–87.
[20] Ibid., Part II, 202.
[21] Ibid., 87.

Christians in Palestine is not only no better, but has actually worsened by the new civil arrangements established
there, which aim at evicting Christianity from the positions
it hitherto occupied to replace it by the Jews.[22]

It would be unwise to interpret this as anti-Semitism, because the
pope's real concern was the defense of the Holy Places. The pope com-
plained that these were already being profaned by the introduction of
places of entertainment and worldly festivals, and went on to say
specifically that Jewish rights should not be restricted, but that on the
other hand neither should the rights of Christians be diminished.[23]

Benedict was not afraid to make a public plea for pressure to be
brought at the League of Nations, mentioning the organization by
name when he stated,

In this matter, We earnestly ask *(vehementer rogamus)* the
rulers of all Christian peoples, even of non-Catholics to
intervene with the League of Nations *(Nationum Soci-
etatem)* which reportedly has the task of fixing the terms of
the British Mandate, so that these rights will not be
infringed.[24]

It should be noted that Benedict's complaint was not with the League
of Nations, but with Great Britain. In effect, he was appealing to the
former about the actions of the latter, thus expressing for the first
time the theme that will be echoed and echoed again in later papal
teaching: that it is the proper function of an international organization to protect human rights threatened by the action of a nation-
state.[25] Also worthy of note is that his exhortation was directed to
leaders of non-Catholic as well as Catholic states. Benedict's remarks

---

[22] "Allocution *Causa Nobis Quidem* to the College of Cardinals, June 13, 1921,"
in Carlo Falconi, *The Popes in the Twentieth Century: From Pius X to John
XXIII* (Boston: Little, Brown, 1967), 142.

[23] Collin, supra note 2, at 206.

[24] Ibid.

[25] "Pope Criticizes Jews for Acts in Palestine; Urges Appeal to League to Define
Mandate," *New York Times* (June 14, 1921): 1; Koenig, supra note 15, ¶715,
Allocution *Causa Nobis Quidem* to the College of Cardinals, June 13, 1921.

received prominent coverage in the press. The *London Times* reported on June 15 that the pope's criticism of British policy in Palestine "caused considerable sensation in diplomatic and other quarters," and that diplomacy had few instances of such plain speaking.[26]

True to the intent of its founder, the Catholic Union of International Studies represented the views of the Holy See to the League concerning the mandate. In September 1921 the Secretariat in Geneva received a petition from the Union asking that (1) nothing be changed in the traditional statute of the Holy Places without the prior agreement of the Holy See, and (2) an international control commission presided over by a representative of France should supervise and guarantee the exercise of Catholic rights in Palestine despite British favoritism to Protestant and Jewish interests. Specifically these rights included the right to establish hospitals and schools, to retain the protection of the flag of their choosing, to teach in their own language, and to receive pupils of all languages and faiths—in short, all the freedoms enjoyed under the Ottoman regime.[27] This petition had been prepared and sent to arrive at the time of the second Assembly, which was to have taken up the question of mandates. For a number of reasons, however, the matter had to be postponed once more. The basic notion of this petition would appear the following spring in an *aide-memoire* from Cardinal Gasparri to the League Secretary-General.[28]

With the accession of Pius XI, Vatican policy became even more energetic regarding Palestine and the Holy Places. In the spring of 1922, Pius accepted the assistance of the Italian government, which

---

[26] See "Stirred by Pope's Appeal—Diplomats in Rome Find Criticism of Palestine Mandate Sensational," *New York Times* (June 15, 1921): 2, which stated, "A dispatch to the *London Times* from Rome says that Pope Benedict's criticism of Great Britain's policy in Palestine, as outlined by the Pontiff Monday in his allocution to the secret consistory, caused a considerable sensation in diplomatic and other quarters. It is maintained, said the dispatch, that diplomacy has had few instances of such plain speaking as the Pope's appeal to the Christian world to insist that the League of nations examine into the British Mandate."

[27] Yves de La Brière, SJ, *L'Organisation Internationale du Monde Contemporain et la Papauté Soveraine, Series I* (Paris: Editions Spes, 1924), 83–84.

[28] Ibid., 101.

was seeking increased influence in Palestine. Foreign Minister Carlo Schanzer made representations to Winston Churchill concerning the positions of Italy and the Holy See on the Palestinian Mandate.[29] Dissatisfied with the result, the pope then requested the Latin Patriarch of Jerusalem, Msgr. Barlassina, to visit London and explain in greater details these concerns and positions to the British government. But the patriarch was poorly received. Neither Balfour nor Churchill would see him. This may be attributed to the fact that Msgr. Barlassina had mentioned in a lecture in Rome that the goal of Zionism was to resettle Jews in Palestine and expel people of other nationalities. He had also pointed out that some Zionists were supported by funds from abroad and were buying the lands of the Moslems impoverished by the war. He further said that European Catholic circles were uninformed about the state of affairs and that the Arabs could not understand why so little was being done to protect the Holy Sites.[30]

In an attempt to combat the influence of the patriarch, Professor Chaim Weizmann, the leader of international Zionism, had two conversations with Cardinal Gasparri in the month of May 1922. He reported that the cardinal seemed more concerned with the British administration than the Zionists, complaining, for example, that members of religious orders were encountering difficulties in getting visas. Weizmann was able to explain the goals of Zionism and give some account of the work being done in Palestine with regard to development. The cardinal indicated that this caused him no anxiety, but he expressed some fear of the influence of the Hebrew University. Weizmann believed that Gasparri prevented his seeing the pope, despite every possible effort.[31]

The diplomatic offensive waged by the Holy See in the spring of 1922 included a long letter written by Cardinal Gasparri to Sir Eric Drummond. It was in the form of a memorandum intended

---

[29] Maurice Pernot, *La Saint-Siège, l'Eglise Catholique et la Politique Mondiale* (Paris: Armand Colin, 1924), 117.

[30] *Cronaca Contemporanea, Cose Romane, Civilta Cattolica,* 11–23 May 1922, II, 461–62; Minerbi, supra note 12, at 175.

[31] Lapide, supra note 10, at 271, 275; Chaim Weizmann, *Trial and Error* (New York: Harper, 1949), 285–86.

for the League Council, which had decided to discuss the Palestinian Mandate at its July meeting in London.[32] The cardinal stated that the Holy See had no objection to the assignment of the mandate to Great Britain, but proposed several changes that would also be in the interests of the British nation, which undoubtedly wanted the mandate to be exercised peacefully. He also wished to avoid upsetting the religious sentiments of the populations involved. The memorandum also raised objections to specific articles: to Article 4, recognizing the Zionist organization as the official Jewish Commission; to Article 6, favoring Jewish immigration; to other articles favoring the Jewish community; and most of all to Article 14, providing for a Commission on the Holy Places. Gasparri said that the entire project (he called it "the Balfour project") aimed at an absolute Jewish preponderance in Palestine that violated the rights of other nationalities and, therefore, Article 23 of the Treaty of Versailles. His greatest objections, however, were reserved for the proposed Commission, and in this regard he submitted a counter-proposal from the Holy See.[33]

The Gasparri memorandum criticized Article 14 of the draft mandate on several counts: the number of members on the proposed Commission was not fixed, and their character was left unstated; the scope of the Commission's responsibility was too vague and there were no limits placed on its control; the right of the Commission to designate Holy Places with the approval of the Mandatory gave Great Britain excessive power, an apparent violation of Article 95 of the Treaty of Sèvres. The cardinal indicated that Catholic representatives should look after Catholic interests. As he argued,

> Now it is obvious that the Holy See cannot consent to the interests of Catholics being delegated to representatives

---

[32] Oliver Earl Benson, *Vatican Diplomatic Practice as Affected by the Lateran Agreements* (Liège: Georges Thone, 1936), 196.

[33] Collin, supra note 2, at 209–11. See "Mandate Favors Jews, Vatican Says— Gives Absolute Preponderance to Them in Palestine, Papal Protest Asserts— Predicts Conflict There—Cardinal Gasparri's Letter to League Also Says Great Britain Would Get Excessive Power," *New York Times* (June 16, 1922): 10.

who have not been selected by the competent hierarchical authorities.[34]

Nor could the Holy See accept that the Commission could call into question the ownership of sanctuaries which had for centuries been in Catholic hands. The Commission would most likely become involved in bitter disputes between different faith communities having an interest in the same shrine; therefore, all religious groups would have to be represented on it and the resulting dissension would prevent it from achieving any concrete results.

Consequently, the Holy See suggested to the League Council that the Commission be composed of the consuls in the Holy Land of those powers that were members of the Council. The states members of the Council having no such consul could appoint a member to the Commission. Gasparri acknowledged that according to the Treaty of Sèvres the Commission should be appointed by Great Britain, but the Holy See hoped that the League Council would see the necessity of adopting the proposed changes so that the decisions of the Commission might be more impartial. In addition, Gasparri pointed out that the Holy See was not opposed to the idea that representatives of the various religious confessions should also belong to the Commission, on condition that they have a consultative voice only.[35] It is significant that according to the plan proposed by the Holy See, the Commission would have been composed of two Protestant powers (the United Kingdom and Sweden), three Catholic powers (France, Italy, and Spain), and one Orthodox power (Greece).[36]

The Gasparri memorandum was sent to Geneva in anticipation of the July meeting of the League Council, and so was a statement from the Catholic Union of International Studies. But these efforts were anticipated by the British and very nearly circumvented when, on May 11, Lord Balfour surprisingly asked the Council, then meeting in its eighteenth session, to take up the Palestinian and Syrian

---

[34] *New York Times* (June 16, 1922): 10.
[35] Collin, supra note 2, at 211.
[36] Benson, supra note 32, at 196–97.

Mandates at once. Conceding that they were not on the agenda, Balfour noted that serious obstacles to these mandates, principally American objections, had suddenly been overcome, so that there was no reason for further delay. But France and Italy were unwilling to go along with this unusual move and the agenda was observed and followed.[37] Six days later, in another speech to the Council, Balfour endeavored to appease the anxieties of Catholics regarding the mandate. He noted the fear in certain circles, but said it was surprising that anyone could imagine Christian interests in Palestine suffering from the transfer of authority from a Moslem to a Christian power, especially Great Britain. True, Britain was a Protestant country, but there was no country, Catholic or Protestant, where the Catholic religion was treated more equitably or generously than in the British Isles.[38] While this assertion may have been made in good faith, it was also clear that Catholics did not enjoy equal status in Great Britain, for example, the prohibition against a Catholic succeeding to the throne.

By the end of May, Gasparri's protest had been received by the League Secretariat, and it was soon made known to the press. Debate then moved to the public forum. The British Palestine Committee issued a rebuttal on May 27 and said that the Catholics wanted to steal a march on the Greek Orthodox, the Zionists being neutral, and that the Vatican charges were ridiculous, amounting to civil disobedience.[39] The question was widely discussed. On June 21 the House of Lords practically endorsed the Vatican objections by a vote of 60 to 29, despite the efforts of Balfour.[40] It was also revealed that Pius XI had protested the terms of the Mandate to the Genoa Conference (April 10–May 19), but this communication was not made public. An American correspondent promoted the view that the dispute was essentially between Catholics and Orthodox, one of the

---

[37] *Monthly Summary*, II (May 1922): 101.

[38] Collin, supra note 2, at 88.

[39] Walter Littlefield, "Behind the Pope's Palestine Note—Growth of a Policy First Questioned by the Crimean War—A Rivalry of Churches," *New York Times* (July 2, 1922): sect. 2, 12.

[40] Ibid.

causes of the Crimean War, and that Jews and Arabs did not care how these matters were settled.[41] Such an analysis missed the central import of Gaparri's memorandum, which was that Zionism was a threat to the peace of the Holy Land and that Article 14 of the mandate proposed machinery for solving problems connected with the Holy Places that was incapable of dealing with this threat. It also failed to understand that the proposal was incompatible with treaties that were in force and established Catholic rights.

The British government replied to Gasparri indirectly, through a note of July 1, 1922, directed to members of the Council. After denying any favored treatment for the Jewish people or the Zionist organization, His Majesty's government suggested an alternative draft of Article 14. The international commission would be composed of at least seven members, named by the Mandatory but subject to the approval of the League Council. The British government would select these members from a panel of candidates of worldwide reputation put forward under some international procedure, but would retain the right to add other names for specified reasons. The commission would be thoroughly representative and include members of the powers interested in Palestine and the three major confessions. The Council of the League would appoint its chairman, and the commission would prepare a report defining existing rights in the Holy Places. This report would be submitted for approval by the League Council, after which it would be binding on the Mandatory. The note added that political interests would be safeguarded by the necessity for Council confirmation of appointments and the commission's report, religious interests by a provision for consultation with the commission by religious bodies and the right of the latter to appeal to the Council, "who may require the mandatory to reassemble the commission."[42]

The League Council meeting at London in July 1922 had all the prospects of a final confrontation between Britain and the Vatican. Both sides prepared carefully for the event. Sir Herbert Samuel,

---

[41] Ibid.
[42] Collin, supra note 2, at 215–16.

the British High Commissioner for Palestine, went to Rome and was received in audience by Pius XI on July 6 for a half hour. He also saw Gasparri and the British Minister to the Holy See.[43] This was clearly an attempt to reach some kind of understanding before the Council met, but it was falsely reported some days later in the *London Daily Telegraph* that the Vatican was fully satisfied with the new draft of the mandate.[44] The Holy See, on the other hand, was soliciting help as well, especially from Italy, and decided to send Archbishop Cerretti, the nuncio in Paris, to London for the Council session. The Council took up the Mandate for Palestine at its eleventh meeting, on the morning of July 22, 1922. The president announced that Archbishop Cerretti had come to London "to be at the disposal of the Council and to explain the views of the Holy See."[45] This was clearly an embarrassment, even a challenge, but the Council reacted diplomatically. Viviani of France proposed that Msgr. Cerretti's presence be noted and that the discussion continue, to see if it were necessary to hear him. If so, other interested parties might also ask to be heard. Lord Balfour agreed, and the Council postponed its decision on allowing the papal emissary to speak.[46]

Discussion at the morning meeting of July 22, 1922, centered around Article 14. Viviani said that the composition of the proposed Commission was far from clear, as was its competence regarding the Holy Places. Would it have a Catholic majority or not? Would it be merely provisional, charged with substituting a new arrangement for the Status Quo? Lord Balfour replied that the Commission could have a judicial character, in which case seven members would suffice. But it might also be composed of representatives of the different national and religious groups, in which case it should be larger. As for the Status Quo, the British government had never intended to replace it with a new arrangement. Britain

---

[43] "Pope Pius Receives Palestine Official—Mutiny of Vatican Carabineers Suppressed a Short Time Before Samuel's Visit," *New York Times* (July 7, 1922): 4.

[44] "Receives Palestine Draft—Vatican Said to be Satisfied with Revised Mandate," *New York Times* (July 17, 1922): 3.

[45] *Official Journal*, II (August 1922): 817.

[46] Ibid., 818.

wanted to avoid the appointment of a permanent commission, creating a kind executive power alongside the Mandatory, which must remain sovereign. The Italian representative, Marquess Imperiali, declared that Italy wanted respect shown for vested rights and favored a permanent commission. The commission should be composed of the representatives of powers with the greatest interest in the country, the majority of which were in fact Catholic. Balfour referred the Council to the international selection procedure in the new Article 14, and a discussion followed of how and when to revise this article, which was blocking approval of the two mandates for Palestine and Syria.[47]

At the afternoon meeting of the Council, Balfour presented still another version of Article 14 (the third), which merely stated that a special commission be appointed by the Mandatory to study and define the rights and claims in connection with the Holy Places and the different religious communities in Palestine. The method of nomination, the composition, and the functions of the commission would be submitted to the Council of the League for approval, and the commission would not be appointed or begin its work without the Council's approval.[48] This of course was merely to postpone any real consideration of Article 14 until after the mandate had been confirmed. The Council agreed to accept this way out of the impasse, although Italy was reluctant, and to approve the mandate formally at its next meeting on the following Monday. The Spanish representative then read a declaration from his government that the traditional position of Spain in the Holy Land obliged it to call attention to its rights and privileges there and that it considered the presence of a Spanish member on the international commission indispensable. The French, Italian, and Belgian representatives made similar statements on behalf of their governments.[49]

After the meetings of July 22, Archbishop Cerretti made a statement to the Associated Press in which he anticipated that the Council

---

[47] *Monthly Summary,* II (July 1922): 155–56; *Official Journal,* III (August 1922): 818–19.

[48] *Official Journal,* II (August 1922): 821–22; Collin, supra note 2, at 91–92.

[49] *Official Journal,* II (August 1922): 822.

would formally approve the Palestinian mandate but not before giving him an opportunity to express the views of the Holy See. He came to London at the telegraphed request of the Holy See, and was naturally disappointed at the Council's failure to hear him before confirming the mandate. In his press statement, he said,

> It is obvious that the revision of Article XIV confirming the composition and authority of the Commission for the custody of the Holy Places was a mere form, and that Great Britain will have the final voice in deciding the personnel and functions of the Commission. The Vatican considers the Holy Places international in character, and consequently the Commission should be international; it should embrace the representatives of all countries which have special interests in the sacred areas. We do not want France or any one country to dictate in these cases. The custody of these places has been under an Italian, a Frenchman and a Spaniard, and recently an Englishman, and it is only just that the Commission should comprise members from these countries.[50]

Cerretti identified the nationality of the Franciscan Custodians of the Holy Places. In a sense he argued that in establishing a Commission for the Holy Places the League should follow the policy of the Church in international administration. His statement penetrated to the heart of the whole issue: Would the Holy Places be either under British or international control?

On the following Monday, July 24, 1922, the Council meeting was public and there was a large number of spectators. Included in this group were Archbishop Cerretti, the Archbishop of Canterbury, members of an Arab delegation, and Mrs. Chaim Weizmann. Lord Balfour presented the good intentions of the British government and said that the Council now had a grave responsibility. Although

---

[50] Quoted in "Council Confirms the Last Mandates—Italy Give Reluctant Assent to Provision for Guarding Holy Places—Papal Nuncio Not Heard—He Expresses Fear that Revised Palestine Agreement Will Not Meet Vatican Wishes," *New York Times* (July 23, 1922): 9.

more discussion on Article 14 was required, the mandate was now settled as far as the League was concerned. Marquess Imperiali said that as a representative of a Catholic country he attached the greatest importance to the question of the Holy Places raised in Article 14, and it was essential that agreement be reached by the Council before the next meeting of the Assembly. A formal announcement was then made by the president that the mandates for Palestine and Syria had been approved.[51] Some may have interpreted this decision as a victory for Balfour and Zionism. Imperiali of Italy had withdrawn as defender of the Vatican's vested rights, and Cerretti had not been allowed to speak. On the other hand, Catholics were pleased that while the entire mandate had in effect been approved, Article 14 was to be further revised. They hoped that this would still present an opportunity to grant the commission a more international character and a greater guarantee of independence.

The Holy See submitted another memorandum to the League on August 15, 1922, which declared that the proposed commission should be permanent. Moreover, since disputes would arise frequently, and since almost all the shrines in Palestine belonged to the Catholic religion, it was sensible for a majority of the commission to be staffed by representatives of Catholic states, especially Belgium, France, Italy, Spain, and Brazil. The Holy See had for many years given responsibility for the custody of the Holy Land to Catholics of various nations thereby demonstrating the non-national or international character of the shrines. In order to be properly informed, members of the commission would reside in Palestine. The simplest solution was that the commission should be made up of consuls, as proposed earlier; the archives of the consulates could thus be easily consulted for documents bearing on disputes. The decisions of the commission should not be submitted to a single power for approval, not even the Mandatory, but should be presented to an international organization, for example, the League Council. Finally, the commission could in no way be authorized to

---

[51] "Council Confirms the Last Mandates," *New York Times* (July 23, 1922): 10; *Official Journal*, III (August 1922): 823–25.

discuss rights already acquired by Catholics in the Holy Places, rights enjoyed peaceably even under Turkish rule.[52]

When the Council next met on August 31, 1922, Balfour was ready with a fourth version of Article 14. Under this proposal, all members of the commission would be named by the League and there would be three subcommissions—Christian, Jewish, and Moslem—each dealing with its own problems and having its own president. The Christian subcommission might have a French president, three Catholic representatives (Italian, Spanish, and Belgian), three Orthodox representatives (one Greek, one Russian, and one other), one Armenian, and one or two representatives of the Abyssinians and Copts. The subcommissions would come together in plenary sessions to discuss common problems under the presidency of an impartial person who would be disinterested in the problems discussed. This official would be empowered to decide questions which had not received unanimous approval by the subcommissions. This proposal would also enable Protestant communities to be represented. The chairman of the commission and the president of each subcommission would be appointed by the Mandatory, and representatives of religious confessions would be appointed in consultation with the heads of the religious denominations involved or with the government concerned. All appointments were to be approved by the League Council.[53]

Lord Balfour presented this plan at the August Council meeting without further discussion. Reactions were solicited for consideration at the next meeting of the Council in October. However, the British did not have to wait until then for Catholics to react. They were appalled because they would have been outnumbered in the Christian subcommission by the Orthodox community. On September 6, 1922, *L'Osservatore Romano* stated that the rights of Catholics were endangered after centuries of non-Catholic possession of most of the sanctuaries of the Holy Land. Moreover, Catholics would constitute a

---

[52] Collin, supra note 2, at 230–32.

[53] *Official Journal*, III (November 1922): 1150, 1153–54; Memorandum Submitted by Lord Balfour to the Council on August 31, 1922, Collin, II, supra note 2, at 233–35.

minority in the Christian subcommission and be set against elements
that for centuries had been a source of continual dissension with the
Catholic Church. Since unanimity was practically impossible in such
a subcommission, the decision would in practice lie with the president of the commission, a Protestant. This, said *L'Osservatore*, was
simply shocking.[54]

During September 1922, the French government developed a
plan for three commissions (Christian, Moslem, and Jewish). The
Christian commission was divided into two subcommissions: a
Catholic subcommission of four members and an Orthodox–
Armenian subcommission of four members. Each dealt with issues
of its own concerns and would meet in plenary session together
under a French president. France claimed the presidency of the
Christian commission on the basis of its historic role and the diplomatic tradition recognized by Article 62 of the Treaty of Berlin. At
the time, a French presidency would likely assure the preponderance
of Catholics on the Christian commission. But Italy claimed the
presidency of the Christian commission, arguing that the Latin
Patriarch of Jerusalem had always been Italian and that the Italian
element traditionally preponderated in the Custody of the Holy
Places. A deadlock ensued.[55] The Holy See did not take sides
between the two countries in this matter, as their positions were
inspired more by national interest than religious zeal.[56]

When the League Council met again on October 4, Balfour
declared that the last plan for the commission was an honest effort,
but "the scheme itself met with great disfavour from those who represented Catholic opinion throughout the world."[57] He gave a
lengthy explanation of the reasons for an American Protestant as
president of the commission, acting as a court of appeals between
denominations, a Christian rather than a Moslem—for which he had
expected some gratitude—and from America, a country unconnected

[54] Collin, supra note 2, at 94; "Protest by Vatican—Balfour Plan for Holy Places
in Palestine Called 'Outrageous,'" *New York Times* (September 7, 1922): 5.
[55] La Brière, supra note 27, at 188–89.
[56] Collin, supra note 2, at 96.
[57] Ibid., 239.

with the subject in dispute.[58] This feature, he said, had shipwrecked the plan, but there were difficulties between the representatives of Catholic countries (an allusion to the French–Italian dispute). The interested powers had to settle the dispute themselves, "for unless we can bring together Catholic opinion upon this subject, I do not see how we can hope easily and quickly to arrive at a satisfactory conclusion."[59] Balfour pledged that in the meantime the British High Commissioner would serve as an interim president and act with absolute impartiality. He also stated that the Mandatory would accept no system that did not give justice to the Orthodox world since it was underrepresented in the League of Nations. France, Italy, and Spain thanked Balfour and gave assurances that they would do all in their power to arrive at the desired agreement before the Fourth Assembly met in September 1923. The practical result of this meeting was that France and Italy had one year to reconcile their differences.[60]

The Holy See was only moderately sympathetic with the French plan for a Christian commission under a French president, who might not be a Catholic or possibly not even a Christian. The same objection held for an Italian president. The aim was to secure a majority that was Catholic, in order to protect its predominant interest in the Holy Places, the vast majority of which were in Catholic hands.[61] The Holy See still preferred its own plan—that the commission should be composed of the consuls in Jerusalem of members of the League Council other than the Mandatory. By this time Sweden and Uruguay had been named to the Council, thus adding a Protestant representative. The Holy See was willing to allow the further addition of the Greek consul to the commission as a representative of Orthodox interests. But realistically the Vatican had to pin its hopes on a French–Italian agreement concerning the proposed commission, even though this perpetuated the concept of European states as protectors of Christians in the Holy Land.[62]

---

[58] Ibid., 240–41.

[59] Ibid., 241–42.

[60] La Brière, supra note 27, at 189; Collin, supra note 2, at 95.

[61] La Brière, supra note 27, at 188, 190.

[62] Collin, supra note 2, at 241–42.

During this period of inactivity by the League Council, the Holy See was concerned to the point that it insisted publicly on the rights of the Church. On December 11, 1922, Pius XI upheld the rights of Catholics in Palestine "vis-à-vis not only Israelites and unbelievers, but also non-Catholics of whatever sect or nation."[63] On May 23, 1923, he spoke out once again with considerable force, saying,

> We have always defended and will always defend to the utmost of Our power the rights of Catholics over the Holy Places, rights which are inalienable as they are evident, and superior to all others. . . .[64]

The thrust of these statements, and the appointment in July of a special papal commissioner for the Holy Places, was to serve notice that in the absence of action by the League, the Holy See would be especially vigilant.[65] It was worried not only about Zionism, but the fact that Britain was trying to replace Russia as protector of the Orthodox, using the Church of England to court Orthodox favor and ultimately achieve Anglican–Orthodox union.[66] The Holy See also objected to the imposition of Anglo–Saxon ideas on Palestinian culture. The source of this objection rested in the refusal of the High Commissioner to recognize legally the canonical decisions on marriage handed down by the Latin Patriarch of Jerusalem, and the institution of non-confessional schools supported by general taxation. This school policy was contrary to the tradition of the country, one of confessional education with no budgetary monopoly by the state.[67]

The continuing French–Italian deadlock was noted by the Council in September 1923 and reported to the Fourth Assembly.[68]

---

[63] Luigi Salvatorelli, *La Politica della Santa Sede dopo la Guerra* (Milano: Instituto per gli Studi di Politica Internazionale, 1937), 99.

[64] La Brière, supra note 27, at 189–90; Koenig, supra note 15, ¶826, Allocution *Gratum Nobis* to the College of Cardinals, May 23, 1923.

[65] La Brière, supra note 27, at 191–93; "Special Papal Agent for Holy Land," New York Times (July 26, 1923): 16; Koenig, supra note 15, ¶¶826–830, Allocution *Gratum Nobis* to the College of Cardinals, May 23, 1923.

[66] La Brière, supra note 27, at 192.

[67] Ibid., 192–93.

[68] Collin, supra note 2, at 96.

France and Italy finally agreed, however, on certain outstanding points concerning the French mandate for Syria. Upon the announcement of this agreement to the Council on September 29, 1923, the Syrian and Palestinian mandates entered ipso facto into full operation.[69] After this, the project for an international commission passed into oblivion and Palestine's only continuing relationship with the League was through the Permanent Mandates Commission, to which Britain was obliged to report annually. Although the League retained a fundamental responsibility for Palestine, and the Council was asked to approve certain extraordinary British decisions, real authority in Palestine had been transferred from the Ottoman to the British Empire.[70] The latter pledged not only to continue the discriminatory policy of the former concerning the Holy Places, but also to create a Jewish homeland in their midst. The Holy See could not help but judge as disastrous the net effect of the League's handling of the entire question of Palestine.

The Holy See had looked to the League for the establishment of an international commission on Holy Places in order to prevent the continuation of the Status Quo, which it considered unjust, and the implementation of Britain's Zionist policy, which it viewed as even more threatening to Christian interests in the Holy Land. But beyond these immediate considerations, the Vatican had learned from centuries of experience that it was dangerous to have the Holy Land controlled by a single power, and had come to favor international administration in principle. It was natural for the Holy See to look to the League for this—as one world institution to another—but the mandate system was not really international in character. The Vatican's innovative effort to modify it in that direction, even through the quiet diplomacy of consuls, could not but threaten the exercise of sovereign power by Great Britain.

The Holy See could blame the League in that the Council failed to recognize the paramount interests of the Catholic Church as the principal administrator of the Holy Places, and did not insist

---

[69] *Monthly Summary,* III (September 1923): 207–8.
[70] Collin, supra note 2, at 97–98.

on a permanent and international commission. The Holy See could also blame the Council for ignoring its warnings that Zionism would endanger the peace in Palestine. But the League was not responsible for the petty jealousy between France and Italy that gave the coup de grace to whatever slight chance there was for an authoritative commission. Nor was it to blame for Britain's insistence on absolute sovereignty and pursuit of a policy that was pro-Zionist, pro-Orthodox, and anti-Catholic in its effect. The net result of the whole affair was to leave the Holy See more skeptical about the real value of the League. There was now more reason than ever to doubt the power of the League in the face of big power intransigence, its effectiveness as an agent for the solving of disputes, its dedication to a truly international approach, its fairness as a forum willing to let all parties express their views, and its basic belief in the protection of human rights. The failure of the League to meet Vatican expectations concerning Palestine was in large measure responsible for the distance increasingly shown by the Holy See toward the League during the interwar period.

The British administration in Palestine established in 1922 was pledged to uphold the Status Quo, and this was affirmed explicitly by the Palestine (Holy Places) Order in Council of July 24, 1924.[71] There were some incidents, such as the failure of British police to keep order in the Basilica of the Holy Sepulchre during the Easter ceremonies of 1924 and the Wailing Wall incident of 1929, when an ad hoc international commission helped regulate the dispute. But in general, the British maintained peace and order in the Holy Places, and their administration was free of the corruption known under the Ottomans.[72] The real danger to peace was the resentment of the Arabs against Zionism and their consequent refusal to cooperate with the authorities. The overwhelming majority of Catholics in Palestine were Arab and the Holy See took their side in the Zionist struggle. On November 1928, a Dutch Catholic newspaper

---

[71] Ibid., 98.
[72] Ibid., 98–103.

reported that Zionism was stirring up Arab hostility and even anti-British opinion, which caused consternation in Vatican circles. The report concluded by stating:

> In this connection the Vatican expressed the desire to have the holiest sites of Christianity removed, as soon as possible, from the daily political turmoil, by an international regulation.[73]

The signing of the Lateran treaty in February 1929 produced strong reactions in Palestine, showing that the unresolved role of the Holy See vis-à-vis the Holy Places was still very much a live question. Catholics celebrated the event and hoped that the pope would name a nuncio to Jerusalem. On the other hand, Zionists were alarmed. A Jewish Telegraphic Agency dispatch from Geneva said it was reported there that with the Vatican as a sovereign state working hand-in-hand with the Italian fascist government, Italy's foreign policy in the Near East would be strongly influenced by the Holy See. It was stated on good authority that the Vatican would receive representation in the League, and there were fears that Italy, with Vatican support, would attempt to acquire the mandate in order to use Palestine as an outlet for immigration and colonization. The Vatican, never satisfied with the settlement of the Palestine question and opposed to the aims of the Zionist movement, would now have increased influence.[74] But this was not a universal Jewish view. *Die Judische Presse,* the official organ of the Orthodox Jewish organization Agudath Israel, praised the Lateran treaty and said it would not affect adversely the rights of the Jewish community. It was thought that peace between Church and state would aid Jewish religious life, and the admission of the Vatican to the League of Nations would "make the influence of the religious point of view more strongly felt in international affairs. . . . "[75]

---

73 Quoted in Lapide, supra note 10, at 276.

74 "Zionists Worried by Accord in Rome," *New York Times* (February 10, 1929): sect. 3, 8.

75 "Jews Praise Rome Accord—Their Official Organ Hopes to See Vatican at League of Nations," *New York Times* (February 24, 1929): sect. 2, 3.

Summing up the attitude of the Holy See toward the issue of the Holy Places, Chaim Weizmann wrote of the interwar period, "Although the Vatican had never formulated any claims on Palestine, it had recognized interest in the holy places. But then practically all of Palestine could be regarded as a holy place."[76] The Vatican feared that the Holy Land would be torn apart by war or at least lose its Christian character. An article in *Civilta Cattolica* of April 2, 1938, expressed the view that since the peaceful existence of Jews with Arabs had turned out to be impossible, the only right thing for the Jews to do was to drop their claims on Palestine.[77] Because it regarded all of Palestine as a Christian Holy Place, the Holy See was naturally alarmed at the growth of Jewish influence there, especially the rapid acquisition of land and the acceleration of Jewish immigration.

Peaceful coexistence between Arabs and Jews was indeed proving to be impossible. Tensions increased and there were frequent disturbances, with four major riots by Arabs between 1921 and 1947 directed against the British administration as well as the Jewish population. Britain tried to mollify the Arabs with restrictions on Jewish immigration and land purchase and the creation of a legislative council with an Arab majority, but the unrest continued. After the Arab riots of 1936, a Royal Commission reported in substance that the terms of the mandate were no longer workable, for the evolution of a single, self-governing state was inconceivable if either Jews or Arabs predominated. The solution recommended was to restrict Jewish immigration and land acquisition and eventually to partition Palestine into two independent countries, keeping Jerusalem and the Holy Places under British mandate. This proposal for triple partition was approved by the British government, and the League Permanent Mandates Commission was also inclined to favor it as an eventual solution, but it was violently attacked by both Arabs and Jews.

The British government attempted once again to induce Jews and Arabs to reach a common agreement on the future of Palestine

---

[76] Quoted in Lapide, supra note 10, at 276.
[77] Ibid.

at a conference called in London in February 1939. When this failed, the government concluded that it had no alternative but to impose its own solution, which it did in the White Paper of May 17, 1939, which proposed a single Palestinian state and restrictions on Jewish immigration, with independence in ten years. But the League Mandates Commission was cool to the plan, and its report to the Council implied that partition would be the wisest solution. It was then the responsibility of the Council to approve or not this recommendation. If it had done so, the Council would have been compelled for the first time since 1922 to attempt a radical solution to the question of Palestine. But before the Council could meet, the Second World War had broken out. The proceedings of the League Mandates Commission in regard to the White Paper were the last act of the League regarding Palestine.

The entry of British forces into Palestine in 1917 marked a turning point in the evolution of the problem of the Holy Places as it had been familiar to the Holy See since the seventh century. From the era of Moslem domination, with its protectorates and capitulations, there remained only the Status Quo, with its continuing but bearable tensions. The League system of mandates, however, posed the problem in a new light. The Holy See hoped for an international solution to the latter problem, but Britain refused and the League hesitated. The novel factor of Zionism as a potential threat to the peace of the Holy Land was perceived far better in the Vatican than in the League of Nations, which largely ignored this movement during the crucial years 1920 to 1923, to its later sorrow. Zionism intensified nascent Arab nationalism, and the ensuing struggle between Arabs and Jews deemphasized conflicts between Moslems and Christians and within the Christian community. The problem became increasingly internationalized. All of this would lead to a subsequent phase in which the problem of Palestine would face the international community in the future at the United Nations.

Pius XI and the League:
Distance and Disappointment

T HE ELECTION of Pius XI on February 6, 1922, brought no sudden or dramatic change in the foreign policy of the Holy See. Pius retained Cardinal Gasparri as secretary of state. As the Genoa Conference opened in April, he echoed the sentiments of Benedict when he wrote: "It should not be forgotten that the best guarantee of peace is not a forest of bayonets, but mutual confidence and friendship."[1] Like his predecessor, he was an interventionist on human rights. A memorandum from Gasparri to the Genoa Conference asked the powers not to readmit Russia into "the association of the civil nations" until it guaranteed full religious freedom.[2] Pius also continued and expanded Benedict's policies on the missions and on the signing of concordats.[3] At the end of 1922, he said specifically that since these same sad conditions existed as in the time of Benedict XV, he had naturally come to make his predecessor's thoughts and solutions his own. There was no true peace in

---

[1] Harry Koenig, *Principles for Peace: Selections from Papal Documents—Leo XIII to Pius XII* (Milwaukee: Bruce, 1943), ¶173, Letter *Con Viva Pacer* to Archbishop Signori of Genoa, April 7, 1922.

[2] Ibid., ¶741, Memorandum sent by Cardinal Gasparri, Secretary of State, to the Diplomatic Representatives at the Genoa Peace Conference, May 15, 1922; see Lord Clonmore, *Pope Pius XI and World Peace* (New York: E. P. Dutton, 1938), 82–86.

[3] Koenig, supra note 1, at 319; Carlo Falconi, *The Popes in the Twentieth Century: From Pius X to John XXIII* (Boston: Little, Brown, 1967), 200.

the world. Public life, he said, was so enveloped by a "dense fog of mutual hatreds and grievances" that the common people could hardly breathe; moreover, there existed the need to temper justice with love.[4]

But there was a basic difference in the thinking of Pius XI that soon became evident. Pius XI had a different style of approaching his work than that of his immediate predecessor. It made him appear more distant from participation and discussion of international affairs. His public pronouncements on such questions did not address disarmament, compulsory arbitration, and economic sanctions. However, the pope expressed his profound concerns about global and European issues in his encyclicals, such as *Quadregesimo Anno, Mit Brennender Sorge,* and *Non Abiamo Bisogno.* Pope Pius was more of a theologian in his approach to the world. Perhaps this is why he chose as his motto "The peace of Christ in the Kingdom of Christ." He viewed the achievement of peace and world organization primarily through the lens of theological reflection. In his first encyclical, *Ubi Arcano Dei* (December 23, 1922), Pius stated that the causes of war are spiritual in nature and that true peace is also spiritual, the peace of Christ. In a disordered society the major need is respect for law, which only the peace of Christ can adequately achieve. But the ideals of Christ, which are essential to human survival, were entrusted to the Church as an infallible teacher and so she is called upon to assume "a singularly important role" in remedying the ills of the day in "leading mankind toward a universal peace."[5]

For Pius XI, the Church was the most competent of all agents to abolish war:

> . . . the Church is the safe and sure guide to conscience, for to her safe-keeping alone there has been confided the doctrines and the promise of the assistance of Christ; she is able not only to bring about at the present hour a peace that is truly the peace of Christ, but can, better than any other agency which We know of, contribute greatly to the

---

[4] Koenig, supra note 1, ¶764, Encyclical *Ubi Arcano Dei* on the Peace of Christ in Kingdom of Christ, December 23, 1922.
[5] Ibid., ¶794.

securing of the same peace for the future, to the making impossible of war in the future.[6]

The phrase "better than any other agency which We know of" is most likely a reference to the League, but Pius becomes more explicit in the next and most famous paragraph of *Ubi Arcano*. His words express the commitment and relevance of Christianity to the family of mankind,

> When, therefore, governments and nations follow in all their activities, whether they be national or international, the dictates of conscience grounded in the teachings, precepts and example of Jesus Christ, and which are binding on each and every individual, then only can we have faith in one another's word and trust in the peaceful solution of the difficulties and controversies which may grow out of differences in point of view or from clash of interest. An attempt in this direction has already and is now being made; its results, however, are almost negligible and, especially so, so far as they can be said to affect those major questions which divide seriously and serve to arouse nations one against the other, No merely human institution of to-day can be as successful in devising a set of international laws which will be in harmony with world conditions as the Middle Ages were in the possession of that true League of Nations, Christianity. It cannot be denied that in the Middle Ages this law was often violated; still it always existed as an ideal, according to which one might judge the acts of nations, and a beacon light calling those who had lost their way back to the safe road.[7]

It was this last paragraph of *Ubi Arcano* that captured the attention of Catholic internationalists. Pius XI contended that the systematic settlement of disputes by peaceful means would not come to pass unless governments obey the moral law ("dictates of conscience")

---

[6] Ibid., ¶797.
[7] Ibid., ¶798.

based on the teachings of Christ. Moreover, he suggested that the League of Nations ("an attempt in this direction") had accomplished nothing significant. Finally, he argued that the League in and of itself (a "merely human institution") could never achieve a world order ("set of international laws") as harmonious as medieval Christendom ("Christianity" is an inferior translation), which despite its imperfect performance was the ideal form of international organization ("that true League of Nations"). What is important to emphasize is that this paragraph can be understood as an appraisal of the League of Nations. It points out the limitations of this international organization and posited an alternative society based on the Church as vital entity capable of preserving world peace.

Immediately after the paragraph on the League, Pope Pius stated that there exists an institution "able to safeguard the sanctity of the law of nations"—part of every nation, but above all nations, and possessing the highest authority: the Church of Christ. The Church alone is adapted to do this great work, for she has a divine commission, and she "cannot but succeed in such a venture where others assuredly will fail."[8] True peace will come when all men obey the law of Christ both in public and private life. It is possible to sum this all up in one phrase: "the kingdom of Christ." In the Kingdom, Christ reigns over not just individuals and the family, but over society as well. This occurs when people recognize his sovereignty, when they accept the divine origin and control of all social forces, and accord to the Church its divinely ordained position as the teacher and guide of every other society whatsoever.[9]

From this and previous passages on the peace of Christ, it is tempting to conclude that Pius conceived of the Kingdom of Christ in purely supernatural and ultimate terms. True and lasting peace is a spiritual and heavenly gift of grace transcending all political efforts and can thus come into being only in a religious society, the Kingdom of Christ. This is the goal of all human history and will finally be established by God only at the end of time. In these terms, there will

8 Ibid., ¶799.
9 Ibid., ¶802.

always be wars on earth until the Kingdom becomes a reality. The League of Nations, as a secular effort at world order, was by the pope's definition bound to fail, for only the Church can organize the world. This interpretation of *Ubi Arcano* leads to a weary attitude toward all secular international organizations. The fact that Pius XI seemed to display such an attitude toward the League only confirmed the view held by some that he was rendering a theological a priori judgment that the Geneva organization was per se unacceptable to Catholics and doomed to fail. The tone and rhetoric of the encyclical as a whole did little to correct this interpretation, but a careful reading of what follows does bring balance into the pope's thinking.

It is in the middle of the last paragraph summarized above that Pius dropped his theological vocabulary and style to be more specific about the role of the Church in the Kingdom. The Church, he said, is

> the teacher and guide of every other society whatsoever not, of course, in the sense that she should abstract in the least from their authority, each in its own sphere supreme, but that she should really perfect their authority, just as divine grace perfects human nature, and should give to them the assistance necessary for men to attain their true final end, eternal happiness, and by that very fact make them the more deserving and certain promoters of their happiness here below.[10]

It is crucial to understand that Pius required for the Kingdom the general recognition by society of three things: the monotheistic view of God as absolute truth and thus the ultimate source of all human authority; the sovereignty of Christ as man over all human affairs, a sovereignty exercised theocratically through the Church; and the role of the Church as moral teacher and guide of secular institutions. To those familiar with the development of Catholic teaching on Church and state, what Pius posits for the Kingdom comes through clearly as an attempt to accommodate his vision of the Church with the classic natural law doctrine. The latter requires the

---

[10] Ibid.

legitimate autonomy and fullest development of secular political institutions as part of the divine plan for mankind.

Pius XI was thinking within a tradition he could not ignore and clearly asserted that the Church cannot usurp the role of any secular society (which includes international organizations) but should rather provide the assistance needed to fulfill its human function. Pius did not argue that secular institutions are part of the Church. As he stated here, they are supreme in their own sphere; however, they are to be perfected by the Church. He concluded that the Church alone cannot build the Kingdom. The Church works by assisting the human and the secular to be what they ought to be. Both the peace of Christ and His Kingdom exist to some degree when this process is going on. The process, directed by the Holy Spirit, is one of a gradual recognition of God, Christ, and the Church by society. This is a process of vibrant interaction between the sacred and the secular, which leads ultimately to the complete realization of the Kingdom and to perfect peace.

A major challenge in understanding of *Ubi Arcano Dei*, and in the thought of Pius XI, is posed by the levels of discourse concerning the peace and Kingdom of Christ. The key paragraph of the encyclical on the League, for example, is preceded by a theoretical discussion of the peace of Christ and the role of the Church that sounds like a proposal for a theocracy. But that paragraph itself then moves immediately to the concrete level of human history. It appears that the pope criticized the League in practice but praised the international legal order of the Middle Ages. In actuality, the criticism of the League was not based on its ideals or its initiatives but for its ineffective impact on the international situation. Pius advanced the view that historical Christendom provided the better model of the "true League." Still, he accepted the real League as another effort to promote global peace but without the same spiritual foundation of Christendom. He displayed his practical wisdom and prudential judgment in acknowledging that even this historical model, built on the spiritual foundation of the Church, achieved only an imperfect peace. He suggested that Christendom was only a partial rather than a complete realization of the peace of Christ.

Medieval Christendom, while not the fullness of the Kingdom, did approach the definition of the Kingdom proposed by Pius, since it was a society acknowledging the divine origin of social forces, the sovereignty of Christ, and the role of the Church as teacher and guide. This definition is on the abstract but not on the supernatural level. Medieval Christendom was for Pius XI a historical example, not yet surpassed, of the Kingdom in process. Pius called for the establishment of the Kingdom of Christ in *Ubi Arcano*, implying its prior historical existence, and this can refer only to Christendom.[11] But he did not call for the restoration of medieval Christendom as such. He seems to have had in mind a more universal system analogous to, but extending beyond, it. It is significant that he did not call for a restoration of the medieval role of the Holy See in international affairs as an alternative to the League. He proposed no concrete alternative, no particular international structure at all. This reflects his poise toward world affairs that differed from the approaches of Leo XIII and Benedict XV, who offered concrete proposals for a strong international organization that the Holy See could engage. Pius offered rather a "reestablishment of the Kingdom," defined by an abstract set of conditions as the basis on which true peace would be possible.[12]

It should be noted that what Pius held up indirectly as a model for the League is not the medieval role of the papacy as arbiter in international affairs, but as guarantor of the legal institutions of Christendom and the respect they engendered. He saw that the role of the Church should concentrate on the teaching of basic religious principles rather than controlling international structures. This stands in contrast to his detailed suggestions for improving the socioeconomic order contained in the encyclical *Quadragesimo Anno*. For him the role of the Church in international organization is the guarantor of "the sanctity of the law of nations" by guiding its development according to true morality and by inducing among the nations a spirit of respect and obedience.[13] The Church can do this

---

[11] Koenig, supra note 1, ¶¶803–809.
[12] Ibid., ¶803.
[13] Ibid., ¶799.

better than any other agency because respect for law must, to be effective and to endure, be based on a true and transcendent moral code. Every political structure needs a solid ideological foundation in the society it attempts to organize. This is what Christendom had and what the League lacked. Pius XI argued that only the law of Christ, in the Kingdom, can adequately clarify and reinforce the natural moral law governing secular institutions—by going beyond it into the supernatural realm of spirit. When the moral law is disobeyed there is no peace because its true spirit is missing.

Despite all this, the phrase "merely human" as used by Pius to describe the League can be easily misunderstood. It is not an indictment of the League as a secular institution. Nowhere did the pope attack the Covenant on the grounds that it was a purely juridical or political instrument. His phrase refers rather to the secular humanistic ideology animating the League and its chief proponents—a utopian naturalism alien to the Christian tradition. He was critical of a purely human faith in the League as ushering in the millennium of eternal peace without God or Christ. For Pius XI, the League was without a solid spiritual foundation of ideological truth and unity. Later events showed this critique to be well-founded, but it was more an indictment of contemporary society than of the League, which Pius disparaged primarily in order to bolster this theological argument that spiritual renewal must underlie all efforts at world organization. Still, the implication is clear that as the Church provided a spiritual foundation for Christendom it could do so once again for a major peace-oriented organization like the League. It would then draw on resources that extended beyond the "merely human." If the Church's role were acknowledged, it could provide the good faith and mutual trust among nations needed to make the League successful.

But there was another reason why the pope criticized the League. It is significant that while Pius insisted that the Church should be the teacher and guide of every human society, he never disparaged the state as a "merely human" institution and thus inferior to some Christian ideal. While he censured the secularist tendencies of the modern state, especially toward totalitarianism, he did not disparage the state as a thoroughly human effort to organize a community politically. Why then did he question the League of Nations? The Church had long since been compelled to relinquish the substitutional exercise of secular authority at local levels, assumed during periods of anarchy, and had formally recognized the legitimate autonomy of the emerging state. This occurred during the age of Christendom. But the Holy See had never formally relinquished its exercise of its international authority. For centuries, no secular claimant to international authority had emerged to demand an end to the Church's dormant but venerable substitutional function through recognition of its own legitimate autonomy—until the League of Nations.

Pius XI reviewed the League and was disappointed that the Holy See should finally have to surrender its once powerful international role to a secular agency, particularly one as weak as the League. What complicated this disappointment was the fact that the League ignored the papal role and would not acknowledge its need for the moral support of the Church or ask for any assistance. There is a reflection of this in *Ubi Arcano*, as the pope asked if the Holy See, with all the spiritual resources of the Church at its command, could only imperfectly keep the peace in a religiously united Europe, how could the infant League, with no true spiritual resources at all, presume to bring peace to a spiritually divided world? Like many contemporary Catholics, Pius thought that international affairs required assistance from religion and the Church.

The nexus between world peace and religion has a historical basis. During the Middle Ages, the Church unified national cultures by providing a source of temporal authority before the nation-state emerged. Christianity provided a moral consensus among mankind and served as a legitimate transnational authority before the rise of secular international organizations. This evolutionary view of world order fits well with the concept of the Kingdom still in process, and may have influenced the attitude of Pius toward the League. But then Pius could have supported the infant League in its struggle toward maturity without being invited. And if he made this kind of judgment, it was not an a priori theological judgment that the League could not survive without supernatural assistance, but a prudential, non-demonstrable, political forecast that the world community was as yet too immature to nurture and sustain such an organization. There is some evidence that Pius had in fact drawn this conclusion when he wrote *Ubi Arcano*.

This interpretation of *Ubi Arcano Dei* reflects the various aspects of the attitude of Pius XI toward the League. It concludes that his basic objection was that the League belonged squarely to the non-Catholic tradition of liberalism, which ignored the moral role of the Church. For Pius XI, as opposed to Benedict XV, ideology was supremely important, while his inclinations and dualistic view of the Church and the world made it more difficult to see the good in an organization that seemed to replace and rival his religious ideal, the Kingdom of Christ as it once existed and could exist again.

This interpretation of *Ubi Arcano* also suggests that Pius XI kept the door open to the natural law approach to international organization pursued by his successor, Pius XII. Pius XI spoke of good faith and mutual trust as the essential virtues required for international organization, calling them Christian principles. They are by no means unique to Christianity. The problem Pius could not solve was how Christ's grace (which causes the "peace of Christ") could operate on humanity to produce such faith and trust among nations in anything but a revived Christendom organized around a Catholic center. This theological dilemma was at the heart of his attitude toward the League. It is strange that Pius underplayed the Church's natural law theory. He was an avid student and admirer of Taparelli, whose *Saggio* he had translated into German.[14] Taparelli's natural law doctrine did not posit the Church, Christendom, or the Kingdom as the underlying principle of world organizations. Nor did St. Thomas Aquinas, whom Pius recommended in his encyclical *Studiorum Ducem* (1923) as con-

---

[14] Yves de La Brière, SJ, *La Conception du Droit International chez les Theologiens Catholiques* (Paris: Centre Européen de la Dotation Carnegie, 1930), 19.

taining "the true foundations of that which is termed the 'League of Nations.' "[15]

Despite the misunderstanding it produced, Pius repeated his approach to peace, especially in the encyclical *Quas Primas* (1925). Here he states that Christ has all temporal as well as spiritual authority: He is King in the true sense, not just figuratively over minds and hearts, but as possessing executive, legislative, and judicial power. Christ's reign is primarily a spiritual thing, but rulers should obey His precepts as they exercise authority, which comes from Him, and respect the rights of the Church. The "Empire of Christ," which Pius said was rejected, embraces all people and has no enemies but Satan, who inspired naturalism and secularism. This language led some of his readers to believe that the pope was reviving the thesis of Boniface VIII in *Unam Sanctam* of 1302 that all mankind must submit to the Roman pontiff.[16]

Given his basic posture toward politics, it is not surprising that Pius XI also differed from Benedict XV in his actions, which show him as much less a mediator and much more a teacher and judge.[17] In his view, the pope's task was to teach truth and to condemn error, whether it be "a species of moral, legal, and social modernism" found among Catholics;[18] the exaggerated nationalism of Maurras's

---

[15] Koenig, supra note 1, ¶846, Encyclical *Studiorum Ducem* on St. Thomas Aquinas, June 29, 1923.

[16] Falconi, supra note 3, at 201. See the papal bull *Unam Sanctum* in which Pope Boniface VIII stated, "We are taught by the words of the Gospel that in this Church and in its power there are two swords, a spiritual, to wit, and a temporal . . . both are in the power of the Church, namely the spiritual and material swords; the one, indeed, to be wielded for the Church, the other by the Church; the former by the priest, the latter by the hand of kings and knights, but at the will and sufferance of the priest. For it is necessary that one sword should be under another and that the temporal authority should be subjected to the spiritual. . . . Consequently, we declare, state, define and pronounce that it is altogether necessary to salvation for every human creature to be subject to the Roman Pontiff." Sidney Ehler and John Morrall, *A Collection of Historic Documents with Commentaries* (London: Burns & Oates, 1954), 91–92. See Luigi Salvatorelli, *La Politica della Santa Sede dopo la Guerra* (Milano: Instituto per gli Studi di Politica Internazionale, 1937), 177.

[17] Salvatorelli, supra note 16, at 94–95.

[18] Koenig, supra note 1, ¶812.

Action Française (condemned in 1925); or the governments of Russia, Germany, Spain, Italy, and Mexico which felt the sting of his criticism when they infringed on the rights of the Church.[19] Under Pius XI the Holy See did continue in the field of mediation and arbitration. In this regard, there was some activity: In 1928 Spain and Peru signed a treaty naming the pope as arbitrator of any differences which might arise between them, but the treaty had not been ratified by either country when the Spanish revolution occurred in 1931.[20] In 1928 Pius XI appealed to the presidents of Bolivia and Paraguay to seek a peaceful settlement of their dispute, which they did.[21] And in 1938 there was a successful papal intervention in the dispute between Haiti and the Dominican Republic.[22]

The pontificate of Pius XI was marked by a withdrawal of the Holy See from the controversies of international politics and a concentration on the spiritual reorganization of the Church. This did not mean, however, that Pius wanted the Church to have no influence on social structures. His dualistic view of sacred and secular led him to see this as the job primarily of Catholic laymen.[23] He consistently encouraged the Catholic elite and Catholic international organizations to further the interests of peace and the rights of the Church rather than involving the Holy See directly. Organized Catholic laity would act as a buffer between the Church and the world, as its temporal power in the struggle to overcome secularism and achieve the peace of Christ in the Kingdom of Christ. The Holy See would retain its authority—and indeed Pius further centralized ecclesiastical power in the hands of the Roman Curia—but

---

[19] Koenig, supra note 1, at 319.

[20] Gordon Ireland, "The State of the City of the Vatican," XXVIII *American Journal of International Law* (1933): 287.

[21] Koenig, supra note 1, ¶883, Letter *Le Notizie Che* to the presidents of Bolivia and Paraguay, December 18, 1928, and ¶884, Allocution to the College of Cardinals, December 24, 1928.

[22] John J. Wright, *National Patriotism in Papal Teaching* (Westminster: Newman, 1943), 326.

[23] Koenig, supra note 1, at 319. This view about the role of the laity in world affairs was again emphasized in "The Pastoral Constitution of the Church," *Gaudium et Spes* (December 7, 1965): nos. 43, 88 & 90.

would act less directly and visibly in the temporal order. This change of policy would affect the role of the Catholic elite in the relations between the Holy See and the League.[24]

Thus Pius XI was consistent when he studiously avoided any close association with the League of Nations. Arès summarized the attitude of the Holy See toward the League as approval of the principle of the League but doubt about the spirit animating it. If the League were to fail, the Church should not be implicated in the League's demise. To the contrary, the Holy See wished to endow the League with an entirely different spirit.[25] Archbishop Cardinale once suggested that Pius XI avoided permanent associations with the League because of possible anticlerical reactions, especially among the Italian representatives who opposed papal influence in international affairs, and because much of the League's activity belonged to the temporal order and was thus considered by many to be outside the competence of the Holy See.[26] Pernot contrasted the attitude of Benedict with that of Pius. Benedict wanted the Church to have an eminent role in world politics and hoped to enter the League. But Pius viewed such a role as more problematic for the Church, whose best recourse was to return to its own ground and undertake the ecclesiastical organization and spiritual conquest required by the times.[27] As Salvatorelli understood the situation, Benedict demonstrated his confidence in the League as constituted but wished for a reform and promised his support. Pius XI, on the other hand, did not speak of such a possibility: the only society of nations possible was one under the direction of the Church.[28]

---

[24] Salvatorelli, *supra* note 16, at 98–99.

[25] Richard Arès, SJ, *L'Eglise Catholique et l'Organisation de la Société Internationale Contemporaine* (Montreal: 1949), 22–23, n. 3.

[26] H. E. Cardinale, "The Contribution of the Holy See to World Peace in the Areas of Diplomacy, Development and Ecumenism," in *The Vatican and World Peace*, ed. Francis Sweeney, SJ (Buckinghamshire: Colin Smythe, 1970), 98.

[27] Maurice Pernot, *Le Saint-Siège, l'Eglise Catholique et la Politique Mondiale* (Paris: Armand Colin, 1924), 41.

[28] Salvatorelli, 93–94. See *Ubi Arcano Dei*.

Even at the beginning of his pontificate, when he was less aloof from world politics, Pius revealed his dim view of the League's significance. While he publicly blessed both the Conference of Genoa in the spring of 1922 and the Lausanne Conference in December,[29] he never sent any kind of greeting or blessing to a meeting of the League. As a political realist, he knew where the power was, and his message to the Genoa Conference criticized the League by indirection. He spoke of

> the happy issue of so great a Congress, including as it does representatives of nearly every civilized nation, will mark an historic date for Christian civilization, especially in Europe.[30]

The only official communications from the Holy See to the League whose existence has been made public were a few memoranda of Cardinal Gasparri on the Holy Places in May and August of 1922; several communications on calendar reform between 1923 and 1926; and a letter on the proposed international convention on slavery in 1926.[31] Although there were informal contacts between the Holy See and the League, this shortage of official communication is a fair index of the attitude of the Holy See toward the League during the pontificate of Pius XI.

Informal contacts with the League, however, were considered more important at the Vatican, since the practical advantages of quietly following and influencing League activities from the sidelines could be had without incurring the supposed disadvantages of presenting a public image of open support for the Geneva organization. The nunciature in Berne was an important channel employed for this purpose, and constituted a kind of informal observer office. Relations with Switzerland had been broken off in 1873, when that country

---

[29] Koenig, supra note 1, ¶756, Diplomatic Note of Cardinal Gasparri, Secretary of State, to the Conference of Lausanne, December 5, 1922.

[30] Koenig, supra note 1, ¶734, Letter *Il Vivissimo Desiderio* to Cardinal Gasparri, Secretary of State, April 29, 1922.

[31] Yves de La Brière, SJ, *L'Organisation Internationale du Monde Contemporain et la Papauté Soveraine, Series II* (Paris: Editions Spes, 1927), 133; Koenig, supra note 1, ¶741.

carried out a kind of *Kulturkampf* of its own. But the nunciature was restored in 1920. The number of legations in Berne had increased due to the Swiss role in the war, making it an even more important listening post. Archbishop Luigi Maglione, already in Berne, was named nuncio. It would seem that Cardinal Gasparri soon entrusted him with the task of unofficial observer at the League.[32] Maglione followed the work of the organization and acted as intermediary for official contacts between the Holy See and Council, especially on the question of the British mandate and the Holy Places.[33] Yet such official contacts were fairly rare and the press amplified Maglione's diplomatic activity vis-à-vis the League. The truth was that

> the nuncio in Berne, conforming to repeated instructions from the Holy See, observed the most prudent and discreet reserve toward the League of Nations and the diverse technical commissions of which it is the center.[34]

Another channel of informal contact was the Secretary-General of the League himself. Sir Eric Drummond made frequent visits to Rome and had several audiences with Pius XI and subsequent conversations with Cardinal Gasparri. These helped to produce a more cordial attitude, but were not publicized.[35] Also, on occasion members of the Catholic elite, clerics and laymen, acted as informal intermediaries. There was no shortage of avenues of communication. What was lacking was the opportunity to communicate more frequently. When such opportunities did not materialize, contacts were at a minimum.[36] The League, on the other hand, had no firm

---

[32] La Brière, supra note 31, at 219–25; Georg Schreiber, "Das Päpstliche Staatssekretariat," in *Historicsches Jahrbuch* (München: Görres-Gesellschaft, 1959, 1960), LXXIX, 194.

[33] La Brière, supra note 31, at 226.

[34] Ibid.

[35] Sir Alec Randall, *Vatican Assignment* (London: William Heinemann, 1956), 48.

[36] Koenig, supra note 1, ¶849, Letter of Cardinal Gasparri, Secretary of State, to Mr. John Eppstein, an Officer of the League of Nations Union, August 11, 1923. Note 82 on page 365 of the Koenig collection states, "Mr. Eppstein had suggested that diplomatic relations might be established, to the mutual advantage of both, between the Council of the League and the Holy See."

or accepted policy on how to deal with the Holy See, much less on how to benefit from more frequent communication. While welcoming Vatican support, some delegates were wary of recognizing the Holy See unless the League benefited in turn. Anticlericals, especially Italians concerned over the Roman Question, adamantly opposed all contacts as Article 15 of the Treaty of London of 1915 demonstrated. Only a few League officials and delegates, largely Catholics, favored more communication and cooperation. Thus relations were characterized by a prudent reserve accompanied by a generally friendly attitude on both sides.[37]

By the end of 1922 when *Ubi Arcano Dei* was issued, the Holy See began to move away from the League, even though in that year it had been involved in several questions under consideration by the organization, particularly issues concerning the Holy Places. This created a real problem for the Catholic elite, which was trying to win support for both of these institutions as sacred and secular agents working for the same goal of world peace. The Catholic elites were necessarily frustrated when one ignored, disappointed, or disparaged the other. *Ubi Arcano* increased the strain between the Holy See and most liberals in the League. Most members of the Catholic elite were thus discouraged by the encyclical, which they rarely mentioned.

The Catholic elite who wanted to work for both the League of Nations and the Kingdom of Christ was indeed a small group. Vaussard wrote in 1924 that there were hardly any more Catholics in Europe who judged human events in terms of being a Catholic first. The confusion produced by the religion of nationalism was such that many Catholics in good faith no longer knew the meaning of the doctrines they professed, the institutions they respected, or even the words they used. Proof of this was the cool reception given to papal international teaching. The papacy had in a sense been reduced to the level of a purely moral authority that had little application to the

---

[37] Gonzague de Reynold, *Mes Mémoires* (Genève: Editions Général, 1963), III, 388, 458–61; George Seldes, *The Vatican: Yesterday, Today, and Tomorrow* (New York: Harper, 1934), 407.

affairs of the world. Its pronouncements, according to one view, could be subordinated to national interest because they seemed to have nothing to do with dogma or religious discipline.[38] This dichotomy between Catholic universalism and real-world politics had negative consequences for the League. Propaganda hostile to it never ceased during the interwar period, even within the Catholic community:

> The Catholic press, with the exception of some publications of democratic inspiration, was almost always critical and mistrustful. In their battle against Geneva the French nationalists were first joined (from 1922 on) by the Italian Fascists, and, later, by the German Nazis. Catholics came under the influence of these groups and accepted their prejudices against the League.[39]

The Catholic elite was forced into an unenviable, cramped, middle position between liberal internationalists and the majority of Catholics. Toward the former, it was militantly Catholic: as Reynold put it, the Catholic Union could not cooperate with the anti-Church of the humanitarians and internationalists who wanted to take over the League and make it a "contre-Vatican."[40] Toward the latter, it was aggressively internationalist, advocating support of the very League it feared would be dominated by its enemies. Reynold reported that despite his attempts to draw up guidelines for Catholic cooperation with the League, he was viewed by the German-speaking Swiss clergy as a liberal ally of the Freemasons, and by the Masons and others of the left as a black clerical and dangerous reactionary.[41] The temper of the times was not conducive to civilized dialogue and fine distinctions. Despite the elite's efforts to win Catholic support for the League, the Geneva organization was attacked as late as 1924 in a textbook on ecclesiastical law used by the Italian clergy as "the daughter of

---

[38] Pierre Renouvin and Jean-Baptiste Duroselle, *Introduction to the History of International Relations* (New York: Praeger, 1967), 213; Maurice Vaussard, *Enquête sur le Nationalisme* (Paris: Spes, 1924), 396–400.

[39] Luigi Sturzo, *Nationalism and Internationalism* (New York: Roy, 1946), 193.

[40] Reynold, supra note 37, III, at 387.

[41] Ibid., 388.

Wilson . . . the apostle of a doctrine impregnated with heterodox, evangelical, and Protestant elements."[42]

The elite was thus restricted by its opponents on the right and left to a hesitant, conservative internationalism that was hardly dynamic. Protecting the League against its enthusiastic supporters left little time for making it more effective. An example of this can be found in the Catholic Union of International Studies. La Brière wrote that one of the tasks of the national sections of the Union was to encourage Catholic participation in associations supporting the League, which were largely composed of strangers to Catholicism and often dominated by Masons and Socialists. He pointed with satisfaction to Msgr. Deploige, who, at two meetings of the federation of these associations, was responsible for the defeat of motions favoring the election of League delegates by universal suffrage and the revision of history textbooks to introduce democratic humanism and proscribe all praise of war heroes. La Brière also urged the Union to demand for the Holy See its rightful share in the League's work. It could contribute more efficaciously than any human power to the improvement of international morality, without which the role of the League would be "perfectly ludicrous" ("parfaitement derisoire").[43]

The hard truth was that the elite was neither intellectually nor politically sure of its own ground. The attitude of the Holy See toward the League, to which the elite had necessarily to appeal, was less than clear under Benedict XV and under Pius XI was described by Reynold in 1922 as an attitude of "suspicious caution" ("prudence mefiante").[44] This papal policy undermined the confidence of the elite on both sides, which steadfastly sought clarification from the Vatican, as will be shown. Essentially, the Catholic tradition had not yet evolved an adequately articulated position on nationalism.

---

[42] Alban de Malezieux du Hamel, Le Pape et la Société des Nations (Albert Mechelinck, 19320, 71, citing Ruffini, Corso di Diritto Ecclesiastico Italiano (Turin: Bocca, 1924), 601.

[43] Yves de La Brière, SJ, L'Organization Internationale du Monde Contemporain et la Papauté Soveraine, Series I (Paris: Editions Spes, 1924), 49–51.

[44] Reynold, supra note 37, III, 387.

The confusion among the elite was clearly revealed by Vaussard's classic *Enquete sur le nationalisme*, published in 1924, which reproduced the attitudes of 160 leading Catholics toward nationalism.[45] The inquiry showed that most of the respondents still clung to an aggressive just war theory, with little understanding of the role of international organization. One said that Catholicism did not exclude wars necessary to vindicate a legitimate right or interest, such as the achievement of "natural frontiers" or economic expansion. Another said that religion could not counsel a nation to "forget an injustice."[46]

In concrete terms, the ambiguity toward nationalism resulted in the same attitude toward the League. Gonzague de Reynold wrote in the Vaussard study:

> In the face of all these ideas, all these trends appealing to our times, we active and thinking Catholics do not always know what our line of conduct should be, how far we should go either in resistance or conciliation. This uncertainty explains why there unfortunately does not exist a united Catholic front with regard, for instance, to the League of Nations.[47]

Reynold said that he supported the official League of Nations but opposed the utopian League, the superstate and superchurch of the Masons, liberal Protestants, Jews, pacifists, and Socialists whose credo was Wilson's Fourteen Points. For a child of the Enlightenment, he said, two obstacles blocked the road, *"les patries, l'Eglise."* The final struggle would be difficult, for this humanitarian internationalism was more dangerous than nationalism.[48] This ideologically militant stance, which allied the Church with the state against internationalism, was representative of a good portion of the elite; but it was not only, as history has shown, a blatant misreading of the situation, it was also a distortion of the Catholic tradition and

---

[45] Renouvin and Duroselle, supra note 38, at 213.
[46] Vaussard, supra note 38, at 371.
[47] Ibid.
[48] Ibid., 366–67.

an implicit rejection of repeated papal warnings of the dangers of nationalism. Lastly, it may help to explain why even thinking Catholics of the period were not united in their resistance and opposition to Fascism.[49]

Despite its problems, the Catholic elite generally continued to press for closer cooperation between Rome and Geneva. One recurring proposal was that diplomatic relations be established between the Holy See and the League Council. In 1923 John Eppstein, the indefatigable Englishman who was an official of the League of Nations Union, submitted this suggestion to the Vatican and received the following reply from the Secretariat of State on August 11:

> The project could be accepted only in the sense that the Holy See would be at the disposal of the League for matters coming within its competence; that is to say for the elucidation of questions of principle in regard to morality and public international law and also to give help to the League's relief work where its [the Holy See's] intervention would be of value to suffering peoples. On this occasion I feel that I must tell you how much the Holy Father appreciates the zeal with which, as an officer of the League of Nations Union, you uphold Catholic principles in all circumstances.[50]

According to Eppstein, private negotiations to establish some kind of diplomatic relations were in fact approved, but were thwarted by Mussolini and Italian interests. Once again the Roman Question confounded the efforts of the Holy See to engage the League through formal diplomatic relations.

It may be that, with a changing climate in Europe, both Rome and Geneva perceived an advantage in diplomatic relations. Had the diplomatic exchange materialized, the Holy See would have gained in international stature, and the League would have acquired new

---

[49] John Eppstein, *Must War Come?* (London: Burns, Oates, and Washbourne, 1935), Chapter 5.

[50] Koenig, supra note 1, ¶849, Letter of Cardinal Gasparri, Secretary of State, to Mr. John Eppstein, An Officer of the League of Nations Union, August 11, 1923.

and valuable popular support among Catholics. The establishment of diplomatic relations between two world institutions which were supranational entities would have been unprecedented. Another type of relationship was later suggested by Catholic writers. It took the form of unilateral representation of the Holy See at the League.[51] This would have been an early form of the concept of a permanent observer that it would eventually hold in the United Nations.

Another effort was made the same year by Gonzague de Reynold, who concluded that "the official League of Nations" was "anxious to have the support of Catholics and the benevolent neutrality of the Holy See."[52] To improve relations between Rome and Geneva, he went to the Vatican in September 1923, describing his mission as a "debut in the ungrateful role of unofficial and sometimes secret ambassador to powers hostile to the League, or at least distrustful of it." He had been encouraged to accept this mission by the nuncio to Switzerland, by Baron de Montenach and Oscar Halecki of the Catholic Union and by Sir Eric Drummond. Pius XI received him briefly, but spoke only in general terms of peace and indicated that Cardinal Gasparri would discuss his mission. That afternoon Gasparri opened the conversation with the words, "Well, this League of Nations won't last." De Reynold replied that the League would last forever, and when the Cardinal asked why, he answered, "Because its employees are extremely well paid." Gasparri laughed and de Reynold told all the amusing stories about the League he could think of, gradually steering the conversation toward serious matters. But when he got to the point of his mission, the Cardinal arose and invited him to call again the next time he was in Rome. Reynold says that it was impossible to get around Gasparri; he was in charge of papal policy from 1914 to 1929 and "everyone knows what happened between those dates."[53]

This incident has already been referred to as persuasive evidence that by December of 1922 Pius XI had made the practical judgment

---

[51] John Eppstein, *The Catholic Tradition of the Law of Nations* (London: Burns, Oates and Washbourne, 1935), 320.

[52] Reynold, supra note 37, III, at 388.

[53] Ibid., 458–61.

that the League would most probably fail. It occurred only a few months later, and Gasparri was quite certainly speaking the mind of the pope as well as his own. Unimpressed with the record of the League as well as its structural deficiencies, he had most likely supported the pessimism of the pope on pragmatic grounds, but restrained himself from attacking the League openly, in the same way that he had earlier restrained the more optimistic Benedict from an unqualified endorsement of the League before it had been put to the test. As principal political analyst of both pontificates, he mitigated the influence of personal papal attitudes toward the League, and successfully promoted a policy of aloofness—not forbidding elite efforts to help the League, but fending off suggestions for direct relations as premature or as a negative influence on the critical factor in papal policy, the Roman Question.[54] The policy may have been prudent from one point of view, but it did not strengthen the League and win new support for it through the mass education of Catholics. Thus the expectation that the League would probably fail ran the risk of becoming a self-fulfilling prophecy.

Despite these rebuffs, internationally minded Catholics continued to propose some kind of official relationship between the Holy See and the League. For example, La Brière noted the suggestion that the Assembly be enlarged to include representatives of the principal international non-governmental institutions. In that case the Holy See would certainly qualify for membership. But he also noted that the Assembly might not be improved, decisions on eligibility would be difficult, and the Holy See would find it demeaning to be classified with institutions lacking recognition as sovereign power in international law. The Covenant would require a slight alteration to admit the Holy See, but state membership would require involvement in worldly political questions it would rather avoid. Hence a special statute would also be needed, allowing the Holy See to participate in certain deliberations while withdrawing from others—a delicate procedure unlikely to win the approval of two-thirds of the

---

[54] See Koenig, supra note 1, ¶849, Letter of Cardinal Gasparri to Mr. John Eppstein, An Officer of the League of Nations, August 11, 1923.

Assembly for some time, to say nothing of the required unanimous vote of the Council. A better arrangement would be an accepted procedure for regular official communication and collaboration. The pope would then no longer suffer a humiliating ostracism from the international community and still be protected from unwanted political involvement, while the League would be saved from debating the thorny question of Vatican membership and would assuredly gain in prestige from the relationship.[55]

The theme of Vatican participation in the League was voiced in several Catholic publications and international meetings, such as the congress in Hanover in September 1924. This gathering resolved unanimously that the Vatican should have "full power and equal rights with the big nations of the world in the League," and that Germany should defer its entry into the League until the latter invited the pope to send a representative.[56] A similar resolution was passed in England by the Catholic Council for International Relations in March of 1925. While League officials did not welcome Vatican membership, they did hope for greater moral support from the Holy See, and one can only conclude that there was disappointment in Geneva at the attitude of Pius XI. This help would have been especially appreciated during the consideration of the Geneva Protocol in 1924, certainly a question of basic principle similar to those dealt with forthrightly by Benedict XV in 1917. In any event, the protocol failed, and nothing came of the other proposals insofar as official relations were concerned.

Attention would first be given to another issue which involved the League and the Holy See directly. Though a peripheral issue itself, it was one in which the League needed the cooperation of the Holy See as a religious force, a cooperation extended reluctantly at the level of expert consultation and then withdrawn. That issue was both secular and sacred—the revision of the calendar. When the League took up the question in 1922, it soon discovered the need

---

[55] La Brière, supra note 43, at 296–307.

[56] "Vatican Wants In League—German Catholic Convention Would Keep Germany Out Otherwise," *New York Times* (September 4, 1924): 2.

for the cooperation of the major religious leaders, especially the Holy See.

In almost every civilization the calendar has had religious significance, situating man in his cosmos and marking the times of fast and festival in the rhythm of life. In the West, the calendar reform of 1582 by Pope Gregory XIII was possible because of the past role of the pope as leader of Christendom. The papacy then functioned as both a central religious institution and the only extant transnational actor in European civilization. The reform was threatened by challenges to the pope's religious authority even though it was demonstrably an improvement from the scientific viewpoint. Germany and Denmark did not accept the Gregorian calendar until 1700, Great Britain and its colonies in 1752, Japan in 1873, China in 1912, and Russia in 1918. This resistance showed that the Holy See was no longer in a position to innovate unilaterally on the question. Nevertheless, it retained a practical veto, due to the influence of world Catholicism, over the success of any further efforts at calendar reform. The same was true of the leaders of other major world religious bodies, especially those with numerous adherents in the West.

As the Enlightenment and Industrial Age increased human desire for symmetrical regularity in the measurement of time, proposals were made to improve the Gregorian calendar. Modern thinking on calendar reform was initiated in 1834 by an Italian priest, Marco Mastrofini, who was also a mathematician and a philosopher. Mastrofini proposed a year of 364 regular days of the week plus an "extra-calendrical" day not counted as a day of the week (in leap years two such extra days). This device, also called the stabilizing or intercalary day, was used later by Auguste Comte in his thirteen-month Positivist Calendar and had the great advantage of making the calendar perpetual, that is, the same date fell on the same day of the week every year. It became the most popular proposal in the organized campaign for calendar reform begun in 1887 by Camille Flammarion, president of the French Astronomical Society.[57]

---

[57] Elizabeth Achelis, *Of Time and the Calendar* (New York: Hermitage House, 1955), 67.

A question intimately related to calendar revision was the agreement on a date for Easter, which had varied according to the phases of the moon, a venerable tradition confirmed by the Synod of Whitby in 664 A.D. The director of the Berlin Observatory, Professor Foerster, worked out a plan for a fixed Easter and in 1897 received a rather encouraging note from Cardinal Rompolla, stating that if a change in the determination of Easter did not hinder Christian unity and was universally demanded, then "the initiative for such a reform could be considered by the Holy See, especially in a general council."[58] The next year the Catholic liturgical journal *Ephemerides Liturgicae* published a series of articles favoring reform, and in 1907 the superiors of all the Benedictine congregations, meeting to discuss the reform of the monastic breviary, unanimously favored calendar reform and a fixed Easter. Thus the Catholic world was by no means opposed to change on principle.[59]

The real impetus for the revision of the calendar, however, came from the secular world of business, which saw it as an aid to economic life. The International Chamber of Commerce urged reform at its conventions of 1910, 1912, and 1914, and presented the question to the Vatican. The secretary of state replied that the Holy See had no objection in principle, but that the matter belonged to the civil authorities. The Church would, however, adapt its religious year to any new calendar agreed upon. After the First World War, the International Astronomical Union revived the issue, forming a committee headed by Cardinal Mercier, which in 1922 approved the perpetual, twelve-month, equal-quarter plan with extra days. Proponents of reform were powerful enough to bring the question before the League that same year.[60]

The League's Advisory and Technical Committee on Communications and Transit took up the question and quickly decided that it was necessary to secure the views of religious authorities, especially

---

[58] A.J. Vincent, "A New Calendar," *Journal of Calendar Reform*, XVII (First Quarter, 1947): 35.

[59] Ibid., 35–36.

[60] League of Nations and Reform of Calendar, 5–6, Genoa (1928); League Minutes, 12, 29–33.

on the stabilization of Easter and the introduction of days outside the week. On June 27, 1923, the Committee asked the Holy See, through the nuncio in Berne, to designate a competent person to attend a meeting in Geneva that August. On July 23, Maglione informed the Committee of the appointment of Reverend Giuseppe Gianfranceschi, SJ, professor of physics at the Gregorian University and president of the Pontifical Academy of Sciences, but with the reservation that his mission did not constitute any pledge on the part of the Holy See regarding decisions to be made. Also invited to the meeting were astronomers designated by the Ecumenical Patriarch of Constantinople and the Archbishop of Canterbury.[61]

The Advisory Committee met with these experts from August 27 to September 1 and reached agreement that calendar reform did not meet with insuperable dogmatic difficulties. But change would not be practicable without the consent of high religious authorities and would be justified only if demanded by public opinion as a means to the improvement of public life and economic relations. It decided to establish a special Committee of Enquiry, composed of its own chairman, the three religious representatives, a representative of the International Astronomical Union, and the president of the International Chamber of Commerce. Governments and religious authorities were to be notified of these decisions and invited to submit any remarks or suggestions by March 1, 1924.[62]

The Advisory Committee reported that it was pleased at the cooperation of religious authorities when it stated:

> The Committee is highly gratified that it has contributed to bring about a rapprochement and cooperation between the high religious authorities and the League of Nations, and it earnestly hopes that, in a matter which is of such general interest, public opinion, enlightened by the various Governments, will be able to render the assistance which is indispensable to these efforts.[63]

---

[61] League of Nations Publications, VIII, Transit, 1923.
[62] Ibid.
[63] Ibid., 4–5.

The mission of Father Gianfranceschi also raised the hopes of the Catholic elite. He was in the choir of the church at the Mass for the opening of the Fourth Assembly on September 2, 1923, leading La Brière to write that the presence of a papal representative was a symbol of collaboration between the Holy See and the League. This participation with the League was still modest but yet official and positive, and the significance would grow with immense benefits to the international order.[64]

In November the League polled governments and religious authorities for their views, and on March 7, 1924, Maglione wrote to Drummond, transmitting the reply of the Holy See. The letter expressed satisfaction that the League had explicitly recognized the need for reform of the calendar, particularly the necessity to address the Easter issue, and that any changes would involve the abandonment of deeply rooted traditions. Change would be neither legitimate nor desirable, except for weighty considerations connected with the common good and general interest. The reply stated,

> The Holy See does not, however, consider that there is sufficient reason for changing; in regard to the fixing of ecclesiastical feast-days, notably that of Easter, what has been the perpetual usage of the Church, handed down by immemorial tradition and sanctioned by councils from early times. Even if, therefore, it were shown that some change in these traditions was demanded by the general good, the Holy See would not be prepared to consider the question except on the advice of an Ecumenical Council.[65]

Replies from other churches and religious groups generally expressed interest in calendar reform, although a good number rejected the idea of an intercalary day. The Federal Council of Churches of Christ in America and the Federation of Swiss Protestant Churches requested representation on the Committee.[66] Replies

---

[64] La Brière, supra note 43, at 133.
[65] Report on the Reform of the Calendar, Publications, VIII, Transit, 1926, 86.
[66] Report of Reform, 86–103.

were received from eleven religious authorities, and in comparison to these communications the reply of the Holy See seems more unyielding, aloof, and uninterested in the calendar question. The replies from governments, 27 in all, showed that they had consulted only scientific bodies and not other groups in the population; generally these replies expressed some interest and a favorable attitude.[67]

When the Special Committee of Enquiry held its first session in Paris in May 1924, all the replies had not yet been received, and so no action could be taken. Father Gianfranceschi voiced his agreement with the Greek Orthodox member of the Committee that Jewish and other non-Christian leaders should be consulted, lest it seem that the Committee should consider the interests of Christians alone. He also stressed that he did not in any way represent the Holy See, and since the Holy See had referred the calendar question to the next ecumenical council, he thought there was no further reason for his remaining on the Committee. He said that the Church saw no reason for disturbing the ancient tradition, but desired to place no obstacles in the way of the investigation launched by the League that concerned the welfare of humanity. The members appointed by the Patriarch and the Archbishop of Canterbury made similar disclaimers of official capacity, the latter stressing that the Church of England could take no step toward reform unless other churches were in agreement. The chairman said he hoped that all three representatives would remain on the Committee, which fully understood their role as intermediaries and did not interpret their private views as binding.[68]

This was the first and last session of the Special Committee which Gianfranceschi attended, and it marked the end of the Holy See's collaboration with the League on the calendar question. At the next session of the Committee in February 1925, Gianfranceschi and the Greek Orthodox representative were both absent, although the former wrote a letter saying that they could meet without him, since he could always send his opinion in writing. The discussion

---

[67] Ibid., 36–85, 103–63.
[68] Minutes of First Session, 3–4.

revealed that the Special Committee wished to hold on to its religious representatives, although it refused to accord representation to other religious bodies, despite their requests.[69] The third session of the Special Committee was held in June 1926, when it adopted its final report. All members were present except Gianfranceschi. His absence may have indicated reluctance on the part of the Holy See to become identified with the Committee's work.[70] The Advisory Committee then resolved that the calendar question should be put before public opinion through the medium of national organizations formed for the purpose. The Assembly approved this in September and two years later noted that national committees on calendar reform were in the process of being formed in several countries.[71]

In the years after 1926, there was considerable activity by proponents of calendar reform. Included was the intensive campaign of George Eastman in the U.S. and the founding of the World Calendar Association, which favored the twelve-month, equal-quarter calendar with the perpetual feature of extra days. This plan, called the World Calendar, emerged as the most popular among reformers, but it also provoked the most opposition because of those intercalary days, which were not counted as days of the week. The resistance was especially strong from Orthodox Jewry, which held the seven-day week as sacred. To admit the extra days into the religious calendar was out of the question, while accepting them in the secular calendar would have put the Sabbath on a different day of the civil week each year. The other principal plans—for a thirteen-month year, or for merely regularizing the months without the perpetual feature—were religiously acceptable to Jews and Seventh-Day Adventists, but drew less support from reformers. All of this led to the League's decision to convene the Fourth General Conference on Communications and Transit for October 1931, devoted exclusively to the question of calendar revision.[72]

---

[69] Minutes of Second Session, 5–7.
[70] Minutes of the Third Session, 23–24, also 6.
[71] League of Nations and the Reform of the Calendar, 16–17, 21.
[72] Achelis, supra note 57, at 70–74.

The League Council decided that invitations to the Fourth General Conference on Communications and Transit should be sent to those states invited to the Third Conference, and that authorities or organizations named by the Chairman of the Advisory Committee should be invited to be present in an advisory capacity or to appoint observers.[73] The Holy See was not eligible for an invitation either as a "power" or as the State of Vatican City which had come into existence two years previously. In fact, it chose not to be present in any capacity, although several religious bodies sent observers, for example, the Church of England, the General Conference of Seventh-Day Adventists, and the International Israelite Committee concerning the Reform of the Calendar. Moreover, there were no observers from any Catholic NGOs.[74] The Holy See was thus conspicuous by its absence. The Conference declared itself in favor of stabilizing movable feasts and asked the League Council to bring this to the notice of the "religious authorities concerned," quoting the response of the Holy See on March 7, 1924. It also decided that the time was not favorable for any modification of the Gregorian calendar, but asked the Advisory Committee to follow future efforts in this direction.[75] The net effect was postponement of calendar reform and requesting that the churches indirectly fix the date of Easter.

The disengagement of the Holy See from the question of calendar reform had nothing to do with the League as such. The Vatican had become aware of the opposition of the Eastern Orthodox Churches to any changes in the calendar and feared that innovations by Rome would be divisive. This became more widely known in 1934, when Msgr. Pizzardo, the Vatican Under secretary of State, replied to a letter from the World Calendar Association. He stated clearly that since the Eastern Church had reproached Rome for departing from ancient traditions by considering calendar reform, such a move would only widen the divisions already existing in the Christian religion. He went on to say that:

[73] *Official Journal* (February 1931):148–49.
[74] Fourth General Conference on Communications and Transit, Geneva, 12–24 October 1931.
[75] Ibid., 259.

Any eventual civil law which would attempt to change the date of Easter would evoke a protest from the Holy See, and the said law would not have any effect except to introduce a new Easter different from both that of the Eastern Schismatics and from that of the Catholic Church, with what advantage to peace, to union and to civilization, it is impossible to say.[76]

Clearly, the Vatican wished to avoid the issue. Again the following year, in response to a memorandum to the Vatican from societies favoring the perpetual calendar, the Holy See said that it was still "premature for the League of Nations or the governments to endeavor to obtain an official decision from the Holy Father."[77]

The last effort to achieve calendar reform through the League originated among the Latin-American members of the International Labour Organisation, who in 1936 unanimously recommended the World Calendar. The following year the representative of Chile on the League Council submitted to the League a draft convention requesting the adoption of this calendar. The Advisory Committee on Communications and Transit went to work and the proposal was submitted to both member and non-member states. However, only fourteen (later seventeen) states approved the convention, and in December 1937, the Council withdrew the item from its agenda.[78] International calendar revision would be moribund for ten years until raised again in the United Nations.

It seems clear that the calendar reformers failed because they had been unable to muster sufficient support to overcome religious objections—tactical on the part of the Holy See, absolute on the part of Orthodox Jewry. A member of the League Secretariat commented,

---

[76] *The World Calendar and Public Opinion,* 212.

[77] Conrad Morin, "Will the Jubilee Year 1950 Open the Era of a New Civil and Religious Calendar?" *Journal of Calendar Reform* XVIII (First Quarter 1948): 41; see Oliver Earl Benson, *Vatican Diplomatic Practice as Affected by the Lateran Agreements* (Liège: Georges Thone, 1936), 197, n. 2.

[78] Achelis, supra note 57, at 75–76.

There was strong opposition on the part of such different religious quarters as the Vatican on one side and Orthodox Jewry on the other. But whereas the Orthodox Jewish attitude was absolute and unconditional, the Vatican repeatedly underlined that it would not oppose a reform demanded "by the common good."[79]

In the last analysis, the opposition of both inhibited League action. Although the same member of the Secretariat said that the Advisory Committee discontinued its labors because of Vatican opposition, the *American Hebrew* declared in 1938 that calendar reform was "opposed and defeated chiefly through the efforts of Chief Rabbi G. H. Hertz, who represented English and American Jewry."[80] But the relative truth of such claims is of far less significance than the fact that in the whole calendar question both of these venerable transnational religious forces had to confront, each in its own way, a new kind of threat to their interest in the status quo, one rendered more potent by the effective use made by the forces of change of a new world forum, the League of Nations.

This was an issue that forced the Holy See to calculate its priorities carefully. There was a widespread movement for calendar reform, which had its clear advantages and to which there were no dogmatic objections. In addition, the intrinsic value of a notable and enduring accomplishment by the League, enhancing its stature and manifesting the support of the Holy See, was urged by the Catholic elite. But ecumenical rapprochement with the Eastern Churches, themselves very tradition-oriented, counted for a great deal. Moreover, Jewish appeals for assistance on this religious issue commanded sympathy and respect. The result was that once these factors became clear, the Holy See may have regretted both its initial cooperation and the fact that the League had taken up the question in the first place. However, the experienced paved the way for subsequent, enduring collaboration between the United Nations and the Holy See.

---

[79] Laurence J. Kenny, SJ, "Calendar Reform," *Journal of Calendar Reform* XVII (Fourth Quarter 1948): 168.

[80] Ibid.

Signs of Rapprochement with the League: The Role of International Catholic Organizations

A S HAS BEEN INDICATED, the practice of the Holy See under Pius XI was to remain more distant from international politics than his predecessor while encouraging engagement by Catholic laymen and lay organizations such as Catholic Action. This policy fostered the participation of the Catholic elite in the activities of the League. Although the isolated involvement of individuals was important in certain cases, this participation was exercised most significantly by the elite as organized into international Catholic non-governmental organizations (NGOs). Relationships between Catholic international NGOs and the League were not extensive and their importance should not be exaggerated. Yet they are interesting for what they were—the budding contacts between the first international organization to attempt the incorporation of world society and the first specialized international organizations to emanate from and represent the world's largest and best organized transnational religious force. While the impact on NGO activity during the interwar period is difficult to assess, it is possible to discern something about the relevance of Catholic NGO collaboration with League organs to Catholic attitudes toward international organization.

This treatment is not a claim of preeminence for Catholic international NGOs as opposed to other religiously oriented or completely secular organizations. In point of fact, the Catholic organizations, whose origins have already been described, represented only a small part of the large number of NGOs then in existence, even of the religiously oriented. One cannot quarrel with Lyman White's impression that while the Roman Catholic Church is undoubtedly the most important international or world organization, Protestant groups have been more active in the great movement for international organizations which began about the middle of the nineteenth century.[1] The Young Men's Christian Association (YMCA), founded in 1855, was probably the first true international NGO.[2] But world Protestantism was hardly a well-organized transnational force, and its NGOs were not at that time coordinated, as they would be in later years.

The earliest international NGOs were religious and humanitarian. However, this trend changed toward the secular as the NGO movement gathered momentum after 1865.[3] By one count, the number of international NGOs rose from 7 in 1860 to 49 in 1900, and 133 in 1920. This figure, in turn, doubled during the interwar period to 269.[4] Of these mostly secular organizations, only some ten percent were Catholic, depending on the criteria employed to determine NGO status. Yet the real question is not one of quantity but of quality (that is, effectiveness), and here the great majority of religiously oriented NGOs tended to lag behind most of the secular organizations. Still, in their own unique area of interest, the influence of religion on international life was promoted by these Catholic groups.

International Catholic NGOs came to be called "international Catholic organizations" or ICOs. They consisted of academic or professional organizations possessing a certain secular competence to their work. It was always obvious that the ICOs were Catholic and enjoyed a relationship with the Holy See. The question arose as to

---

[1] Lyman C. White and Marie R. Zocca, *International Non-Governmental Organizations: Their Purposes, Methods and Accomplishments* (New Brunswick, NJ: Rutgers University Press, 1951), 134.

[2] Ibid., 4.

[3] Ibid., 4–5.

[4] E. S. Tew, "The Organizational World," *International Associations* XII (December 1960): 732.

how this relationship affected their attitudes, policies, and freedom of action. Msgr. Beaupin, the secretary-general of the Catholic Union of International Studies acknowledged that the Union was a private association composed of Catholic groups and individuals from different countries. The Union, while acting on its own, remained in contact with the Holy See, which did not involve itself directly with the Union but did provide advice on the organization's activities.[5]

Hindsight shows that the Union was a successful effort at formulating a productive and cooperative relationship between the Holy See and an ICO. This model not only governed relations between the Vatican and Catholic NGOs generally during the League period, but it survived that period (which the Catholic Union did not) to remain operative during the early period of the United Nations. It thus merits some examination at this point.

The Catholic Union, and thus the typical ICO, is described by Beaupin first as a private association. From the secular point, it was private in the sense of non-governmental, but it was also private from an ecclesiastical standpoint in that it was not part of the ordinary Church structure. As a voluntary association, it was founded by its members and depended upon them for its continued existence. Furthermore, its purpose was specialized, and is thus subsidiary and ancillary to the aims of the Church. The term "private" connotes a freedom from hierarchical direction greater than that possessed by Church functionaries. On the other hand, as an ICO, it was composed of Catholic national associations or sections and individuals who were loyal to the Church and dedicated to furthering its mission in the international environment. These characteristics gave it a distinctive religious dimension and allied it to a larger transnational force, the Holy See.

It is significant that the ICO had member sections from different countries (in fact, they were usually national organizations in their own right), making the ICO truly international. It did not

---

[5] Msgr. E. Beaupin, *La Coopération Internationale dans la Vie Intellectuelle, Le Problème de la Vie Internationale* (Paris: Gabalda, 1927), 417–29.

rely solely on the supranationality of the Church for its international character. Furthermore, each ICO acted independently. It took the initiative in formulating positive programs agreed upon by its membership. It was a source of ideas and action for which it alone was accountable. The competence for such responsibility implied a claim by the ICO to an expertise in its specialized field.

The right of the Holy See to exercise supervision over ICOs is not found in Canon Law. It is derived ultimately from its right to approve any organization as Catholic, that is, to permit the use of the term "Catholic" in its title.[6] Since this approval can and should be revoked if the organization operates contrary to the Catholic faith, the Holy See is obliged to exercise some general oversight of its activities. But such supervision is the application of a passive norm, not a positive input into the ICO's decisionmaking process. This process operates independently of the Holy See. The Vatican is not responsible for its actions, and can thus disavow them as Church policy if necessary. The ICO does not officially represent the Holy See or the Church. On the other hand, the ICO can act as a spokesman for Catholic attitudes, which it is expected to know, and it is generally accepted in this capacity by the international forum. Unless Church authority contradicts the statements of the ICO, its tacit approval is presumed.

The loyalty of Catholic ICO personnel to the Church and their devotion to effective and unified Catholic participation in interna-

---

[6] A recent illustration of this principle comes from the action of the United States Conference of Catholic Bishops and its May 10, 2000, statement on the status of the organization that calls itself Catholics for a Free Choice, a pro-abortion advocacy organization. In part this statement says, "On a number of occasions the National Conference of Catholic Bishops (NCCB) has stated publicly that CFFC is not a Catholic Organization, does not speak for the Catholic Church, and in fact promotes positions contrary to the teaching of the Church as articulated by the Holy See and the NCCB. . . . As the Catholic Bishops of the United States have stated for many years, the use of the name Catholic as a platform for promoting the taking of innocent human life and ridiculing the Church is offensive not only to Catholics, but to all who expect honesty and forthrightness in public discourse. We state once again with strongest emphasis: 'Because of its opposition to the human rights of some of the most defenseless members of the human race, and because its purposes and activities deliberately contradict essential teachings of the Catholic faith. . . . Catholics for a Free Choice merits no recognition or support as a Catholic organization.' "

tional organizations is presumed, as is the encouragement and appreciation of these efforts by the Holy See. In practice, this has not been lacking. ICO work attracts only dedicated Catholics for the most part, since it offers little in the way of monetary or other reward. The Vatican has responded appropriately with respect for this spontaneous service. As for the direction of the Holy See, it consists largely of the authoritative teachings of the Church on questions of faith and morals, largely its social teaching, which for the ICO is an automatic and convenient framework for policy formation. As a rule, the Holy See issues general pronouncements, which the ICO is free to apply to particular social situations, formulating its own policies and strategies and translating them into action within the particular international organizations to which it is affiliated.

By the time the Beaupin statement appeared in 1929, it had become clear that Rome avoided issuing concrete directives on policy to ICOs. It preferred the discreet suggestion, rarely needed or employed, to steer a maverick ICO in the desired direction or incite a sluggish ICO to action. It was also clear that ICOs welcomed and even solicited direction from knowledgeable Roman officials and the Holy See's valuable guidance on complex issues of importance to the Church. This does not deny the distinction between the roles of the Holy See and ICOs. While the ICO generally wishes to preserve its independence and reputation in the NGO world, the Holy See usually seeks the coordination of all NGO activity so that the Catholic community might speak with one voice and function more effectively as a transnational force. Beaupin envisaged both this tension and its resolution when he said that the NGO is to respect the direction of the Holy See.

It should be remembered that in certain matters the Holy See prefers to remain detached, at least for a time, and observe developments, letting the ICOs adopt and present their positions. In such cases, the Holy See does not necessarily desire that the NGO position be the same as its own. Relations between ICOs and the League are a good illustration of this. This is precisely how the

Catholic Union and other ICOs carried on with the League in the early pontificate of Pius XI.

Generally, the ICO informs the Holy See of its initiatives through regular channels of communication as well as informal contacts with Roman officials. Effective liaison of this sort is essential to supervision. But it is also extremely important to the function, at times assumed by the Holy See, of coordinating ICO policies and activities in order to prevent duplication of effort and waste of scarce resources. The Vatican has encouraged ICOs to coordinate their own policies and programs, and it has in turn wished to be kept informed of these efforts as well. The ICO cannot intelligently inform the Holy See of its initiatives without also informing it of the situations and events that inspire these moves. While not an official arm of the Vatican in international organizations, ICOs can and do serve as a source of news. Such is the observer function of ICOs, which is never entirely supplanted even when a papal observer is present on the scene. In that case, he can avail himself of NGO-collected data and partially fulfill the liaison function with the Holy See.

The ICO is thus a step removed from the official apparatus of the Holy See, standing midway between the Church and the world as an expression of the Christian involvement of the laity in temporal affairs. This is reflected in the pronouncements of the Second Vatican Council, where it was declared that lay groups such as NGOs would apply in specific situations the social teachings which the Church proclaims.[7] The function of the ICO in this process is essentially one of mediation and education.

It is now time to consider the relations that existed between ICOs and the League of Nations. A reference in Article 24 of the Covenant to "international bureaux" made some observers of the League conclude that there existed a juridical basis for relationships between the League and NGOs. In its first years the League adopted a broad interpretation of this article. But in July, 1923, the Council decided that Article 24 referred solely to international organizations

---

[7] See "the Pastoral Constitution on the Church," *Gaudium et Spes* (December 7, 1965): nos. 43, 88 & 90.

established by treaty.[8] In practice, NGO relationships with the League were essentially unwritten and informal. Some NGO representatives were attached to the social, economic, humanitarian, and cultural committees of the League, but the rules of procedure varied from one committee to another.[9] There were common features: most NGO representatives to a committee were a small number of experts in their fields called "assessors." Though they were without vote, they participated openly in the work, and on most committees could propose resolutions, offer amendments, be appointed to subcommittees, present reports, and defend themselves before the delegates.[10] They thus had considerable input into committee decisions.

A good part of the NGO activity in Geneva pertained to social and humanitarian questions of interest to Catholic organizations, for example, the protection of children and the suppression of obscenity, drugs, the traffic in women, and slavery.[11] The Catholic Union supplied the League Secretariat and advisory committees with documents and statistics on these questions.[12] In 1921 the League Council established the Advisory Committee on the Traffic in Women and Children. One of its ten assessors accredited in 1922 was a representative of the International Catholic Association for the Protection of Young Women.[13] In 1924 the Council restructured the Committee into the Advisory Commission for the Protection and Welfare of Children and Young People, which included the Advisory Committee on the Traffic in Women and Children and the Advisory Committee on Child Welfare. The International Catholic Association for the Protection of Young Women continued

---

[8] League of Nations, *Official Journal,* Geneva, 8 (1925): 858. See Neal Malicky, "Religious Groups at the United Nations: A Study of Certain Religious Non-Governmental Organizations at the United Nations," unpublished Ph.D. dissertation, Columbia University, 1967, 56.

[9] Malicky, supra note 8, at 55.

[10] Ibid., 58.

[11] M. Marcel Prelot, "Organisation and Activity of the League of Nations," in *International Relations from a Catholic Standpoint* (Dublin: Brown and Nowlan, 1932), 160, n. 2.

[12] Ibid.

[13] *Ten Years of World Cooperation* (Geneva: League of Nations, 1930), 291–92.

to send an assessor to the former, and the International Union of Catholic Women's Leagues to both.[14]

The assessors were not that numerous: In 1930 the Committee on Traffic had five; that on Child Welfare, eight.[15] As a result, the Catholic assessors had, as one of them reported to her own NGO, a significant influence on the resolutions sent to the Council and Assembly, which in turn influenced the policies of member states.[16]

But the NGO representatives who were committee assessors constituted a privileged few. Prior to 1932 no special facilities as to seating or documentation were provided for most NGO personnel. They had to arrive early at meetings in Geneva before tourists occupied the available seats not taken by delegates of state members. In time, however, the ongoing presence of representatives of certain NGOs, together with the contribution of their specialized information, advice, or operational support, which aided the League, won them the confidence and respect of League officials and delegates. This confidence and respect constituted a kind of informal recognition.[17] In addition to these more outstanding NGOs, the League Secretariat kept in touch with a number of private national and international organizations interested in some or all of the aspects of the League's work. Consequently, an official of the Secretariat was sent to their conferences when necessary.[18] A special department of the Secretariat, called the International Bureaux Section, kept a list of NGOs and published a handbook of international organizations from 1921 to 1938.

In addition to specialized work with the advisory committees, ICOs performed another function that was valuable to the League vis-à-vis the Catholic community. This was the giving of moral sup-

---

[14] Ibid.

[15] Malicky, supra note 8, at 59.

[16] *Union Internationale des Ligues feminins Catholiques, Huitième Conseil International tenu à Rome* (Bruxelles: G. Bothy, 1930), 57, cited in Jeremiah Newman, *Change and the Catholic Church: An Essay in Sociological Ecclesiology* (Baltimore: Helicon, 1965), 55.

[17] Carnegie Endowment Consultation, 12.

[18] *Essential Facts* . . . 10th Ed. Rev. (Geneva: League of nations Information Section, 1939), 314.

port to the League. The International Union of Social Studies, founded by Cardinal Mercier, provides a good example. At its annual meeting in 1925, Mercier himself moved that the Union send a message to the League. As adopted, the message affirmed that "the brotherhood of men implies the brotherhood of nations," and that "the idea of giving a permanent form to the natural society of nations is both just and good." Tribute was paid to the efforts of the League in the areas of social progress and labor legislation, with the wish that "similar efforts might be successful in favor of Christian minorities in those countries where they are threatened." Finally, all Catholics were urged to "both follow and support the work of the League of Nations."[19] This kind of statement was extremely valuable to Geneva. It would have been more welcome coming from Rome, but it was still an important solution to counteract anti-League propaganda among Catholics.

One organ of the League of Nations with which the Catholic elite collaborated in a significant way was the International Committee on Intellectual Cooperation, the forerunner of UNESCO. At first it did not appear likely that Catholics would have anything to do with this body. The idea for such a committee dated back to 1919 and originated from the same secularistic individuals and groups whose utopian concept of the League idea so alarmed Catholic opinion, for example, men like Leon Bourgeois and Albert Thomas, and the powerful Union of International Associations. Even Catholics as levelheaded as La Brière feared their belief in the League as a world superstate with a ministry of public instruction to supervise the education of youth by suppressing all teaching about war and spreading democratic pacifism and the cult of a liberated humanity.[20] The First Assembly of the League passed a resolution favoring international action in the realm of intellectual cooperation, and the Second Assembly, after hearing a report from

---

[19] Maurice Vaussard, "La Coopération Internationale des Catholiques," in *Le Problème de la Vie Internationale* (Paris: Gabalda, 1927), 598–99.

[20] Gonzague de Reynold, *Mes Mémoires,* III (Genève: Editions Général, 1963), 384–85; Yves de La Brière, SJ, *L'Organisation Internationale du Monde Contemporain et la Papauté Soveraine, Series I* (Paris: Editions Spes, 1924), 125.

Leon Bourgeois (whom Reynold called *"ce pape laique"*) charged the Council with naming a committee of twelve to carry on the work. According to Reynold, it was understood that Belgium and Switzerland would each have a representative on the Committee. It was desired that one member be Catholic because of the perspectives of the Vatican. Though Cardinal Mercier was mentioned for the Belgian seat, it was impossible not to reward Jules Destrees, a leader of the Socialist party, with this position. Thus the twelfth to be named should be Swiss and a Catholic, and so Reynold was named.[21]

The International Committee on Intellectual Cooperation held its first meeting in Geneva in August 1922, and its distinguished members included such notables as Henri Bergson, Gilbert Murray, and Madame Curie. La Brière said that after this first meeting Catholic fears were allayed and that the proceedings were a disappointment for some secularist ideologues. He noted that the extremely diverse backgrounds of the Committee's members led them to avoid controversial questions and seek a common ground. Their common outlook as professors or directors of scientific laboratories led them to avoid the empty debate so beloved by politicians. The Committee concentrated on questions that offended no one, such as international organization of bibliography, exchange of publication, and collaboration in research. The Committee also put aside potentially divisive projects that would have exceeded its competence. Lastly, the Committee agreed to treat state and private universities on an equal basis, considering only the character and importance of the services they might render to education and the diffusion of knowledge. The presence of two men in particular at that first meeting of the International Committee helped to overcome Catholic hesitation. Gonzague de Reynold was the rapporteur of the Committee and Oscar Halecki, a professor at the University of Warsaw and member of the Catholic Union of International Studies (like Reynold), was a member of the League Secretariat. These two members of the Catholic elite, working with the

---

[21] Reynold, supra note 20, at 386–87.

Committee, performed a very valuable mediatory function between the League and the Holy See.[22]

At its Milan meeting of 1923, the Catholic Union of International Studies established the International Catholic Committee on Intellectual Cooperation to follow the work of the League Committee. Reynold told the latter body at its fourth session in 1924 that Catholic circles were following the work of the Committee of the League and the Committee's activities had a positive effect of unifying Catholic forces in the intellectual and university world. Reynold said that the Catholic Union would be glad to establish relations with the League Committee.[23] The League Committee agreed to accept this offer of collaboration, provided that the difference between the Catholic Union's Committee and its own national committees was emphasized.[24] There remained a question of organizing modes of collaboration between these two committees.

The Catholic elite was genuinely interested in the question of international intellectual cooperation. Msgr. Beaupin of the Catholic Union told his listeners at the Catholic Social Week of 1926 in Le Havre (which was devoted to international questions) that the Church had always favored and practiced intellectual cooperation. Medieval universities had students from many nations, the *"studia generalia"* being erected by papal bulls, and the degrees conferring the *"jus ubique docendi,"* the right to teach anywhere in Christendom. The Church's institutions of learning in Rome had always had an international basis. Consequently, Catholics should be loyal to this tradition and study how it could contribute to the work of the League. Beaupin praised the work of the League Committee and mentioned the role of Gonzague de Reynold, who upheld Catholic religious interests in the group, and of Oscar Halecki, who directed the League's bulletin on university relations, in which activities of Catholic universities and scientific institutes organized by the Holy See received prominent notice. Beaupin favored an attitude of

---

[22] La Brière, supra note 20, at 126–30.

[23] League of Nations, Committee on International Cooperation, Minutes of 4th Session, Geneva, 25–29 July 1924 (A, 20. 1924 XII), 11.

[24] Ibid.

cooperation on the part of Catholics and participation in such projects as developing methods of teaching youth their international obligations. He decried the international secularism of the Socialists and Communists which substituted the compartmentalization of men into classes for national loyalties, pitting them against one another. He also deplored the pacifist internationalism which opposed all use of force instead of establishing the necessary distinction between the just and unjust use of force. But he said that Catholics must teach a Christian internationalism that reflected a harmonious synthesis of national and international duties. He said it had been proposed to Catholics that they should teach young people about the League of Nations and its ideal of cooperation in all areas of human activity. Catholics should not refuse this duty, said Beaupin, for it was an opportunity to show how much this ideal was in accord with their own. They should take the League as it is and work to make it what it should be. Intellectual cooperation, he concluded, was a great movement, which Catholics could neither ignore or abstain from and leave open to others. They should oppose this movement when it went against their doctrines, and take part in it by parallel or cooperative action as the situation demanded.[25]

The Catholic Union served as a model of the ICO during the interwar period, since it reached a fairly high degree of development. Beginning with national sections in France, Italy, and Switzerland in the early years, the Union added others in Germany, Great Britain, Austria, Hungary, Poland, Czechoslovakia, Yugoslavia, and the U.S. by 1926. In addition, corresponding members were recruited in other countries—Spain, the Netherlands, Ireland, Canada, and Peru—with the idea of founding national sections in those states. The Catholic Union held nine international conferences between 1920 and 1931, all in European cities, and had three general committees: a Committee on Intellectual Cooperation (1923), on Catholic Minorities (1925), and on Humanitarian Causes (1923).

---

[25] Beaupin, *La Coopération Internationale dans la Vie Intellectuelle,* supra note 5, at 417–29.

There were also temporary committees—those composed of jurists and missionaries—which dealt with such questions as conventions on forced labor and polygamy at its meeting in Paris in 1931.[26]

The Catholic Union's Committee on Humanitarian Causes was the result of the participation by several members of the Union as observers at the second opium conference in Geneva in 1924. The conference had heard proposals from the Catholic Union at its session of November 24, 1924, and a few days later received from that organization a copy of the directives issued by the vicars apostolic in China to the Catholic faithful against the use of opium. The same Committee of the Catholic Union worked with the League's temporary committee on slavery, supplying it with data based on documentation furnished by missionaries. A memo was also sent on May 9, 1925, proposing reforms for the emancipation of women. In September of 1926, the same committee supported the position of the Holy See on certain clauses in the international convention on slavery, which was voted by the Assembly during its seventh session. When the International Labor Organization (ILO) took up the question of forced labor in 1928, this Catholic Union Committee on Humanitarian Causes prepared an answer to its questionnaire and sent a memo to the International Labor Conference of 1929 and another in 1930. The committee dealt with other questions as well: immoral propaganda, children born out of wedlock, and population (a Catholic committee of experts to study population problems was established). The Catholic Union, being involved in all of these matters, had to coordinate its efforts with those of other international NGOs, which brought it into the mainstream of international life. Again, the Catholic Union's Committee on Minorities sent to the Assembly in December in 1924 a statistical note on the Christian population of the Mosul region, to draw the attention of the Council to the plight of Christians there. In November 1925, when the Council was to render a decision on the Mosul problem, the Committee sent a detailed report on the deportations and massacres of Chaldean Catholics by the Turks. This documentation was

---

[26] Reynold, supra note 20, at 501–4.

communicated officially by the Secretariat to all members of the
Council. Thus the Catholic Union, through its committees, communicated with the League on a broad range of problems.

In general, the Catholic Union took a position toward the
League of Nations of objective good will ("bienveillance objective"),
which enabled it to intervene in the deliberations of that body
whenever it thought useful. The Union did not give up in these and
other efforts. If it had not been present and participating, Catholics
would in many cases not have had the means to be heard. It is no
exaggeration that the Union played an important role in the development of international Catholic relations around the world, by
helping establish international Catholic specialized secretariats. In
this way it filled certain gaps in the presentation of Catholic interests at Geneva. During the Seventh Assembly of the League in
1926, members of the Catholic Union met together in several gath-
erings. All agreed on the necessity of creating at Geneva, as soon as
the resources could be gathered, a permanent office of the Union to
follow the work of the League which affected the interests of
Catholicism. It was noted that since 1921 a permanent office of the
International Masonic Association had been furthering the cause of
universal secularization at the League.[27] The high point of the activity of the Catholic Union was at the international Catholic Week of
Geneva in 1929 (Semaine Catholique Internationale de Geneve).
Msgr. Beaupin wrote that in the city of the League of Nations,
where doctrines of every sort were exhibited to a cosmopolitan and
diverse public, the Union had made clear what principles Catholics
proposed to solve the great international problems of the age.

Its work with League bodies gradually brought the Catholic
Union in contact with other international organizations, some
Catholic and some not. It cooperated with these organizations and
groups in specific cases where there was a common interest. In this
way the Union came to be represented in a larger committee composed of groups interested in the education of youth for peace, and

---

[27] Yves de La Brière, SJ, *L'Organisation Internationale du Monde Contemporain et
la Papauté Soveraine, Series II* (Paris: Editions Spes, 1927), 183.

members of the Union joined national groups supporting the League of Nations, especially in intellectual cooperation and social service. The participation of the Union or its members in these organizations was as far as possible a concerted effort, with generally good results. Their involvement and participation demonstrated that Catholics would not refuse their collaboration with a good cause, provided that their religious principles were respected. Sometimes Catholics had to defend these principles, for example, at the population conference held at Geneva in the fall of 1927, where certain population control theses were advanced that brought vigorous reaction from members of the Union and other Catholics. As a result of this controversy, the Union contributed to the creation of the International Association for Life and the Family (Association Internationale pour la Vie et la Famille), and set up its own committee of experts on population.[28]

The education of youth in international affairs, in which the Catholic Union collaborated, was one of the principal ventures of the League's international Committee on Intellectual Cooperation. Governments and NGOs were consulted for their views, and the ICOs responded. The International Secretariat of Catholic youth, which reported on its own international educational activities, indicated a desire to cooperate with the League.[29] The Holy See was not contacted as a government or as an NGO, but a communication from League circles did reach the Roman Curia. Msgr. Georg Schreiber reported that the norms which had been established by Geneva seemed to exclude religious and even moral influences in education, and made the Curia very cautious. Despite the invitation to cooperate, the Holy See did not take part in the program. In a conversation with Msgr. Giuseppe Pizzardo, the Undersecretary of State at the Vatican, Schreiber urged the Holy See to respond to such invitations when possible through intellectual circles close to

---

[28] Beaupin, "Les Singulières d'un Congress," *Chronique Sociale de France* (Janvier 1928): 27.

[29] Instruction of Children and Youth in the Existence and Aims of the League of Nations, Report Submitted by the Secretariat to the 6th Assembly (A.10.1925, XII), Geneva, 25 June 1925, 40.

Rome, since the League was beginning to show greater broadmind-edness in humanitarian questions. Pizzardo seemed interested and asked for a memorandum dealing with modalities for cooperation by Vatican scientific and cultural bodies.[30] There seemed to have been at Rome a cautious desire for a limited collaboration by the Holy See tempered by a healthy suspicion of the secularist ideology associated with the League of Nations.

In 1925 and 1926 the League's Committee on Intellectual Cooperation went through a structural metamorphosis from being a solely consultative body to becoming the governing body of the International Institute of Intellectual Cooperation in Paris. The International Organization for Intellectual Cooperation maintained relations with NGOs, some of which were Catholic. The work of international pedagogy continued especially in the publication of manuals of instruction on the League and intellectual cooperation. The Catholic Union was stimulated to publish a book of its own in 1928, titled *La Societe Internationale*, which included chapters on Christian principles and international relations, the work of the Church for peace, the organization and activity of the League of Nations, and the international organization of labor.[31] The work was translated into various languages by sections of the Catholic Union. As a consequence, *International Relations from a Catholic Standpoint* was published by the Irish section of the Catholic Union in 1932.[32] The Irish section, called the Catholic Union of International Studies, added to the work a program of studies which provided an informative index to attitudes toward the League held by the Catholic elites.

Thus the League of Nations, through its Committee on Intellectual Cooperation, had a stimulating effect on international thinking generally, and within the Catholic community itself. From the earliest days of the Committee, the French government called for more

[30] George Schreiber, *Das Päpstliche Staatssekretariat in Historicsches Jahrbuch* (München: Görres-Gesellschaft, 1959, 1960), LXXIX, 196–97.
[31] Msgr. Beaupin, "Introduction," in *International Relations from a Catholic Standpoint* (Dublin: Brown and Nowland, 1932), 1–10.
[32] Ibid., v–vii, Foreword.

detailed instruction on the existence, work, and goals of the League. But it encountered strong resistance among Catholic and nationalist leaders who opposed "the Wilsonian catechism."[33] By 1928, however, there was a general acceptance by the teaching profession in both government and religious schools of the need for adequate instruction on the League and the exclusion of hostile, anti-German material.[34] The problem Catholics had with the League's international pedagogical efforts is well described by Msgr. Beaupin in his introduction to *La Societe Internationale*, where he stated,

> Thus it became a question for French educationalists, in what way and to what extent they were to join in the efforts called for by the League. In France this is still a moot question. "Pacifist" education, if given bluntly and without qualification, can hurt not only lawful and sane patriotism, but even the faith itself; on the other hand, if imparted properly, it may be quite in accord with love of country and with the demand of the strictest orthodoxy. The League of Nations is a fact which cannot be ignored, and there exists a philosophic body of teaching on the duties and rights between nations. Finally before long all these vexed questions will probably be a matter for investigation. For all these reasons the Catholic Union of International Studies, a private association founded in 1920, numbering now adherents in some twenty countries, decided on this little book at its meeting in 1926. It entrusted its drawing-up to its own Committee of Intellectual Cooperation.[35]

The Catholic Union was always friendly toward other international Catholic organizations, which had in almost every case members who were also in the Union, and most Union members also belonged to other Catholic NGOs. This situation made the exchange of documentation and joint action easier for there was a

---

[33] John Eppstein, *Ten Years' Life of the League of Nations* (London: May Fair Press, 1929), 79.

[34] Ibid.

[35] Beaupin, supra note 31, at 3–4.

coordination of Catholic participation in the international conference on social service held in Paris in 1928. The Catholic Union
also helped to foster the growth of other Catholic NGOs during the
interwar period and shared its officers with several of them. The
Union thus functioned as a kind of interlocking directorate
amongst the Catholic elite. This system had its disadvantages. For
example, the Catholic Union and Pax Romana shared the same secretary-general, a distinguished cleric of Fribourg, full of good will
but so loaded down with other duties that he could not work fully
for either organization. Nevertheless, the system also tended to draw
together the various ICOs in an effort to better coordinate their
activities vis-às-vis the League of Nations.

In 1925 the British Catholic Council for International Relations, led by John Eppstein, sponsored a conference in Oxford in an
effort to establish a unified Catholic organization, thereby avoiding
duplication of effort and dispersal of forces. Representatives of the
Catholic Union for International Studies, the International
Catholic League (IKA) of Austrian origin, and the International
Office of Catholic Organizations (L'Office Internationale des Organizations Catholique) came together in Rome in the early 1920s
and published a *Manual of Catholic Organizations* in 1924. The
subject of this gathering was Catholic teaching on race and nationality, but the center of interest was the discussion of the question of
why there should be three Catholic internationals. Representatives
of organizations from 27 nations were present, and they formed a
new overall organization called the *Confederatio Internationalis
Catholica*, which unified Catholic action throughout the world for
the promotion of peace.[36] The *Confederatio* did not function very
effectively, and two years later another, less formal effort was made
to coordinate Catholic international organizations.

---

[36] Stephen J. Brown, SJ, "Catholic Internationalism," *Studies* XIV (September
1925): 479. The provisional constitution of the *Confederatio* had two principal
goals: (1) "to labour to preserve and to render more effective the unity of
Catholic action throughout the world;" and (2) "to promote International
peace based upon Justice and Christian Charity, according to the desire and
direction of the Holy See."

Of all the organs and agencies in the league system, the Holy See enjoyed the best relations with the International Labour Organisation, founded by the treaty of Versailles in 1919. It is significant that this cordial relationship was with a largely autonomous organization linked to the League, rather than with the League itself. The Holy See was better prepared to deal with an organ performing a social or humanitarian function than with an organ basically political in nature, such as the League Assembly or Council. This was true basically because the Holy See wished to avoid involvement in political disputes whenever possible. But there was an additional factor in this case: The Catholic social movement since 1869 had prepared the Vatican and the Church in general for action in the labor field. It had already established a pattern of ideological detente and regular cooperation with secular organizations favoring international action to improve the condition of the workingman.[37] The ILO was attractive to the Holy See and the Catholic elite, since it was an intergovernmental organization possessing the widest possible range of membership and a high degree of competence and authority. Moreover, its constitution, contained in Part XIII of the Treaty of Versailles, bore a striking resemblance to the principles of Catholic social doctrine set out in Pope Leo XIII's encyclical *Rerum Novarum*.[38] Lastly, the whole approach of the ILO toward building peace, through the cultivation of social justice at both national and international levels, was in accord with the papal emphasis on justice as the necessary foundation of peace.

Despite this fundamental compatibility, however, there was still opposition to the ILO among some Catholics. George Shuster writes that, "For many years, for example, Catholic bishops in Latin America were persuaded that the ILO was a subversive organization, even as there were conservative Protestants in Germany who looked on the League of Nations as an invention of 'Liberalism.' "[39] Other

---

[37] See Albert LeRoy, SJ, *The Dignity of Labor*, x.

[38] Boissard, *La Coopération dans le Domaine Social: Le Bureau International du Truvail et les Associations Internationales de Politique Social* (Semaines Sociale, 1926), 459.

[39] George N. Shuster, *UNESCO: Assessment and Promise* (New York: Harper and Row, 1963), 74.

early fears of the ILO, however, were based on more solid and specific grounds that impressed Catholics who supported the organization in principle. Although the International Federation of Christian Trade Unions (IFCTU) founded under Catholic inspiration and representing some three and a half million workers had favored the establishment of the ILO, its members were dismayed when it soon became evident that the majority of the trade unions represented there opposed the participation of Christian trade unions. Also, many Catholics were disturbed that the first Director-General of the ILO was a genuine Socialist, Albert Thomas, who had been a minister in two leftist cabinets when the left was trying to reignite the fires of religious persecution in France. They had reason to believe that the ILO favored close ties with the very political parties that Catholics were battling at home.[40] Fortunately, these two important objections were soon overcome.

But it was Albert Thomas himself who overcame the principal Catholic objection to the ILO. He was a dynamic and visionary individual who made a genuine effort to win the support of the Christian Social movement for his organization. He was wise enough to take the advice of Gaston Tessier, Christian trade union leader and technical expert with the French governmental delegation to the ILO, that it would be a good idea to have a priest on the staff of the secretariat, that is, the International Labour Office, and let him oversee the relations with Catholic authorities and organizations.[41] Moving against the wishes of the majority of the unions in the ILO, Thomas visited the pope and invited the collaboration of the Holy See with the ILO, specifically asking for a priest to be attached to his staff to follow the Christian social movement. The Holy See approved this plan, and Father Andre Arnou, SJ was appointed to the International Labour Office in 1926, a procedure that has been followed ever since.[42] Father Arnou and his successors, all Jesuits,

---

[40] Joseph Joblin, SJ, "Le Pere Albert Le Roy," in *Etudes,* Tome 317, 5 (May 1963): 252–53.

[41] Ibid., 254; see E. J. Phelan, *Yes and Albert Thomas* (London: Cresset Press, 1936), 247.

[42] Le Roy, supra note 37, at 63.

have functioned as observers of the Christian social movement and performed liaison functions with Catholic national NGOs, as well as providing an informal link between the ILO and Rome.[43] Albert Thomas and the ILO received high praise from speakers at the French Catholic Social Week of 1926. The ILO was called "the international ministry of social justice," and Thomas was viewed as a man of confidence in his own socialist creed, yet profoundly respectful of the convictions of others and desirous of collaboration with all social-minded people.[44]

Thomas desired mutual comprehension and union among men of divergent ideological tendencies, but without suppression of particularities and differences. For him, no movement that could strengthen the ILO or the cause of social justice was to be kept at arm's length. The Christians were free to advance their ideals. At Munich in 1928, for example, Thomas told the representatives of Christian trade unions to strengthen their own beliefs and to act upon them. He said the ILO did not wish any group to restrain its own particular beliefs. He hoped that each group would elevate its own ideals in order that everyone might achieve thought and action in union with one another. It was possible to work together only in complete honesty.[45] In his annual *Report of the Director Presented to the Conference* for 1928, Thomas paid a remarkable tribute to the Catholic social movement since *Rerum Novarum*. He emphasized the statements and actions of bishops in recent years; he noted their condemnations of laissez-faire, their emphasis on the social duty of property owners, the just wage, the rights of workers, and the trade union movement. Thomas particularly praised the 1919 statement of the National Catholic Welfare Conference's administrative committee remarking, "Once again the fundamental conception of the Christian economic system is emphasized. Profit is not the chief end of industry, and riches are only held in trust. . . . Economic activity should be a social mission." The Report stated that it was

---

[43] Ibid.
[44] Boissard, supra note 38, at 466–67.
[45] Joblin, supra note 40, at 254–55.

not difficult to understand how Catholics could support the ILO program, citing examples of ILO representation at various Catholic meetings. It further stated that the International Labour Office had cordial relations with the Catholic International Union of Social Service and had, during 1927, increased its contacts with other Catholic organizations. In the Report, the Catholic social movement received five columns to the Protestants' one and a half columns.[46]

The generous praise given by Thomas to Catholic involvement in the social question was reciprocated by Pope Pius XI in his encyclical of 1931, *Quadragesimo Anno (On Reconstructing the Social Order)*, Pope Pius XI wrote that Pope Leo XIII's encyclical *Rerum Novarum* had "impelled people themselves to promote a social policy on truer grounds and with greater intensity, and so strongly encouraged good Catholics to furnish valuable help to heads of States in this field that they often stood forth as illustrious champions of this new policy even in legislatures."[47] At the promulgation of this encyclical in Rome, a message from Thomas was read, in which he said that the ILO was the outcome of prolonged effort and active collaboration of many; that the seed fell on fertile soil which had been carefully prepared by those determined to achieve social justice including those who based their convictions on *Rerum Novarum*.[48] Visible testimony to the harmony between the Holy See and the Catholic social movement, on the one hand and the ILO on the other, was provided by a mural painted by Maurice Denis and given to the ILO in 1931. It portrays Christ as a youth in Nazareth next to the workbench of St. Joseph, and around him are

---

[46] "Report of the Director Presented to the Conference," International Labour Conference, 11th Session, Geneva, 1928 (English ed.), 56–59.

[47] Harry Koenig, *Principles for Peace: Selections from Papal Documents—Leo XIII to Pius XII* (Milwaukee: Bruce, 1943), ¶945, Encyclical *Quadragesimo Anno (On Reconstructing the Social Order)*, May 15, 1931.

[48] Le Roy, supra note 37, at 6, where Thomas said, "The International Labour Organisation is not a spontaneous creation, but rather the outcome of prolonged effort and close and active collaboration on the part of all who are inspired by ideals. The seed feel on fertile soil, which had been carefully prepared by workers who were determined to achieve social justice, including those who based their convictions on the Encyclical *Rerum Novarum*."

Jews of the period, some twentieth-century workmen, and the Christian trade union leaders, Joseph Serrarens and Gaston Tessier.

On his death in 1932, Albert Thomas was eulogized by the Catholic press all over the world. He was praised for giving the Christian trade unions the same rights as others in the ILO, for paying public tribute to the leadership of the Catholic Church as a moral force, for smoothing the difficulties that had hampered collaboration between Christian and other organizations, and as a sincere supporter of social justice.[49]

The principal mode of contact between the Holy See and the ILO was through the Jesuit priests employed by the International Labour Office. An important indirect relationship existed, however, through the mediation of the Christian trade unions, members of the IFCTU, who participated in the work of the organization. This relationship was primarily academic, in the sense that it inspired a particular policy line on the one hand and provided a forum for discussion and implementation on the other. In this case, the Holy See as director of a transnational force was able to find a mechanism for delivering its message through the IFCTU, a Catholic international NGO. The unions which were members of IFCTU provided both Workers' Delegates and technical advisers to the ILO, from the Netherlands, Czechoslovakia, and Poland.[50] In the same category of relationship, but on a different level, was the participation of outstanding Catholic laymen and clerics in their capacity as individual delegates. The part played by supporters of Christian social movements at the International Labour Conference depended on their importance in their own country. If a political party drew inspiration from Christian principles, then it was usual for some of the government delegates or technical advisers to be chosen from a strong religious background. This was the case with several West European countries. For example, Msgr. W. H. Nolens, the Dutch labor priest, at one time minister of state for the Netherlands,

---

[49] International Labour Office, *Albert Thomas, 1878–1932* (Geneva: ILO, 1932), 48, 49, 67, 71, 93, 94–95, 105, 109.

[50] Le Roy, supra note 37, at 59–61.

served as a government delegate to the ILO from 1919 to 1931. He also served on numerous committees, and in 1926 he was elected president of the Conference. The Reverend D. Brauns, a former minister of labor, was a member of the German delegation to the Conference in 1929.[51] At the NGO level, the IFCTU had the highest rank of consultative status at the ILO and could thus intervene in debates. Some Catholic employers' associations affiliated to the International Union of Catholic Employers Associations played a limited role in the Conference as well. More informally, the International Labour Office entered into relationships with any private organization that wished to do so or that needed its help. Many Catholic organizations benefited from this contact—the French Social Week, the International Young Christian Workers, Pax Romana, Catholic Institutes of Social Order, and various trade union associations throughout the world.[52] Thus relations between the ILO and the Holy See were excellent. That this was so seems attributable to the following factors. First, there was ideological agreement, and absence of mutual suspicion, and the assumption of Catholic participation through individuals and groups as normal and expected. Second, the head of the secular organization was friendly to religious groups, above and beyond a mere toleration, so that they were encouraged to be themselves and surrender no principles. Third, the participation of Catholic NGOs was not hindered after the legal battle had been won, and they assumed a full role in the organization. Finally, a mode of direct contact was worked out between the Holy See and the secretariat of the organization, in this case through a permanent employee who fulfilled the function of an ambassador or observer without the title—although later an official relationship would be established, as in the case of other specialized agencies of the United Nations.

The year 1926 not only marked the appointment of Father Arnou to the staff of the International Labour Office, but also

---

[51] International Labour Conference, 8th Session, Geneva, 1926, vol. I, 4–11; Le Roy, supra note 37, at 60

[52] Le Roy, supra note 37, at 60–63.

brought evidence of a change in the attitude of the Holy See toward the League of Nations. Signs of a change had appeared and the way prepared during the previous year by the pope's condemnation of *Action Française,* the narrowly nationalistic group of Charles of Maurras in France, which was bitterly opposed to the League. In March, 1926, there appeared in *Civiltà Cattolica* an article on Tapparelli as a herald of the League. Although critical of the "airy idealism of Wilson" and of the League as resembling a group of victorious powers more anxious to hang on to the fruits of victory than to prevent armed conflict, the article did situate the League in a tradition having parallels in Catholic roots, and thus tended to legitimate the organization as compatible with the Catholic tradition.[53] The same month, *L'Osservatore Romano* denied that the Holy See had backed Brazil in its stand in the League Council which blocked the admission of Germany, contending for a seat on the Council. This had appeared in the British press and *L'Osservatore* took pains to state,

> As the Holy See has never been requested to participate in the League of Nations, it has been careful to refrain from hindering the work of the League. Instead, all its activities— as numerous reiterated Pontifical documents demonstrate— always have been directed toward the pacification of souls, so as to lessen the unhappy consequences of war, and therefore to facilitate by spiritual preparation the task of the League.[54]

The Holy See wished to see Germany enter the League, thereby ending the impression that the organization was a club of victors. Another factor was the threatened resignation of Spain from the League in 1926, which provided an opportunity for the pope to give Geneva some much needed support.

In April, a German cleric reported to Foreign Minister Stresemann, after conversations with Cardinal Gasparri and Msgr. Pizzardo,

---

[53] "Un Precusore Italiano della Societa Delle Nazioni," *Civiltà Cattolica* (March 3, 1926): 395; (March 26, 1926): 28.
[54] *L'Osservatore Romano* (March 27, 1926).

that in the Curia there was definitely the impression that the League was a forward-moving, growing power, making the distinction between the political sphere on the one hand and the social and cultural on the other. He reported that impression to the ILO and to certain commissions of the League, as well as the Institute for Intellectual Cooperation.[55] At the French Catholic Social Week of 1926, Eugene Duthoit suggested in his opening paper that the Holy See might establish diplomatic relations with the League if it so desired, but that the decision was up to the Vatican as to how this might be done. The context of his statement was that the League could receive from the Church the same services that states have so received in establishing relations with the Holy See.[56] There began in the summer a series of rumors that the Holy See was indeed seeking such an arrangement. This impression was strengthened by another article in *Civiltà Cattolica* in August which had kind words for the League saying that,

> Catholics, like all men of good-will, cannot remain indifferent in the face of such a great moral issue as is presented by the League, and, if there are forces at work for its destruction it is essential that all who love peace should band themselves together in its defence, for the League must not be destroyed but strengthened and improved.[57]

The article then recounted the history of the papacy in international relations and concluded by saying that religious peace facilitates and secures political peace among nations. Moreover, the Church would betray its own spirit by refusing to support those

---

[55] Schreiber, supra note 30, at 195–96.

[56] Eugene Duthoit, "Comment le Catholicisme Concoit et Harmonise le Devoir national et le Devoir International," in *Le Problème de la Vie International* (Paris: Gabalda, 1927), 71, n. 2.

[57] "Lo Spirito della Chiesa e l'Organizzazione Internazionale dei Popoli," in *La Civiltà Cattolica* III (August 12, 1926): 305. The original Italian reads as follows: "I cattolici, come tutti gli uomini di buon volere, non possono essere indifferenti di fronte al gran de problema morale che s'impernia oggi sulla Società ginevrina. Se delle schiere l'assediano per abbatterla o indebolirla, bisogna che essi, propugnatori dell pace, ne piglino risolutamente la difesa, perchè non muoia la Società delle Nazioni, ma *si corregga e viva*." [Italic in original.]

international institutions, however imperfect, which were working for peace.[58]

In September, *L'Osservatore Romano* denied reports in the Italian press of an increased interest in the League of Nations and plans to use the nuncio in Switzerland as an observer. As was reported by the *New York Times*, the Vatican paper declared that the Holy See had not in any way changed its attitude toward the League and that reports to the contrary were "fantastic."[59] In November there came another denial, this time of reports that a Geneva office would be created to observe the work of the League, in the form of an international organization. The paper stated that neither the Holy See nor any other competent ecclesiastical authority was connected with the rumored project and that such an organization would have no right to use the designation "international Catholic."[60] The organization or office referred to in this denial was undoubtedly the ICO office envisioned by the representatives of Catholic NGOs who had met during the Seventh League Assembly and proposed just such an institution.

Further light was shed on all the rumors of the year by an article in the French Jesuit magazine *Etudes* written by La Brière and published on December 5, 1926. La Brière stated that contrary to a rumor that had circulated since the summer, he could guarantee, on the basis of the most authentic sources, that the pope in no way desired to take a place in the League, and even if he were offered membership he was resolved to decline it definitively. La Brière said that the position that the papacy would necessarily have to occupy, by the same title as the fifty other powers already represented, would not be fitting to the dignity of the Holy See. In addition, most of the questions discussed by the League were of a profane nature, in which the Holy See had serious reasons for not intervening, and thus compromising its moral and spiritual authority. Furthermore, he said that the Holy See did not want to participate in the coercive measures envisaged by Article 16 of the Covenant, which were repugnant

---

[58] Ibid., 317.

[59] "Pope Not Watching League: Vatican Organ Denies Reports of Increased Interest," *New York Times* (September 4, 1926): 2.

[60] "Vatican Denies Geneva Bureau," *New York Times* (November 16, 1926): 2.

to its religious mission. La Brière argued that not only did Pius XI not seek to enter the League, but he did not at that time envisage some form of permanent and official representation of the Holy See in Geneva that would follow and observe events of the League.

Even though this kind of relationship did not present the same difficulties as membership, the pope wished to avoid any appearance of moral solidarity and regular collaboration with the League. He wished to remain independent of any relationship with the League and its operations. It was not that the pope was uninterested in the work of international collaboration for peace, nor did he disapprove of Catholic personalities and institutions which participated in the League and allied organizations, but those represented their own interests rather than those of the Holy See. Pius XI did not repudiate in advance all contact with the League but foresaw only intermittent contacts arising from particular problems, such as religious minorities, the rights of missionaries, the mandate of territories, the repression of illicit traffic, aid to distressed populations, and so on. If the League desired the collaboration of the Holy See on particular issues, nothing was easier for it than to address a request to the Vatican, which would give it favorable consideration. There were certain questions no doubt, such as calendar reform, in which the pope did not favor formal intervention. But in many other questions, positive collaboration appeared both possible and desirable. The pope would take care of the matter through negotiations with the League through the nuncio in Berne or some other papal diplomat. La Brière concluded that Catholics should not be hostile to the League simply because the pope was not a member. Rather they should work with tact so that in questions of interest to the Church the League could solicit the cooperation of the Holy See through the participation of Catholic NGOs.[61] This disavowal of any papal interest in an observer status, official or unofficial, was the reverse of La Brière's own early suggestions.

It was a distinct pleasure for Catholic supporters of the League to learn that the papal nuncios in Paris and Berlin, in their tradi-

---

[61] La Brière, II, supra note 27, at 266–67.

tional speeches of greeting given as deans of the diplomatic corps, had on New Year's Day, 1927, praised the Locarno Accords and the work of the League.[62] This surprising development lent support to La Brière's description of the new Vatican policy as one of support at a distance. Rumors of efforts to bring the Holy See into the League still persisted, however, eliciting in March the comment from the legal section of the League Secretariat that since it would be preposterous to consider the Vatican a self-governing state, a change in the Covenant would be necessary for its admission. The Geneva correspondent who reported this concluded,

> What all State members desire is the friendship and cooperation of the Vatican with the League and the Vatican already has evidenced the greatest interest in the League's efforts.[63]

This highly publicized interplay of rumor and denial, amid surprisingly favorable statements from the Vatican about the League—following upon the numerous proposals by the Catholic elite for observer status, membership, or some other form of collaboration between the Holy See and the League—caused misunderstandings, no doubt. But they all had one positive effect in that they stimulated Catholic interest in international affairs, especially in international law and the League. There were nationalist groups which certainly did not favor the League or any form of collaboration with it, especially in France and Germany. But now the great majority of Catholics followed a new line. Evidence of this was seen at a meeting sponsored by the French Federation of League of Nations Societies held in March 1927, attended by the Bishop of Arras and principal Catholic internationalists. They all commented on the importance of the League, considering it a truly Catholic institution, leading non-Catholics and even atheists in attendance to observe that Catholicism was no longer synonymous with reaction and nationalism and

---

[62] Alban de Malezieux du Hamel, *Le Pape et la Société des Nations* (Albert Mechelinck, 1932), 104; Maurice Vaussard, "L'Eglise Catholique, La Guerre et la Paix," in *Guerre et Paix* (Lyon: Chronique Social de France, 1953), 138.

[63] "Geneva Hears Vatican Would Join the League: Obstacles Are Seen as Only Self-Governing States Are Eligible," *New York Times* (March 9, 1927): 4.

that the Catholic elite was on the other hand firmly behind the cause of the League of Nations.[64] The image of the Church in international affairs began to undergo a distinct change away from nationalism and toward internationalism.

Another effect of this rapprochement, which took place in mid-decade, was that Pope Pius XI moved a bit more into the international field. In June, for example, he received Dr. Nicholas Murray Butler and promised him support for the campaign by the Carnegie Endowment for International Peace for world peace agreements between various countries.[65] The new climate was analyzed by Count Carlo Sforza in a lecture given in the United States on August 23, 1927. Sforza declared that the speeches of the nuncios in Paris and Berlin the previous January were highly significant as to the attitude of the Church toward the League. He noted that the League had survived and developed, especially with the admission of Germany the year before, which partly explained the difference between the coldness of 1920 and the warmth of 1927 in the Church's attitude. But the greatest factor in deciding the Church in favor of the League, he declared, was the appearance of extremist views exemplified by ultranationalist groups, such as the *Action Française.*

An additional factor was also responsible for this change in attitude. The Church, he said, had taken sides in the one quarrel that mattered for future civilization, understanding that extreme nationalism and communism might endanger the peace, and that there would either be peace—uncertain but with a future, or war—with the destruction of civilization.[66] The analysis of Sforza is quite perceptive. One last factor responsible for the change in attitude can be added, namely that negotiations on the Roman Question were at that time going forward and appeared likely to suceed. This may very well have been responsible for the upsurge of international

[64] Giorgio Cansacchi, *Il Papa e la Società delle Nazioni* (Turin: Bocca, 1929), 24.

[65] "Pope Promises Dr. Butler Aid of Church in Campaign for World Peace Agreement," *New York Times* (June 26, 1927): 1.

[66] "War Debts Debate Enlivens Institute—Sforza Lectures on Church and the League," *New York Times* (August 24, 1927): 11.

activity in Rome and the improvement of the attitude of the Holy See toward the League.

By way of conclusion, the Holy See's interest in developing some regular relationship with the League was met in part by the participation of Catholic NGOs. Yet, this was not the same as ongoing formal participation by the Holy See in the organization. The Holy See neither controlled nor directed the work of these ICOs. By the same token, these Catholic organizations did not consider themselves to be official representatives of the Holy See. All in all, however, the work of the ICOs with the League of Nations would establish a precedent for the formal provisions for consultation with the Economic and Social Council under Article 71 of the Charter of the United Nations.

Epilogue

THE PRESENT VOLUME has surveyed the role of the Holy See as an actor in different international systems, which can be understood as forms of international organization in the wide sense, from the medieval *republica christiana* in Europe, through the expansion of the Westphalian nation-state system to the dawn of the age of international organization in the strict sense, the first years of the League of Nations. During these centuries, the scope of activity of the Holy See, as the central administrative organ of the Roman Catholic Church, broadened geographically as that Church gradually became more universal—keeping pace with the secular phenomenon of globalization. The Vatican began to play a bigger role on a larger world stage. The nature of its international activity also underwent a change. After the full-scale presentation of the social teaching of the Church in *Rerum Novarum*, Rome began to take a much greater interest in the socioeconomic and cultural questions now being increasingly discussed in the secular global forum and came to be seen as an important participant. The loss of its temporal power over the Papal States, while complicating the international legal debate and incurring the temporary enmity of the new Kingdom of Italy, actually enhanced the Holy See's international position by lifting it out of the nation-state category and into that of a unique, global, spiritual, and moral authority, still endowed with international juridical personality and thus able to operate in the system of states and international organizations.

The results of this evolution have been illustrated concretely in the Vatican's relationships with the League of Nations and its "specialized agency," the International Labour Organisation, in the first decade of their existence. The key factor here was the discovery of issues of common concern and the development of communication and cooperation in working for solutions. Between the League and the Holy See, the principal examples were shorter-term issues such as the Palestine Mandate, calendar reform, intellectual cooperation, and various humanitarian questions. What linked the Vatican and the ILO, on the other hand, was a deeper shared vision of social justice in the world of work. The informal arrangement for ongoing contact and cooperation worked out by these two bodies in 1926 would continue after the League was replaced by the United Nations.

Relations between the League of Nations and its committees on the one hand, and the Holy See and international Catholic organizations on the other, peaked in the late 1920s and developed no further. Reasons for this are to be found in the deterioration in the general climate of international relations. It was becoming ever more obvious that the peace of Versailles was not a true peace after all, as Pope Benedict and others had feared, but had sown the seeds of future conflict. The advent of communism and fascism were challenging democracy and the rule of law. The financial crash of 1929 and the subsequent global economic depression was another factor. The decade from 1929 to 1939 was a gathering storm in world affairs and constituted an epilogue to the earlier Vatican–League relationship. During this period, the two bodies continued to share the same deep concern for the peaceful solution of disputes, particularly that between Italy and Ethiopia, but they operated independently of one another, from different perspectives and in very different ways.

Before considering the Italo–Ethiopian conflict of the 1930s, however, at least a brief mention should be made of that major event in the international life of the Holy See that had taken place a few years earlier, namely, the signing of the Lateran Treaty with Italy on February 11, 1929. Since much has already been written about this accord, and because it did not impinge upon the subject of the present study, it will not be treated here. Suffice it to say that Pope Pius XI and Premier Mussolini both found it advantageous to negotiate a definitive answer to the "Roman Question." The Holy See was financially compensated for the loss of property, the State of Vatican City was established politically as an independent sovereign state, and a concordat was signed that regulated the role of the Catholic Church in the life of Italy. The tiny State of Vatican City (108.7 acres) was still large enough to provide the pope with an independent platform and to counter the positivist legal argument that sovereignty required territory. The Lateran Treaty was an extremely important achievement for the Holy See: Although it was not itself a state, it now "possessed a state," and with it all the required attributes of sovereignty. The distinction between the Holy See and Vatican City State was then, and still is, essential, but a certain subtlety is necessary to grasp it, as became evident decades later, when the Vatican came into close contact with the United Nations system. But that encounter will be treated in the next volume of this series.

A critical issue that drew papal diplomacy once again into the quest for international peace was the Italian attempt to establish an empire in Ethiopia. The Holy See's reservations with and concerns about Italian expansion began after the finalization of the Lateran Treaty of 1929. In 1930 a papal diplomat, Msgr. Valerio Valeri, the apostolic delegate for Egypt, Eritrea, and Abyssinia was tapped to represent Pius XI at the coronation of Emperor Haile Selassie. In addition to being a gesture of goodwill, the Holy See's attendance provided an opportunity for the Holy See to strengthen relations with the Christian community in East Africa. Although some believe that he did not sufficiently condemn Italian ambitions in Ethiopia and may have even tacitly approved of them,[1] the pope was gravely

---

[1] See, e.g., John McKnight, *The Papacy: A New Appraisal* (New York: Rhinehart and Company, 1952), 255.

concerned with the aspirations Italy expressed through its African goals. Pius XI had communicated much earlier his concerns for peace and tranquility in Italy when, in 1922, he exhorted the bishops of Italy to work for the pacification of their country.[2] Now, it was hoped that the Lateran Treaty would contribute substantially to this effort. The pope conveyed these sentiments in an address that he gave at the Catholic University of Milan a few days after its signing.[3] But the progress toward peace in Italy was frustrated with the consolidation of power by the fascists. In response to this political development, Pius XI issued his June 29, 1931, encyclical *Non Abbiamo Bisogno* condemning those actions pursued for the exclusive advancement of the fascist party. While avoiding specific references, he undoubtedly had Italy in mind when he delivered his December 24, 1934, allocution *Felicemente Tutto* to the College of Cardinals lamenting the preparations for war.[4] In his July 28, 1935, discourse *Il venerabile Servo*, on the occasion of honoring the first apostolic delegate to Abyssinia, Giustino de Jacobis, the pope again urged his appeal for peace. In guarded language, he pleaded that nothing be done in this growing conflict "that is not in accordance with justice and charity."[5] As disinterested parties of the period noted, the pope was in a "delicate position" because of his devotion to the Ethiopians (Pius XI had established the Ethiopian College within Vatican City—the only national college for priestly formation within the Vatican walls) and his need to maintain cordial relations with the Italian government that had cooperated in resolving the Roman Question.[6] It is important to remember that the Vatican did not always reflect views in accord with those of the Italian government, nor was it reluctant to

---

[2] See Harry Koenig, *Principles for Peace: Selections from Papal Documents—Leo XIII to Pius XII* (Milwaukee: Bruce, 1943); *Il Disordini* to the Bishops of Italy, August 6, 1922, ¶¶745–50, and *Ora Sono Pochi Mesil* to the Bishops of Italy, October 28, 1922, ¶¶752–55.

[3] Ibid., ¶887, "Address," *Vogliamo Anzitutto* (February 13, 1929).

[4] Ibid., ¶¶1120–21.

[5] Ibid., ¶1130.

[6] "Pope Believes Italy Will Seize Ethiopia—Pontiff in Delicate Position, As He Is Friendy Toward Both Nations and Opposes Force," *New York Times* (August 5, 1935): 4.

disagree publicly with Mussolini.[7] Any criticism of the pope that he was "too neutral" fails to take account of the fact that as head of the universal Church, he is obligated to "maintain strict neutrality in secular disputes" because of the presence in most nations of the faithful whom he shepherds and for whom he is responsible.[8] In addition, his situation was made more difficult when his sovereign territory was surrounded by a belligerent military force that could expressly or implicitly pressure him.[9] Other states plotting their own mischief were not adverse to exploiting the pope's position. For example, Germany's Nazi regime attacked the pope for seemingly ignoring the Fifth Commandment prohibition against killing.[10] But these unwarranted assaults did not dissuade him from his labors of peace.[11] When some member states of the League began to pursue sanctions against Italy that wiser political observers of the day considered dangerous, he took the initiative of asking members of the League to postpone those sanctions, in the hope of promoting peace and avoiding world economic disorder.[12]

At the same time, it became increasingly clear that the League of Nations was fighting for its life. While many world leaders expressed both their hope that the League would survive, and their belief in the potential of the League to promote peace,[13] this experiment in international organization was, in the opinion of many,

---

[7] See "Mussolini and Pope Disagree on Holidays—Il Duce's Order to Banks to Stay Open on Sunday Draws a Rebuke From Pontiff," *New York Times* (October 29, 1935): 10.

[8] See "Vatican Disturbed by Geneva Move," *New York Times* (October 15, 1935): 15.

[9] Ibid.

[10] See "Nazi Paper Attacks Pope," *New York Times* (December 17, 1935): 17, wherein the Nazi Labor Front's official organ, *Angriff,* was quoted as saying the pope "is wise for silence is golden and speeches in Geneva and other places are just so much lead. Every Catholic must, however, be much surprised that His Holiness wastes words on 'anti-Catholic actions' in Germany, since his tongue could not be set free by murder and arson in East Africa."

[11] "London Hears Pope Has Peace Plan—Laval and Nuncio Discuss Idea Italy Taking Lowlands and Province of Tigre," *New York Times* (October 16, 1935): 1.

[12] See "Vatican Said to Be Helpful," *New York Times* (November 16, 1935): 17.

[13] F. P. Walters, *A History of the League of Nations,* II (London: Oxford University Press, 1952), 646–47.

already doomed.[14] It was particularly unable to contribute to the peaceful resolution of the Italo–Ethiopian crisis, which the pope had been attempting to resolve through the exercise of Vatican diplomacy. Pius XI expressed his concern that certain activities in the League of Nations might be leading toward, rather than away from,[15] war. In relying on the Church's teachings, he spoke out in September of 1935 against "the crime of war" and "war of conquest" and very likely spoke to Mussolini about these matters.[16] Pius XI was clearly less attracted to the League of Nations than his predecessor, Benedict XV. But like the League he was very interested in a peaceful and equitable resolution of the Italo–Ethiopian conflict. So, he quietly labored independently for peace in East Africa. While some critics viewed him as an Italian partisan in the conflict,[17] his words and deeds amply demonstrated that he was an international leader of high moral stature who was immersed in a most precarious situation.

As the press noted, the likely Italian seizure of Ethiopia put the pope in a "delicate position," in which he strived to be responsive to both states.[18] As the press further indicated, the pope observed that if Italy were to be involved in Ethiopia, its presence "should be achieved peacefully" rather than through armed conflict and aggression. As he said in a discourse in August of 1935, "We hope for peace; indeed We pray the good God to spare Us from war."[19] There was little doubt that Pius was speaking of the growing tension in East Africa when he specified events "outside Italy," and mentioned a "war of conquest . . . of aggression."[20] While he did

[14] Ibid., 647.

[15] See "Vatican Disturbed by Geneva Moves—He Regards the Present Crisis as Tragic Diplomatic Failure and Deprecates All Wars," *New York Times* (October 15, 1935): 15.

[16] Ibid.

[17] For example, Prof. Walters suggested that the pope's expressions for peace "could not embarrass the Fascist government, nor did they prevent many Italian prelates from giving their enthusiastic support to the war policy of Mussolini." Walters, II, supra note 13, at 647, n.1.

[18] See supra note 6.

[19] Koenig, supra note 2, ¶1133, Discourse *Voilà un Coup d'Oeil* to the International Congress of Catholic Nurses, August 27, 1935.

[20] Ibid., ¶1134.

not preclude legitimate involvement by one country in the affairs of another if they were intended to promote the common good,[21] the pope unmistakably condemned any possible war of expansion; that would be "unjust" or "unthinkable," and he would "deliberately reject it."[22] Nevertheless, he also indicated that any war in which Italy might be involved could be acceptable if it were "a war of defense."[23] He hastened to acknowledge and warn that "the right of defense has limits and restrictions which cannot be ignored without culpability."[24] Again, the popular press confirmed the pope's opposition to Italian expansion in late August of 1935.[25]

As the end of the summer approached, the pope continued to manifest the hope that any conflict should be peacefully resolved before the partisans resorted to war.[26] On September 7, he addressed a group of war veterans and stated that in spite of the threats of war there also appeared a "rainbow on the horizon."[27] In the new year of 1936, the pope asserted his optimism for a peaceful resolution of the East African conflict in his address to the Pontifical Academy and reiterated the content of his September 7th address.[28] An Associated Press report of January 12, 1936, reported that Cardinal Verdier, the Archbishop of Paris, had called for support of Premier Pierre Laval's effort to end the Ethiopian conflict; moreover, the Cardinal reiterated that self-defense was the only legitimate justification for war.[29]

---

[21] Ibid., ¶¶1136–37.

[22] Ibid., ¶1134.

[23] Ibid., ¶1135.

[24] Ibid.

[25] See "Pope Pleads Strongly Against African War; Questions Italian Talk of Need to Expand," *New York Times* (August 29, 1935): 3, describing the pope's address as a "strong appeal against recourse to war as a means of solving the Italo-Ethiopian dispute."

[26] See "Pope Hopes Italy Will Avoid War" and "Truce While League Talks Reported Pledged by Italy; Pope Sees Hope for Peace," *New York Times* (September 8, 1935): 1.

[27] Koenig, supra note 2, ¶1140, Address *Cari Combattenti* to a Pilgrimage of War Veterans, September 7, 1935. See "Pope Hopes Italy Will Avoid War," *New York Times* (September 8, 1935): 1.

[28] "Pope Predicts Peace; Paris Expects Move—Cardinal Verdier Reveals Pontiff's Hope that France Will Avoid Conflict," *New York Times* (January 13, 1936): 11.

[29] Ibid.

Contrary to the assertions of some critics, Pius XI continued his own quiet diplomacy to end this conflict. In February 1936, he asked the Czech president, Eduard Benes, to serve as an intermediary between Mussolini and the member states of the League who were in the vanguard of imposing sanctions against Italy.[30] A few months later, in April, he again turned to France and sought its assistance and good offices to end the war in East Africa and to encourage states such as the United Kingdom to end sanctions against Italy.[31] In the following month, the pope publicly expressed his gratitude for the end of the Ethiopian hostilities, and he urged all, especially those Europeans present in East Africa, to return humanity to "wisdom and comprehension."[32]

With the end of the war in Ethiopia, papal attention for world peace was diverted to concern about persecutions in Germany and Russia.[33] By the late summer, the pope extended his apprehension of the state of world affairs to Spain, in his allocution to Spanish refugees.[34] In retrospect, it becomes understandable why Pius XI did not place much hope in the League for resolving the growing tensions around the world. After all, the League was established by the victors of the First World War and admitted only those states that it wished to welcome. The political issues that emerged from this process of admission of new members and the corresponding

---

[30] "Pope Seeks Peacemaker—Reported to Have Asked Benes to Act as a Negotiator," *New York Times* (February 22, 1926): 6.

[31] "Pope Appeals to France—Asks Intercession to End War Between Ethiopia and Italy," *New York Times* (April 15, 1935): 15.

[32] "Pope Gives Thanks to God for End of African War," *New York Times* (May 6, 1936): 17. See Anne O'Hare McCormick, "The Pope Steers a Course Amid Storms," in *Vatican Journal* (New York: Farrar, Strauss and Cudahy, 1957), 69–81, regarding this correspondent's firsthand observations of the pope's ongoing concern about the desperate need to establish peace in East Africa.

[33] "Pontiff Condemns Red and Nazi Curbs—He Decries Interferences with Religion in Russia and Reich—Assails Communism Anew," *New York Times* (May 13, 1936): 1. With regard to concerns about the silence of some Catholics toward the German move into Austria, see Luigi Sturzo, *Nationalism and Internationalism* (New York: Roy Publishers, 1946), 195–96. See encyclicals by Pius XI, *Mit Brenneder Sorge* and *Divini Redemptoris*.

[34] Koenig, supra note 2, ¶¶1150–60, Allocution *La Vostra Presenza* to the Spanish Refugees, September 14, 1936.

administration of the League interfered with its universal mission to establish world peace. Its actions, according to some, were based not on internationalism but on the rather parochial views of specific states.[35] As Joseph Bernhart concluded in 1939 about an international "community of peoples," what the Catholic Church was able to establish and maintain during the era of Christendom, the League of Nations could not—its efforts to reestablish such an order were an "illusion."[36] As the world edged closer to international armed conflict, Pope Pius strove to keep alive some hope for international structures of cooperation and the promotion of peace, declaring that he was willing to sacrifice himself for the cause of world peace.[37]

As the decade of the 1930s was drawing to a close, the high probability of a major war was becoming more and more evident. The League of Nations, which had failed to prevent aggression against Ethiopia, was now generally considered to be an ineffectual instrument for preserving peace and security. The Holy See therefore increased its efforts for peace through the bilateral channels of papal diplomacy. But there were no illusions at the Vatican. The Secretary of State, Cardinal Eugenio Pacelli, who was a seasoned papal diplomat and former nuncio in Germany, had already voiced his concern about the drift toward war in a speech delivered in May of 1938.[38] He was to become pope himself, after Pius XI died in February of the following year, and would reign as Pius XII until 1958. He would be widely admired for his tireless pleas for peace, especially his Christmas messages, and his humanitarian efforts to relieve suffering during the horrible conflict that marked the first years of his pontificate and led to a new period in the history of world order. These activities for peace would prepare the Holy See

---

[35] Sturzo, supra note 33, at 257.

[36] Joseph Bernhart, *The Vatican as World Power* (London: Longmans, Green and Co., 1939), 382.

[37] Koenig, supra note 2, ¶¶1298–99, Radio address, "*Mentre Lilioni di Uomini* to the Whole World," September 29, 1938.

[38] Koenig, supra note 2, ¶¶1282–89, Address of Cardinal Pacelli, Secretary of State, to the Thirty-Fourth International Eucharistic Congress at Budapest, May 25, 1938.

to enter the next phase of its relationships with international organizations in the postwar period.

But already with the beginning of the Second World War, the League of Nations had ceased to function effectively and so the present study has now reached its logical and chronological conclusion. However, it is not the end of the story. It should be seen rather as an introduction to the much larger and richer story of the relations of the Holy See with the United Nations and its specialized agencies, to be presented in a second volume.

Index

Holy Places in Palestine. *See* Palestine, British Mandate for

Holy See. *See also* more specific topics, including individual popes

apostolic mission of, 3–4, 9–12, 17–18

arbitrator/mediator, role as. *See* arbitrator/mediator between states, Holy See's role as

communication/collaboration with League. *See* communications/collaboration between League and Holy See

definition and etymology of term, 2–3n2, 3

ILO, relationship with, 241–46

international Catholic organizations, relationship with, 224–28

international juridical personality. *See* international juridical personality of Holy See

membership/exclusion from membership in League. *See* membership of Holy See in League, question of

neutrality viewed as essential to, 259

Vatican City distinguished from, 257

Holy War, concept of, 28

House, Colonel, 101

humanist tradition of League of Nations, 123–24, 198, 231, 237–38

humanitarian concerns. *See* social justice

Hungary, 145, 234. *See also* Austria and Austria-Hungary

I

IALL (International Association for Labor Organizations), 88–89

ICOs. *See* international Catholic organizations

IFTCU (International Federation of Christian Trade Unions), 144–45, 242, 245–46

IKA, 145, 240

ILC (International Law Commission), 12–13

ILO. *See* International Labour Organisation (ILO)

immigration practices, 118–19

Imperiali, Marquess, 179, 181

India, 41, 84

Indians of New World, Vitoria's defense of rights of, 30–31

infallibility of pope, dogma of, 55

Innocent III (pope), 21

Intellectual Cooperation, International Committee on, 231–34, 237–39, 256

Internacio Katholika (IKA), 145, 240

International Association for Labor Organizations (IALL), 88–89

International Association for Life and the Family, 237

International Astronomical Union, 215, 216

International Catholic Association for the Protection of Young Women, 85, 229

International Catholic Committee
on Intellectual Cooperation,
231–34
international Catholic elite. *See*
Catholic elite and the League
International Catholic League
(IKA), 145, 240
international Catholic organizations, 223–53. *See also* Catholic
Union of International Studies,
and other specific organizations
"Catholic," titular use of, 225,
249
communications/collaboration
between League and Holy
See, 202, 227–28, 232–33,
237–38, 250
Holy See, relationship with,
224–28
ILO, 241–46
interaction between, 235,
236–37, 238–40, 243, 244
League, relationship with.
See international Catholic
organizations and League,
relationship between
national member sections,
225–26, 234
nineteenth and early twentieth
centuries, 84–89
Pius XI's relations with League,
202
private nature of, 225
unified international Catholic
organization, attempt to
establish, 240
WWI and founding of League,
143–46

international Catholic organizations
and League, relationship
between, 227–40
assessors, 229–31
Catholic Union, 229, 234–37,
238–40
interaction between organizations, 235, 236–37, 238–40,
243, 244
International Committee on
Intellectual Cooperation,
231–34, 237–39, 256
moral support, 230–31
social and humanitarian
concerns, 229–30
International Catholic Union
for the Study of International
Law According to Christian
Principles, 83
International Chamber of Commerce, 215, 216
International Committee on Intellectual Cooperation, 231–34,
237–39, 256
International Congresses of
Catholic Youth, 145–46
International Federation of
Catholic Associations of
Doctors, 146
International Federation of Christ-
ian Trade Unions (IFCTU),
144–45, 242, 245–46
International Institute of Intellec-
tual Cooperation, 238
International Israelite Committee
concerning the Reform of the
Calendar, 220

minority rights, protection of,
47, 146–47, 152–54, 235
Palestinian conquest, 164–65
WWI defeat of, 166–67

U

Ubi Arcano Dei (Pius XI), 192–97,
205
ultramontanism, 81
Unam Sanctam (Boniface VIII),
201
UNESCO, 231
Union Catholique d'Etudes Inter-
nationales. *See* Catholic Union
of International Studies
Union Internationale d"Etudes
Sociales, 144
Union of International Associa-
tions, 231
United Kingdom. *See* Britain
United Nations, 190, 211, 222,
253, 257, 264
United States. *See also* Wilson,
Woodrow
Benedict XV's WWI peace pro-
posals, 96, 101
calendar reform, 217, 219
Catholic Association for Inter-
national Peace, 144
Catholic attitudes towards
League of Nations, 122–23,
126–27, 137
Catholic social justice and labor
movements, 87
Catholic Union of International
Studies, 234
immigration practices, 117–19

League of Nations, ultimate
nonparticipation in, 127, 135
Leo XIII's relationship with, 63,
68, 69
National Catholic Welfare Conference, 155, 243
Palestine and Holy Places, 176,
177, 183
recognition of Holy See by, 7
Washington Conference,
154–57
Universal Peace Congress, 1897,
68–69
universalism vs. nationalism. *See*
nationalism and the nation-state
Upper Silesia, 143
Urquhart, David, 53–55
Uruguay, 184

V

Valeri, Valerio, 257
Valignano, Alexander, 41
van Karnebeek, H.A., President,
147
Vanderpol, Alfred, 82–83, 144
Vatican City, State of, 257
Vatican Council I, 52–55
Vatican Council II, 11–12, 226
Vaughan, Cardinal Herbert, 69
Vaussard, Maurice, 52, 142, 205,
206, 208
Venezuela, 68, 69
Venizelos, Eleutherios, 118–19
Verdier, Cardinal Jean, 261
Verdross, Alfred, 115–16
Versailles, Treaty of, 121, 129, 150,
174, 241, 256
Victor Emmanuel I of Italy, 55

About the Authors

FR. JOHN LUCAL served in the Permanent Mission of the Holy See to the United Nations some thirty years ago. He was also an editor and contributor to *America Magazine*. He subsequently served as a Professorial Lecturer at Georgetown University. He is now engaged in English language pastoral ministry and Christian/Muslim Dialogue in Ankara, Turkey.

FR. ROBERT JOHN ARAUJO is a Professor of Law at Gonzaga University, on an academic leave of absence serving as an attaché to the Permanent Mission of the Holy See to the United Nations. His articles on international law have appeared in the *Notes et Documents*, Institut International Jacques Maritain; *St. Thomas Law Review*; *Georgetown Journal of Law & Public Policy*; *Ave Maria Law Review*; *Tulane Journal of International and Comparative Law*; *Evangile et Justice*; *Fordham Urban Law Journal*; *Fordham Journal of International Law*; *Catholic University Law Review*; *American University International Law Review*; *Vanderbilt Journal of Transnational Law*; and *Across Borders*.